Critical Sermons of the Zen Tradition

Dr Hisamatsu Shin'ichi, at age 87. Photograph taken by the late Professor Hyōdō Shōnōsuke in 1976, at Dr Hisamatsu's residence in Gifu.

Critical Sermons of the Zen Tradition
Hisamatsu's Talks on Linji

translated and edited by
Christopher Ives and Tokiwa Gishin

University of Hawai'i Press
Honolulu

First published 2002 by
PALGRAVE MACMILLAN
Houndmills, Basingstoke, Hampshire RG21 6XS

Published in North America by
University of Hawai'i Press
2840 Kolowalu Street
Honolulu, Hawai'i 96822

Library of Congress Cataloging-in-Publication Data

Hisamatsu, Shin'ichi, 1889–1980
    [Rinzairoku shōkō. English.]
    Zen talks on the Record of Linji / translators and editors Tokiwa Gishin, Ives
    Christopher.
        p. cm.
    Includes bibliographical references and index.
    ISBN 0–8248–2383-4 (cloth : alk. paper) – ISBN 0–8248–2384-2 (pbk. : alk paper)
    1. Linji Yixuan d. 867. 2. Zen Buddhism. I. Linji-lu
    Ives, Christopher, 1954– II. Tokiwa, Gishin III. Title.

BQ9399.I554 L55335 2000
294.3'85—dc21

                                                                    00–033778

Printed and bound in Great Britain by
Antony Rowe Ltd, Chippenham, Wiltshire

Together with Hisamatsu Shin'ichi,
the translators dedicate this book to
All Humankind in their Depth Humanity of No-Rank

Contents

Acknowledgements

Like other projects of similar magnitude, this publication received support from numerous directions. Soon after the death of Dr Hisamatsu in 1980, Abe Masao played an instrumental role in initiating the translations of Hisamatsu's talks on the *Record of Linji*. Norman Waddell, a member of the *Eastern Buddhist* editorial board, kindly holed up with Chris Ives for several days back in 1980 to help polish the translation of the first two talks. Over the following years, as the first fifteen talks were published serially in *The Eastern Buddhist*, Wayne Yokoyama provided – with his characteristic generosity – extensive editorial input and bibliographical help. Dan Yukie, also formerly of *The Eastern Buddhist*, followed suit with her unstinting administrative and logistical support. At several points Jeff Shore at Hanazono University provided editorial and logistical assistance as well.

In 1990 the Japan Foundation awarded Chris Ives a fellowship that enabled the translators to work together on this book for three months in Kyoto. The University of Puget Sound provided him with a travel grant for a short trip to Kyoto in 1997 as well as a long-term typing grant; Carol Avery in the Department of Religion at Puget Sound deserves high praise for her superb typing – and retyping – of the manuscript through its many incarnations and her adroit handling of diacritics software, file exchanges, and reformatting.

This project has also benefited from the generosity of Hanazono University and its two outstanding Zen Studies institutes: the Zenbunka Kenkyūsho (Institute for Zen Studies) and the Kokusai Zengaku Kenkyūsho (International Research Institute for Zen Buddhism). While teaching at Hanazono and working on this translation, Tokiwa Gishin wrote the annotations for Hisamatsu's talks and Yanagida's introduction.

Kitahara Ryūtarō served as the main editor when Hisamatsu's talks on the *Record of Linji* were first published by the Risōsha Publishing Company. The foreword to this volume, which is an abridged translation of Kitahara's postscript to the volume of Hisamatsu's collected writings in which the talks were first published, as well as the preface by Abe Masao and introduction by Yanagida Seizan, outline Hisamatsu's approach to Zen and the classical Zen text he explores in this book.

The editors wish to thank Mr Kamibeppu Shigeru, Chief Editor of Hōzōkan Publishing Company, for granting permission to publish this translation of Hisamatsu's talks, for which Hōzōkan currently holds the copyright; Mr Hisamatsu Sadaaki, inheritor of the author's rights, for agreeing to this publication; Professor Inoue Takami, Secretary of the Eastern Buddhist Society, for permission to republish the translations of the first fifteen talks; and Professor Hirano Sōjō, Director of the Zenbunka Kenkyūsho, holders of the copyright of Ruth F. Sasaki's *The Record of Lin-chi*, portions of which were excerpted and adapted for this volume.

Any mistranslations, or inaccuracies in the annotations, are the full responsibility of the translators, who hope they have given Hisamatsu's words the faithful and dynamic rendering they deserve.

Japanese name order

The translators have followed the Japanese convention of ordering Japanese names with the surname followed by the given name, even when following an honorific: e.g. Professor Hisamatsu Shin'ichi.

Notes on the Contributors

Hisamatsu Shin'ichi (1889–1980) studied philosophy at Kyoto Imperial University from 1912 to 1915. After his graduation, he followed the advice of Nishida Kitarō, the professor in charge of the Department of Philosophy at that time, and in November 1915 began Zen practice with Ikegami Shōzan of the Myōshinji monastery. In the December retreat of that year he reportedly attained Awakening. He remained a layperson throughout his life.

From 1919 Dr Hisamatsu gave lectures on the philosophy of religion at private universities in Kyoto. In 1935 he became a full-time lecturer in the Department of Letters at Kyoto Imperial University, and from 1937, as an assistant professor, he offered courses in Religious Studies and Buddhist Studies. In January 1941 he started the Kyōdai Shincha-kai, a Kyoto University student association for the study of "heart tea." In April 1944 he founded Gakudō Dōjō, an association of Kyoto University students and alumni for the "study and practice of the Way." He was promoted to full professor in 1946, and the following year he was awarded the degree of Doctor of Literature. In 1949 he retired from Kyoto University. From 1952 to 1963, as a professor at Kyoto Municipal University of the Fine Arts, he gave lectures on philosophy and religion.

In the autumn of 1957 Dr Hisamatsu gave lectures as a visiting professor at Harvard Divinity School. During this period in the United States and then while traveling in Europe and India he had conversations with philosophers, theologians, and specialists in other fields. In April 1960 he changed the name of Gakudō Dōjō to FAS Society, by which it has been known ever since. In January 1964, when the Zenbunka Kenkyūsho (Institute for Zen Studies) started in Kyoto, he served as an academic advisor together with D.T. Suzuki and Nishitani Keiji.

In the 1970s and 1980s the Risōsha Publishing Company in Tokyo published *Hisamatsu Shin'ichi Chosakushū*, an eight-volume collection of his writings. Between 1990 and 1991 Hōzōkan Publishing Company in Kyoto put out a four-volume collection of his lectures on Buddhism, *Hisamatsu Shin'ichi Bukkyō Kōgi*. Hōzōkan also published a revised and enlarged collection of his collected writings in nine volumes from 1994 to 1996.

Dr Hisamatsu's *Zen to bijutsu* (Bokubisha Publishing, 1958) was translated into English by Tokiwa Gishin and published as *Zen and the Fine
Arts* (Kodansha International, 1971). Translations of other writings
have appeared in several journals, including *The Eastern Buddhist*, and
several members of the FAS Society are compiling an anthology of his
writings that have been translated into English.

Kitahara Ryūtarō is a senior member of the FAS Society. Starting in
1946, when he was student majoring in philosophy at Kyoto
University, he devoted himself to Zen practice under the guidance of
Dr Hisamatsu and acquired deep trust in him. Over the years Kitahara
has contributed extensively to promoting the FAS Society's practice of
mutual self-investigation. From 1980 to 1988 he devoted himself to
compiling a complete collection of works by his father, Kitahara
Hakushū (1885–1942), a prominent poet of modern Japan; collabora-
tion with poetry experts and his father's disciples resulted in *Hakushū
Zenshū* (Complete Works of Hakushū; published by Iwanami Shoten in
39 volumes together with one additional special volume). Recently he
has turned to the elucidation of the religious core of his father's poetry.

Abe Masao is Professor Emeritus of Nara University of Education. He
has taught widely in the United States and Europe and played a central
role in Buddhist-Christian dialogue over the past four decades. His
numerous publications include *Zen and Western Thought* (Macmillan
and University of Hawai'i Press, 1985), *Buddhism and Interfaith Dialogue*
(Macmillan and University of Hawai'i Press, 1995), and *Zen and
Comparative Studies* (Macmillan, 1997). His religio-philosophical standpoint and responses to it by Christian and Jewish theologians can be
found in *The Emptying God: A Buddhist-Jewish-Christian Dialogue* (Orbis
Books, 1990) and *Divine Emptiness and Historical Fullness: A Buddhist-
Jewish-Christian Conversation with Masao Abe* (Trinity Press
International, 1995).

Yanagida Seizan is a renowned Zen text scholar, Professor Emeritus of
Kyoto University, and researcher at and former director of the
International Research Institute for Zen Buddhism at Hanazono
University in Kyoto. His many books include *Shoki-Zenshū shisho no
kenkyū* (Studies on Historical Texts of the Early Chinese Zen), a six-
volume collection of his writings (Hōzōkan, from 1999), and a three-
volume concordance of the *Zutan-ji* (Kor. *Chodanchip*, J. *Sodōshū*,
Records Collected from the Chan Founding Masters' Halls).

Tokiwa Gishin is Professor Emeritus at Hanazono University in Kyoto. He has taught at the University of Michigan and the University of Leiden (Holland). He is a specialist in Mahāyāna texts and philosophy as well as Japanese Zen Buddhism. He has published English translations of Hisamatu's *Zen and the Fine Arts* and the *Jueguan-lun* (A Dialogue on Contemplation Extinguished; a Chinese Zen text of the Tang dynasty, discovered in the caves at Dunhuang). He has translated into modern Japanese the Sanskrit text, the *Laṅkāvatāra Mahāyāna sūtram*, and the *Sokkōroku Kaien-fusestu* (General Remarks on the Occasion of Taking up the Record of Sokkō), a work by Hakuin Ekaku (1685–1768) in Chinese.

Christopher Ives is Professor of Religious Studies at Stonehill College, in Easton, Massachusetts. In his scholarship he focuses on Zen Buddhism and ethics, especially modern Zen ethical thought and political dimensions of Buddhism in Japanese history. In the 1970s he studied Zen for four years with the FAS Society at Myōshinji in Kyoto. His publications include *Zen Awakening and Society* (Macmillan and University of Hawai'i Press, 1992).

Foreword
Kitahara Ryūtarō

In his talks at the first FAS Society[1] retreat in July 1947, Dr Hisamatsu avoided terms from traditional Zen practice, such as *dai-sesshin* ("great mind-concentration," i.e. a Zen retreat), *teishō* ("presentation and advocacy [by a master]," a Dharma-talk), *zazen* ("sitting zen," seated meditation), *kōan* ("universal case"), *sanzen-nisshitsu* ("practicing zen through attending the master," koan interviews), and *kinhin* ("going by," walking meditation). In their place he coined new expressions, like *betsuji-gakudō* ("a special period for learning the Way," an FAS Society retreat), *teikō* (explained below), *tanza-jikkyū* ("upright-sitting for practical inquiry"), *sōgo-sankyū* ("mutual self-inquiry"), *gyōdō* ("going along the path," i.e. walking meditation), and *kyūdai* ("investigating topics"). In short, he was not wedded to old modes; he incorporated something novel, creating new forms as he went. He tried to establish the most universal, straightforward, unerring, and unprecedented method of bringing about Awakening.

The word *teikō* has been used for centuries. A *teikō* is no ordinary lecture, for it is similar to a *teishō* in a Zen monastery. Dr Hisamatsu has given the expression the new meaning of "bringing out (**tei**-*ritsu*) guiding principles (**kō**-*ryo*)," which corresponds to "ascending the platform," a term used in the *Record of Linji* (Ch. *Linji-lu*, J. *Rinzairoku*) and other Zen texts. Moreover, to erase possible hints of the established connotations of "*teishō*," he ascribed additional meaning to the term *teikō*. He construed it as the person of master-rank, the true person of no rank, the bottomless, boundless, infinite, formless, original self, straightforwardly talking about itself. At *betsuji-gakudō* retreats held three times a year, over eighteen years, ending in December 1964, Dr Hisamatsu delivered such *teikō* every other day. On the other days participants engaged in mutual inquiry, *sōgo-sankyū*, and the lively contents of that practice found vivid reflection in the *teikō*. Throughout the week-long retreats, we member practitioners engaged in vigorous *tanza-jikkyū*, full-lotus zazen, for ten hours a day and in that samadhi[2] we listened to the Dharma he conveyed through the *teikō*.

His *Rinzairoku-shōkō*, the *teikō* he gave on passages he selected from the *Record of Linji*, constituted the final, crowning moment of the talks he had delivered over those eighteen years. This is not to say that he gave no other important talks. One other set of *teikō*, the *Yuima-shichisoku* ("Seven Cases from the *Vimalakīrti-nirdeśa-sūtra*"), with its quality and quantity, could constitute a separate monograph in itself. But Dr Hisamatsu considered the *Record of Linji* to be the best of all Zen texts, and he gave talks on this one work during eight consecutive retreats over three years.

I believe Dr Hisamatsu exerted himself throughout his life to give *teikō* on Zen texts because he wanted to have member practitioners get awakened directly to their own formless, true self. This warm compassion flows through his Zen talks on the *Record of Linji*, and he expresses it beyond mere words in ways that extinguish all workings of consciousness.

On 8 October 1955, at one of the weekly meetings called *heijo-dōjō* ("the locus of Awakening in ordinary life"), Dr Hisamatsu began a series of talks on the *Chuanxinfayao*,[3] which is the record of Huangbo, Linji's master. According to notes I wrote later that year, on December 25, the next-to-the-last day of the 26th retreat, Dr Hisamatsu concluded that series of talks:

> The *Chuanxinfayao* is a classic that clarifies the source of Zen, and as such it is indispensable for the confrontation of East and West. But its way of exposition is conceptual. In contrast, the *Record of Linji* operates prior to conceptuality; in it the one mind that goes beyond discrimination is throbbing with life. Making itself felt there is the living breath of Zen.
>
> As records of the sayings and doings of various persons, the *Bi-yan-lu* (J. Hekigan-roku, "Blue-Cliff Record") and the *Wumenguan* (J. *Mumonkan*, "Gateless Barrier") do offer variety. But in that variety I sense disconnectedness. In contrast, the *Record of Linji*, based on the life of Linji, exhibits a concrete consistency, and I regard this text as the foremost Zen record. If you read it over and over you'll feel something different from other Zen texts. And if you continue to read it patiently, you can feel it, so to speak, breathing. From there you can better penetrate it and see it from within. Ultimately, the text will come to life as your own speech and conduct.
>
> The *Chuanxinfayao* provides a conceptual exposition of the *Record of Linji*. These two texts share a number of expressions, with all the important ones in the *Record of Linji* already present in the *Chuanxinfayao*. For that reason, as preparation for the *Record of Linji*, I recommend reading the *Chuanxinfayao*.

On 25 August 1957 I had a conversation with Dr Hisamatsu at his residence, *Hōseki-an*, in the Myōshinji monastic compound. With a broad smile he explained, "As for the *Chuanxinfayao*, I feel like I wrote it myself." He pointed out the oneness of the two texts: "The *Record of Linji* and the *Chuanxinfayao* are like the inside and outside." According to my diary, on 30 July 1956 we had another conversation at *Hōseki-an*; thinking along the lines of the saying, "In the morning one hears the Way; in the evening one can die," I said, "If I truly understand only the *Record of Linji*, I think that will suffice." Frowning, Dr Hisamatsu responded with severe advice: "It won't do to read only that. Read widely." His words still echo in my ears.

In his studies on the history of Zen thought, Dr Suzuki Daisetsu detected originality in Linji's idea of "Person," and Suzuki emphasized that Linji's idea went beyond his master Huangbo's traditional notion of "one mind." Though Suzuki was correct in pointing out this discontinuity, we can also discern perfect continuity between Huangbo and Linji. While diverging in their modes of expression or manifestation, they share a single root, as seen in the case of two contemporary masters, Sunshin (Nishida Kitarō) and Hōseki (Hisamatsu Shin'ichi).

Dr Hisamatsu's talks on the *Chuanxinfayao* were so clear and exhaustive that it seemed like he was looking at his own palm. It was as if Huangbo himself were appearing before us. Peixiu (797–870), a former prime minister of the Tang dynasty who compiled Huangbo's record, praised Huangbo: "His words are brief; his logic is straight; his path is steep; his practice is solitary." Between the words of Huangbo and the daily exposition of our old man Hōseki, there is, I believe, complete agreement.

Despite repeated requests from people around him, Dr Hisamatsu seemed to avoid giving talks on the *Record of Linji*, which made me wonder if even he had reservations about taking up that text. Finally, however, he dared to do so, and, to the unexpected delight of us all, unsparingly he laid bare the FAS of the living Linji.

From 13 July 1962 through 3 February 1963, right when he was starting his talks on Linji, Dr Hisamatsu gave lectures each month at FAS plenary seminars on the *Liuzu-tanjing* (J. *Rokuso-dankyō*, "The Sixth Founding Teacher's Platform Sutra"). After that, he gave lectures on the *Dunwu-yaomen* (J. *Tongo-yōmon*, "Essential Gate for Immediate Awakening") by Dazhu Huihai (dates unknown; a disciple of Mazu Daoyi, 709–88).

As the immediate presence of the clear Awakening of the Formless Self, Dr Hisamatsu elucidated these classic Zen texts in accord with the standpoint of FAS. Through his lectures the practitioners in attendance gradually secured a clear understanding of what was running through these texts.

Dr Hisamatsu's talks on the *Record of Linji* link closely with the contents of his earlier *teikō* and his more academic lectures. To deepen our understanding of difficult parts of his talks on Linji, we should refer to Dr Hisamatsu's writings, to any lectures of his that might be published in the future, and to classic Zen texts. More than anything, however, we need to have our own formless self awaken immediately, here and now. If that hasn't happened, we need to devote ourselves wholeheartedly to exploring the place where neither reasoning nor non-reasoning will do. Otherwise, we'll never find a way to clarify our formless self and realize it truly and ultimately.

Dr Hisamatsu presented talks on the *Record of Linji* during eight *betsuji-gakudō* from September 1962 through December 1964. As one of the compilers of the talks, I gave them tentative titles. At first the titles were simpler, in Chinese characters alone. Later, following suggestions from my co-editor, Professor Fujiyoshi Jikai, I changed the titles to phrases in mixed Japanese and Chinese characters, and obtained Dr Hisamatsu's consent. I chose not to reorder the talks, deciding instead to leave them in the order in which they were given. For an easy grasp of the whole, I have divided the talks according to the retreats in which they were given.

Forty-fifth FAS retreat:
1. I Simply Couldn't Open My Mouth (*Kore kaiku-futoku*); 9 September 1962
2. Who is Pure and Direct in His Behavior? (*Gyōgō-jun'itsu wa dare*); 13 September 1962

Forty-sixth FAS retreat:
3. There's Nothing Special in the Buddha-Dharma (*Buppō tasu nashi*); 18 December 1962
4. After Realizing the Great Block of Awakening (*Daigodan no ato*); 20 December 1962
5. Leaving after the Summer Retreat (*Ge o oete saru*); 22 December 1962

Forty-seventh FAS retreat:
6. The One True Person without Rank (*Ichi-mu'i no shinnin ari*); 2 April 1963
7. Speak! Speak! (*Ie ie*); 4 April 1963

8. The Mind-Dharma is without Form and Pervades the Ten Directions (*Shinbō mukei, jippō ni tsūkan su*); 6 April 1963

Forth-eighth FAS retreat:
9. You, the Follower of the Way Right Now before My Eyes Listening to the Dharma (*Mokuzen genkon chōbō-tei no hito*); 1 September 1963
10. Independent of All Things (*Mono ni yorazushite idekitare*); 3 September 1963
11. Not at all Thus (*Sō ni fuyomo*); 5 September 1963

Forty-ninth FAS retreat:
12. I Do Not Pay Homage to the Buddha or the Founding Teacher (*Busso tomo ni raisezu*); 17 December 1963
13. True Insight (*Shinshō no kenge*); 19 December 1963
14. The Meaning of the Founder's Coming from the West (*Soshi-seirai no i*); 21 December 1963

Fiftieth FAS Retreat:
15. The Three Vehicles' Twelve Divisions of Teachings (*Sanjō jūni-bunkyō*); 1 April 1964
16. The Instant You Open Your Mouth You're Already Way Off (*Kuchi o hirakaba mokkyōshō*); 3 April 1964
17. No Dividing into Categories (*Konki o hezu*); 5 April 1964

Fifty-first FAS retreat
18. The Four Classifications: A General Outline (*Shi-ryōken, 1, gaisetsu*); 1 September 1964
19. The Four Classifications: First Half (*Shi-ryōken, 2, zenhan*); 3 September 1964

Fifty-second FAS retreat:
20. The Four Classifications: Second Half (*Shi-ryōken, 3, kōhan*); 17 December 1964
21. On the Way and at Home (*Tochū to kasha to*); 21 December 1964
22. The Buddha-Dharma is Deep and Mysterious (*Buppō yūgen nari*); 23 December 1964

Based on their written notes, several people wrote out Dr Hisamatsu's talks and checked them relative to tape recordings. Kawasaki Yukio handled talks 3–7 and 18; Kimura Kiyoko, talks 8 and 11; Nemoto Katsuko, talks 9, 12, 13, 14, and 20; Ogihara Yasuko, talk 10; Imai Fujio, talks 16 and 17; Shimomura Eiji, talk 19; and myself, talks 21 and 22. I'm not sure who did it, but talks 1, 2, and 15 were transcribed by someone a while back and published in the journal *FAS*. I collated all of the manuscripts in light of the written records I kept in my notebooks. In the early stages, I also consulted transcripts of the talks made by Hamatani Yukihiko, Hoshi Masae, Doi Michiko, and Honda Masako. These transcriptions varied. Of the talks on the Four Classifications (*shi-ryōken*), for example, there were three transcriptions, each reflecting the recorder's personality. Certain recorders tried to arrange the style logically; others tried to keep Dr Hisamatsu's "voice" as they had heard it. In compiling the talks, I followed the latter approach, knowing full well that the meaning would be hard to grasp in places or repeated in complicated ways. My chief concern, though, was transmitting accurately to posterity the lively manner in which the Formless Self gave talks.

In short, by comparing the transcriptions, I tried to capture the gist of the talks. As the sayings go, "One who stays with words is lost," and "Don't consult words; consult meaning." Along these lines, I chose not to retain each and every one of Dr Hisamatsu's idiosyncratic ways of speaking. Indeed, one who clings too much to particular verbal constructions will end up "a crazy dog that runs after a clod of dirt," or "a blind mule that chases after a team."

To determine which passages in the *Record of Linji* Dr Hisamatsu was quoting, I referred to various texts. While I appreciate the scientific rigor in the new approach to reading texts that has been generated by recent developments in Chinese linguistics, what matters here is how Dr Hisamatsu read the passages. I regarded everything else as minor details in the face of the grave matter at hand, especially given that the talks emerge from the Awakening of the Formless Self as an immediate presence, which is the place to which all problems return. For example, an utterance like "This weed patch has never been spaded" has received divergent interpretations even in the traditional approach to Zen texts. Some construe the expression as indicating the absolute affirmation of the direct presence of unruly weeds. I would rather interpret it as pointing to the aspect of reality in which both persons and surroundings have been taken away, which is characteristic of Hōseki's way of being in which he is at once an extricated Linji and a vitally active Linji. This aspect is completely free from any outflowing of verbal defilement. As far as Hōseki's realm is concerned, "not taking away surroundings" is where the great functioning of "taking away surroundings" presents itself.

Restoration from the recorded tapes was first attempted by the Risōsha Publishing Company. They encountered great difficulty and with good reason. Even those of us who for thirty years have been accustomed to hearing Dr Hisamatsu's voice and are versed in his way of thinking find it extremely difficult to catch exactly what he is saying. The tapes record even the reverberating sounds of the temple bell, which, harmonizing with the spiritual voice of the *teikō*, disclose the immediate presence of *genjō-kōan*, "things just as they are, are the very cases that await immediate, ultimate solution." In this respect, the Song of the Jewel-Mirror Samadhi offered by the tapes might even surpass the written notes. The pace at which Dr Hisamatsu talks as he discriminates free from discrimination, though normally quite slow, speeds up when this words become white-hot or spout forth like water and leave human ears, and even machine ears, far behind. Not even formless ears would have any chance of keeping up.

Notes

1. FAS conveys the original True Self that is a dynamic unity of three dimensions of human existence: F, to awaken to the Formless Self; A, to stand in the standpoint of all humankind; and S, to create history suprahistorically. Hisamatsu emphasized the dynamic unity of FAS, arguing that the salvation of humankind is impossible without it.

   The FAS Society began as *Gakudō-dōjō*, "Locus for Awakening," originally a group for *zazen* practice and discussion established at Kyoto University on 8 April 1944. Membership was limited to university students under the guidance of Professor Hisamatsu. Later, when he retired, the organization opened itself up to the outside world, changing its name to the FAS Society. Currently, members meet in Kyoto for *zazen* and discussion on Saturday afternoons, for a summer seminar, for a winter retreat, and for occasional Sunday afternoon discussions. The Society has published journals in Japanese and English (discontinued respectively since November 1994 and after the 1999 issue) and a newsletter in Japanese. It supports itself financially, and it has no property. Though formerly meeting in the Myōshinji compound, these days the group meets at Shōkokuji.
2. This term refers to the calm, pre-reflective attention cultivated in seated meditation.
3. J. *Denshinhōyō*, "Essentials of Transmitting the Mind-Dharma."

Preface
Abe Masao

Goroku (Ch. *yulu*) are a unique form of Zen literature. These texts usually present discourses by a particular Zen master and a record of his life and career. This genre flourished in Tang (618–907) and Song (960–1279) China and to some extent in Muromachi (1333–1573) Japan. The discourses compiled in *goroku* are not doctrinal discussions of Zen Buddhism but vivid and direct presentations of a Zen master's existential Zen awakening.

We can approach *goroku* in at least two ways. The first is the traditional approach in the form of *teishō*, lectures or discourses delivered by a Zen master for his disciples in a Zen monastery. In a *teishō* a Zen master does not discuss or explain a *goroku* objectively as a professor might do with a text in a university lecture. Rather, through his own Zen experience the master tries to elucidate the inner realization expressed by the *goroku*. Identified with the text, he tries to revitalize its spirit while expressing his own Zen awakening. There is no room for modern rationality to enter into this approach.

The second approach is the modern one, which has been influenced by historical, linguistic, and philological methods from the Western academic tradition. Scholars who take this approach deal with the text from the outside, and privilege their approach above the existential, non-objective approach. They insist that the traditional approach, insofar as it lacks an exact reading of the text through historical and philological analysis, is apt to be subjective or dogmatic. In the last five decades the historical and philological study of *goroku* has exhibited remarkable development in Japan and the West, and revised ways of reading these texts have shed important new light on them.

Now we have a translation of Hisamatsu Shin'ichi's "Talks on the *Record of Linji*" (*Rinzairoku shōkō*). In the "Talks" we can discern the salient features of Hisamatsu's approach, which diverges from both of the above approaches. In one sense his approach is similar to the traditional way of reading the text. Paying little attention to linguistic or historical analysis, Hisamatsu emphasizes the internal, existential approach:

The way for us, as religious seekers, to respond truly to the *Record* is to seek it within ourselves. *Right now*, within us, where is it? (p. 4)

Yet Hisamatsu's approach overlaps with the second approach as well. Unlike traditional Zen masters, Hisamatsu was baptized in modern, Western ways of thinking, and his approach is in no way sectarian or anti-intellectual. Early in life Hisamatsu confronted rationality, but this confrontation did not revolve around the issue of the Western emphasis on historical and philological study of texts. Rather, he confronted the unobjectifiable, purely rational realization of the self, and as a result, in at least the following three senses, Hisamatsu's existential approach is more radical and thoroughgoing than the traditional one.

1. To Hisamatsu, the *Record of Linji* itself is beyond words and actions and is inexpressible. Nevertheless, it is presenting itself in living reality, right here and right now. In this living presentation the lecturer and the listener are completely non-dual and identical. In his talks Hisamatsu is neither a lecturer on nor a listener to the *Record*, for he is functioning as the *Record* itself.

2. To Hisamatsu, however, to be one with the *Record* does not mean to imitate Linji, but rather to get rid of him.

To study and practice Linji's Way means to free ourselves from him. His Original Face – the true Linji – must function as our own Original Face. Here, there can be no Linji, any more than there can be a Śākyamuni, Bodhidharma, or Sixth Founding Teacher. We must free ourselves from them all. (p. 5)

To be one with the *Record of Linji* is for us to become the "True Person without Rank" and display its great awakened activity.

3. In Hisamatsu, the "True Person without Rank" was realized more widely and more deeply than in the traditional approach, as evidenced by his Zen poem, "Living Linji." In this poem he advances the original True Self:

Breaking down the divine palace (theism) of medieval heteronomy, slaying the human ego (humanism) of modern autonomy, and breaking out of the old shell of conservative Zen practice, lifting up the original True Self – FAS.[1]

Now, how do you confront Linji in Hisamatsu's talks on the *Record?* How do you get rid of Linji in your encounter with him?

Note

1. Hisamatsu Shin'ichi, *Hisamatsu Shin'ichi Chosaku-shū* (The Collected Writings of Hisamatsu Shin'ichi), vol. 8, *Hasōai* (Tokyo: Risōsha, 1974; Kyoto: Hōzōkan, 1995), p. 331.

Introduction
Yanagida Seizan

Professor Hisamatsu once said, "As for the *Chuanxinfayao,* I feel like I wrote it myself." I believe that this statement is an honest expression of what he thought.

Only when we understand the author's mind thoroughly have we truly read a text, and we master the object of our reading only when we discern the author's opinions, though this does not mean that we have to accept them in their entirety. If we have not read in a way that breaks through the wall separating us from the book, we have not truly read it. Insofar as the author stands outside us, we will end up reading our own views into the text or converting blindly to those of the author. Moreover, our criticism, whether affirmative or negative, will lead nowhere; it might even result in a loss of interest on all sides, or foster arbitrary views and breed delusions. In short, we will labor in vain, generating garbage.

To engage in true criticism is not simply to offer variations on a pre-existing theme, but to pierce through the text and create a new text. At its best, such criticism generates the one argument that is decisive at a particular point in time.

In Hisamatsu's "Talks on the *Record of Linji*" we find a precedent-setting example of this way of reading classical texts. His reading is peerless, and for this reason we can justifiably deem it a model or standard. Though "standard" may connote something to be rigidly followed, something authoritative that runs the risk of becoming an object of dogmatism, Hisamatsu's talks are a liberating standard, and with their unique familiarity they pull us in.

Linji at one point exclaims, "Don't accept what I say."[1] In effect he is saying, "You mustn't take my words to heart. Don't make me into a role model!" He delivers these words nonchalantly, and in that moment there is nothing anyone can do – he has led his listeners to an aporia, to an absolute problem of life and death that cannot easily be transcended. Somehow, though, his listeners must transcend it.

If we respond to Linji's admonition literally by not accepting what he said, we will already have accepted it. Conversely, if we accept it, we will get entangled in him from the start. Whether or not we accept what he said, as long as he is outside of us we will fall into his trap. Or, more accurately, we will snag ourselves in it. Caught in a trap of our own making, we will bind ourselves in knots. If we do not transcend the opposition between self and other and stand on his side, we will fail to appreciate his words and never realize true understanding within ourselves.

From start to finish, the *Record of Linji* is filled with such dangerous traps, with treacherous devices, so we cannot afford to read this text carelessly. A "talk" in Hisamatsu's sense is the key to dismantling these devices in the text. Yet to give a "talk" is not simply to take up a section of one's choice and then offer fitting remarks. On the contrary, whatever section we examine, we must attend to the entirety of the text all at once, and discover the place of a fundamental, liberating, and completely free reading. Expressed in more extreme terms, we must write a new Zen record. To give such a "talk" is to discover the place where to read is truly to write and to write is truly to read, thus making the reader and the writer one and the same.

All books should be like this. Historically, though, writers tend to fall short of this ideal and as a result most books are not worth reading. They are garbage, "waste paper for wiping off privy filth."[2] The *Record of Linji* is an example of a book that seeks the type of reading described here, and Hisamatsu's "Talks on the *Record of Linji*" are the first Zen talks to provide it. In this respect, his "Talks on the *Record of Linji*" constitute an original *Record of Linji*. Not once since the *Record* was compiled in the Song Dynasty (960–1279) has there appeared anything comparable to Hisamatsu's reading. His are comments that "discriminate right from wrong in the past and the present."[3]

Most of the talks were delivered during retreats of the FAS Society[4] and hence they emerged under particular conditions, but they exemplify the type of reading that should be done by every person in every time and place. In clarifying the internal foothold on which one can truly read the *Record*, Hisamatsu's talks stand alone as a peerless inquiry into the text.

The *Record of Linji* consists of the statements and actions of Linji Yixuan (J. Rinzai Gigen, d. 866), and it is his "Treasury of the True Dharma Eye".[5] A Zen record is such a treasury, standing as a text of truth. Truth becomes characters and words in the form of a text. Though it is an historical work written with particular words, such a text is neither a work written on a desk in anticipation of a large, unspecified group of readers nor a record of specific historical events. Nothing conveys the creative, historical location of humanity as vividly as Zen records do. As internal documentation of one-time events, Zen records do not allow for re-enactment or comments, yet for this reason they are truly creative historical records that are available to all people and give rise to limitless comments. And on this basis translation becomes possible.

Set at Linji's temple in Hebei Province at the end of the Tang dynasty, the *Record* is made up of statements and actions by the flesh-and-blood Linji at an unparalleled time and place. For 1200 years this text had been seeking the reading Hisamatsu offered. Hisamatsu's "Talks on the *Record of Linji*" clarify for the first time the essence of the *Record* as a text of truth. His talks are no mere literary production or commentary, for as his "Treasury of the True Dharma Eye" they constitute a new record of truth and a new set of fundamental historical materials.

There is a famous black-ink painting by Liangkai (early thirteenth century) entitled "The Sixth Founding Teacher Tearing Up a Sutra." In this representative work of Zen art, Liangkai depicts Huineng (638–713) with his right hand holding a rolled sutra and his left hand tearing off strips. The painting is paired with "The Sixth Founding Teacher Cutting Bamboo." The dynamic *po-mo* ("flung ink") style of these paintings expresses Huineng's fierce vigor. From early on Hisamatsu liked these paintings, and he used them as illustrations in *Eastern Nothingness*,[6] discussed them in *Zen and the Fine Arts*,[7] and selected them as the frontpiece for the sixth volume of his collected works, which includes his talks on the *Record of Linji*.

The paintings of Huineng cutting bamboo and tearing up the sutra do not stand as materials corroborating historical facts. In a certain respect Huineng's "Treasury of the True Dharma Eye" is independent of words and eludes all recording, and Liangkai is a new type of successor who grasps Huineng's mind and reads his "Treasury." For this reason, Liangkai's paintings are comments in the true sense, and as such they constitute a new edition of Huineng's Zen record.

Huineng's tearing up of the sutras in Liangkai's painting parallels Linji's remark that one gains emancipation only by burning sutras and Buddhist images. One could offer the interpretation that what Huineng tore up was his own *Platform Sutra*, and that in cutting bamboo he provided himself with chips on which to write a new record.

Linji exclaims that the Three Vehicles' twelve divisions of teachings[8] are nothing but "waste paper for wiping off privy filth." As long as these teachings are outside us, we will never finish tearing them up. Our task, however, is not simply to make sure we have torn everything, but to give birth to things as we tear. This holds true for the internal text: when we tear we give birth to it anew. In any case, the illiterate Huineng's fierce vigor and the true reading of the Three Vehicles' twelve divisions of teachings find superb expression in Liangkai's work.

In juxtaposing Liangkai's painting of Huineng with Linji, Hisamatsu penetrates the *Record* and draws a new portrait of Linji. By "new" I mean something that had been hidden, for what is oldest and most fundamental was for the first time brought into view by Hisamatsu, and it is the foundation on which Linji becomes Linji, the fundamental reality from which Huineng becomes Huineng. From long ago it has remained unchanged, and yet it exudes eternal freshness.

The most interesting thing about reading a religious text is this process through which the foundation rises up like invisible ink brought out by heat. In contrast, books geared for general readers and writings with a strategic, proselytizing intent are usually mundane political reflections that offer quantitative treatment of the lives of self and other. They reify racial, national, and class distinctions, and though they may speak of amelioration or liberation, they are simply playing with generic concepts. Clinging dogmatically to universals and to the systems based on them, they entangle us.

The liberation of individual lives comes about only through individual efforts to slay such universals. The power of religious language finds clear expression in the devising of methods for breaking repeatedly through these systems and opening up other systems from within. A Zen record conveys this internal, individual struggle, and it precludes all generalization and generic conceptualization.

There are as many records as there are sentient beings. Certain records avoid seeking externally for universality – which is not attainable there or within – and hence can convey the wonder of conversations in which individuals call out and respond to each other. What I mean by "record," however, diverges from the self-advertisement found in the egotistic utterances and propaganda of what are commonly called records. A record in my sense of the term is a text of truth in which the author transcends and discards himself or herself and yet does not disappear. To use one of the expressions coined by Hisamatsu, a record in the true sense is a record of the Way of Absolute Subjectivity, and through this Way, comments on the *Record of Linji* become possible.

The fourteenth koan in the *Biyan-lu* collection[9] is a question-and-answer exchange (*mondō*) between a monk and Yunmen Wenyan

(864–949) of the Five Dynasties period. The monk asks, "What are the teachings of the [Buddha's] entire lifetime?" Yunmen replies, "Reciprocally to one he talks."[10] "Teachings of an entire lifetime" refers to the "elucidatory classification of facets of the teachings," as found in the classificatory scheme of the Tiantai school. This expression denotes the countless Theravāda and Mahāyāna scriptures written in India and Central Asia, translated into Chinese, and systematized by Chinese Buddhists in an effort to comprehend them as a corpus. These sutras are explanations coming from the "golden mouth" of the Buddha, and the content of each of those talks exhibits distinct individuality. One might ask where, when, and to whom the Buddha explained the Dharma over the 49 years from his Awakening to his death. Luckily, each of the scriptures provides details about where and when the Buddha gave his talks and which disciples were with him.

People have organized Theravāda and Mahāyāna scriptures, coming up with frameworks like the "Eight Teachings in the Five Periods." They have inserted Buddhist scriptures into a framework of five periods in ascending order of truth. The Buddha's exposition of his Awakening in five different periods in eight different ways has been called "exposition that is *upāya*."[11] That is to say, it was in accordance with the capability of his listeners that he framed his remarks about Awakening. Insofar as this is a matter of *upāya*, one might expect true reality to be separate from this, and in fact numerous arguments and sects have emerged from questions about whether true reality is separate from *upāya* or in some sense behind it. Be that as it may, a sect is a standpoint from which people interpret scriptures, and the creation of frameworks for organizing the Buddha's talks originates in the Chinese tradition of formulating typologies in conjunction with Confucian ethical and educational curricula. In short, while the theory of the Three Vehicles' twelve divisions of teachings originated in India as a systematization of Theravāda and Mahāyāna Buddhism, the framework of the Eight Teachings in the Five Periods was produced in China, and it contains philosophy particular to that culture.

Buddha expounded on the Dharma for nearly 50 years, and one might expect his talks to operate at increasingly high levels over time. Some people disagree, claiming that the *Avataṃsaka-sūtra*, the highest exposition, was set forth by the Buddha immediately after he attained the Way, when he talked freely about his state of mind without accommodating the capabilities of his listeners. Either way, what is deemed high is not necessarily acceptable, and what is deemed low should not be denigrated. Kind consideration operates in the low, and danger may lurk in the high.

Catalyzed by the formulation of Tiantai doctrine, Chan and Pure Land Buddhists in China initiated new schema: the notion of a "special transmission separate from doctrinal teachings" and the theory of self-power and other-power, which are both further examples of "elucidatory classification of aspects of the teachings" in a broad sense. From the standpoint of the "special transmission separate from doctrinal teachings," some argue that Śākyamuni did not expound a single word for forty-nine years, yet one of the attractive features of Chan/Zen Buddhism is how it takes the traditions of "personally settled truth [self-realization] as principal penetration," "directive truth as verbal penetration,"[12] and the "Treasury of the True Dharma Eye" as the essence of the "teachings spanning a lifetime." The conversation between Yunmen and the monk illustrates this point.

Cognizant of the Tiantai theory of the Eight Teachings, Yunmen uses the expression, "Reciprocally to one he talks," to indicate the crux of Zen Buddhism, which exists neither outside doctrinal teachings nor within them. A certain dialogue with a certain person at a certain time and place can be the gist of the Eight Teachings in the Five Periods, and one does not need to force a living dialogue into one of the periods.

The point of Yunmen's dialogue with the monk is further clarified by the expression in the fifteenth koan in the *Biyan-lu*, "Reversely to one he talks."[13] In that koan a monk asks, "When it is not about the presence of a subtle function or evidence that I ask, what do you say?" In effect the monk is asking, "Teacher, how do you conceive of the Buddha's teaching when it concerns no particular person or theme?"[14] Here he has put forth something outside the framework of teachings, something that is neither *upāya* nor true reality, and this accords with the period of the *Avataṃsaka-sūtra*. Yunmen's response strikes a clear note with its utmost freshness.

Yunmen replies, "Reversely to one he talks." This expression is hard to interpret. It appears to refer to clearing things away, to discarding in each situation the element of one-on-one in the earlier statement about "reciprocally talking to one." This is the same as Huineng's ripping up the sutra and Linji's "Don't grasp onto my words!" Yet it does not mean discarding everything abruptly; it means to clear away the approach of "reciprocally talking to one," an approach that was necessary in its proper time as a skillful means. Here we have absolute selectivity far beyond the prefabricated framework of the universal individual who does not speak for the sake of the other.

One of the interesting things about Zen records is that they defy all attempts to fit them into a preconceived framework. They can't even be fit into the framework of not fitting into frameworks. They thrive in the wonder of a vital call and response. The words in a Zen record are not a unilateral coercion upon the other, yet in the end there is no coercion this severe. They embody the knack of neither affirming nor negating.

Though both texts made their appearance after the flourishing of the classification of Buddhist teachings, the *Record of Linji* is severe while the *Record of Yunmen* is mild. Hisamatsu tried his hand at giving talks on the *Record*, and through the contrast with the *Record of Yunmen* his talks manifest the noteworthy points of the *Record*.

As a species of the commentary-based scholarship at the heart of Chinese Buddhism, classifications of the teachings are an exemplary scholarly attainment in China, and they have functioned for a long time as part of the cultivation of Chan/Zen Buddhism. They are a type of garbage, but there is no dump for them.

In the preface to *The Way of Absolute Subjectivity* (1948), Hisamatsu set forth a magnificent framework for classifying the teachings. As a metaphor for five ways of being, he wrote about five ways of entering an abyss. The first is when the person who cannot swim enters the deep water, bobs in the waves, feels joy and sadness, and then drowns. Not realizing that this will happen, the person believes unreflectively and blindly in his or her own power. With the body and the mind as negative "moments" confronting the functioning of the waves, the person drowns in the depths.

This first of five ways of being is "human-absolutism," and it is followed by nihilism, existentialism, "absolute-other-power-ism," and "critical absolute-self-power-ism." Each of the first four is overcome in the form of the next, rising up to the fifth way of being, which can also be called the Way of Absolute Subjectivity. As a religion of Awakening, this Way corresponds to Zen. Of course, Hisamatsu's scheme is not a classification in terms of sectarian doctrines, for he is establishing correspondences between the process of his own religious awakening and historical religions.

Prior to his talks on the *Record of Linji* there existed in the back of Hisamatsu's mind a system for tearing through the text, and it is only natural that the Way of Absolute Subjectivity led him to the *Record of Linji*. As the process leading to his talks on the *Record*, in lectures on such Chinese and Japanese Buddhist texts as *Chuanxinfayao*, the *Awakening of Mahāyāna Faith*,[15] the *Jinshizi-zhang*,[16] the *Vimalakīrti-nirdeśa-sūtra*, the *Zhao-lun*,[17] and the *Kyōgyō-shinshō*,[18] Hisamatsu talked "reciprocally" and "reversely" to his audience.

It was not without reason that Hisamatsu said that he felt that he had written the *Chuanxinfayao*. This text is the recorded sayings of Huangbo Xiyun, and under this teacher Linji awakened to his "treasury of truly awakened eyes." The *Record* is seen as a set of subjective comments on Huangbo's text, which is a kind of *ur*-text for the *Record*. Based on textual and historical analysis, however, I have concluded that the *Chuanxinfayao* is a set of comments on the *Record*, but this discussion will have to wait for another occasion.

The sixth volume of Hisamatsu's collected writings, which contains his *teikō* on the *Record*, has a distinctive character not found in the other volumes. It seems to consist of internal material, Hisamatsu's inner sanctum *vis-à-vis* Zen records. These *teikō* were given with meticulous care, either as lectures in his classroom at Kyoto University or as talks at retreats of the FAS society. They have been reconstructed on the basis of notes taken by his listeners, almost all of whom were new to the material. The transcribers were students conversant with the terminology and ideas of modern Western philosophy but with no background in classical Chinese texts. By directly talking to one "reciprocally" and "reversely" for his audience, Hisamatsu gave his talks.

The use of Chinese texts for traditional Buddhist scriptural talks has been a common practice in all East Asian Buddhist sects, so what Hisamatsu did was in no respect rare. In the case of Zen, talks called *teishō*[19] have their own unique flavor and they can be quite interesting, but more often than not they tend to impose dogma and offer arbitrary solo performances that have few rivals for banality. Though one might expect them not to get entangled in texts, Zen talks end up being little more than rearrangements of religious technical terms. This holds true for scriptural talks in other sects as well. Indeed, regardless of the sect, many talks have been cruel linguistic prisons that allow no escape. Nothing has surpassed their tediousness. And given the atheistic bias in contemporary education and curricula, which shy away from classical Chinese texts, it is not surprising that the general audience has a difficult time understanding Buddhist texts, not to mention talks given about them.

From 1936 to 1937 Hisamatsu used the *Awakening of Mahāyāna Faith* as his text for Buddhist Studies lectures in the Faculty of Letters at Kyoto University. Drawing from the "theology of crisis" and existentialism, which were cutting-edge theoretical approaches in European philosophy of religion at the time, Hisamatsu gave a reading of this text from a theoretical standpoint that diverged from historical and philological methodologies. Scholars working on this text had tended simply to contribute further theoretical interpretations to the debate about whether the text was composed in India or in China, but Hisamatsu's lectures began with an admonition against the imposition of preexisting sectarian dogmas and proposed new "eyes for reading sutras." Other Buddhists had talked about "eyes for reading sutras," but from Hisamatsu's mouth this notion had a fresh, captivating ring to it, for he offered a subjective interpretation not found in the domain of ordinary words and ideas.

It was Hisamatsu's understanding that to possess eyes for reading sutras is to stand in – and fully know – the standpoint of the active expression of Buddhism. This is no simple task. Without these eyes, one cannot achieve an internal understanding, and one will unavoidably remain stuck on the outside. From Hisamatsu's perspective, if what we focus on remains "over there," we will never attain true understanding, and for this reason "over there" must become "here." In terms of the internal understanding of the *Awakening of Mahāyāna Faith*, for "over there" to become "here" is for one to awaken to true suchness: *tathatā*. Expressed in terms of ignorance (Skt. *avidyā*), for "over there" to become "here" is for the completely objectified *tathatā* to become subjective by means of "attained awakening" (J. *shikaku*). This point seems to be lost on contemporary Buddhologists. Further, even if one somehow comprehends the text internally, one has simply grasped what it is and has not clarified its significance and value. Such evaluation belongs to the criticism of what is. But what sort of standpoint is most valid for this criticism? *The Awakening of Mahāyāna Faith* is not something criticized but, rather, that which does the criticizing. It stands in the standpoint of the absolute and becomes the subject doing the criticism, not the object criticized.

Hisamatsu articulated this stance in his lectures, which were compiled later in *Problems Posed by the Awakening of Faith*. With the passage of time, some of his absolutist statements have come to concern me a bit, but running through Hisamatsu's scholarship is the method of becoming the subjective agent of the text and criticizing it from within, and I dare say that this method is built upon the *Record*. Hisamatsu reads the *Awakening of Mahāyāna Faith* on the basis of the *Record*, and with this approach he regards them as fundamentally one and the same expression.

Compared with the *Record*, the *Awakening of Mahāyāna Faith* is rather theoretical and hence lends itself to a theoretical reading. If we get caught up in issues surrounding its complicated genesis – such as who wrote it, whether or not it is a translation from a Sanskrit original, and how it has been studied by specialists – we will fail to delve into the text itself. It would be wiser to cast such issues aside and dive straight into the content, which is much more crucial to understanding the text. In turn we will gain a more authoritative voice concerning such external issues as authorship, translations, and the history of research on the text.

It is exceedingly difficult, however, to penetrate the content of the *Record*. We cannot engage in theoretical examination of the "Discourses" and question–answer (*mondō*) sections without considering the leading actor: Linji Yixuan. In the *Awakening of Mahāyāna Faith*, the structure of attained awakening, original awakening, *tathatā*, and ignorance are expounded theoretically. We can perhaps say that the Path to which one awakens is quite evident, but there is, of course, a trap here, for if we should get caught up in a discussion of an absolute structure we will not be able to extricate ourselves. We can, however, take precautions to distinguish the method and the goal. In the case of the *Record*, awakening to *tathatā* is, as always, crucial, but this alone does not constitute a reading of the text. Linji's "true person" is no mere *tathatā*. From within the true person Linji leaves the true person, exhorting his audience, "Do not get caught up in my words." In this regard, there is a particular way of reading the *Record*.

The *Awakening of Mahāyāna Faith* is a treatise but the *Record* is a Zen record. It is the Zen record of Zen records, for it is "solitarily emancipated" and "non-dependent," and it negates theorizing. With no text are the "eyes for reading sutras" as important.

Among the texts taken up by Hisamatsu in the sixth volume of his collected writings, the *Awakening of Mahāyāna Faith* stands at a somewhat introductory level. In terms of the Tiantai classificatory scheme, it probably belongs to the period of scriptures expounding the original teaching (*Āgama-sūtras*). At best, it belongs to the period of scriptures of great extension (*Vaipulya*). The *Awakening of Mahāyāna Faith* has exhausted all theories and broken through them, but it does not expound anything further. The *Record of Linji*, in contrast, springs forth from the point of that breakthrough. This is evident in "this [high] seat," which is the eye for reading sutras and at the same time a negation of taking the high seat to give a talk in the monastery; "this seat" expresses the one-on-one response to each person "right before your eyes listening to the Dharma." It puts on various clothes and takes them off. It is Linji's kind concern, a circumspect preparation for awakening others.

Hisamatsu laid a groundwork for his talks on the *Record* in one other way as well. He read the *Record* in light of Huangbo's *Chuanxinfayao* (*Essentials*), using the method he had followed since his examination of the *Awakening of Mahāyāna Faith*. So when he said he felt it was he who had written the *Essentials*, he was not saying this on some general, theoretical basis but rather in anticipation of his talks on the *Record*, something for which he had prepared over many years.

Huangbo's *Essentials* is a record of Peixiu's questions about the Dharma in Zhongling and Wanling. Editing has given the text a theoretical orientation and hence has made it a basis on which one can read the *Record* theoretically. (As I wrote earlier, it is my tentative conclusion that the *Essentials* was compiled after the *Record*, for the *Essentials* amounts to a commentary on the *Record*.) Because people disliked its theoretical bent, the *Essentials* was not read much, but in some respects, the *Essentials* and the *Record* should be read as two sides of a coin. At the very least, one cannot ignore the *Essentials* in research on the *Record*.

During the 50 years since the war, historical and philological work on the *Record* has generated impressive results in European Asian Studies. While there are several translations of the *Essentials*, the *Record* is exceedingly difficult to translate, in large part because of its colloquialisms. Recently, however, research on colloquialisms as one distinctive characteristic of Zen literature has made great strides. The purpose of this research is to investigate *how* things are written, a stage of inquiry prior to determining *what* is written and what the standpoint of the text might be.

The life blood of texts is language, and we must not force living language into our theoretical molds. As indicated by the expression, "Imitating meaning is easy, but imitating the form [of words] is difficult," we must return to the origin of active expression and intuit the form of living language. When we translate into a modern, foreign language the spoken vernacular that was written down in classical Chinese, what matters most is preserving the original nuance. To find appropriate renderings we must grasp the living whole, which includes the form, structure, sound, and smell of the original.

Unexpectedly, the way of subjective understanding instituted by Hisamatsu was generating similar results in what appears to be a completely different realm of scholarship. By this I mean Paul Demieville's

French translation and Ruth Fuller Sasaki's English translation of the *Record*, as well as the treatment of the *Record* by the first-rate Zen man Suzuki Daisetsu in his English writings. These scholars pulled from broader research on East Asia to generate a way of reading the *Record* that differs from the traditional Japanese rendering of classical Chinese.

Distinct postwar international interest in the *Record* as a representative foundational text of Zen Buddhism guided many of these efforts. These scholars clearly recognized that in rendering the text in a foreign language they could not ignore the results of philological and historical research, and that genuine philological and historical findings inevitably amount to something subjectively engaged (*shutaiteki*) and internal. Now that Hisamatsu's lectures on the *Record* have been translated into English, people are afforded a valuable opportunity to realize that textual research on the *Record* is ultimately inseparable from subjective, internal understanding of the text.

I happen to have been deeply involved in these international efforts, and at this point I cannot avoid conveying some personal details. I was first introduced to the *Record* in April of 1940, when I entered Rinzai Gakuin Senmon Gakkō[20] in Kyoto and heard the *teishō* given by the school's president. In no way I could truly understand what was being discussed, for I was a rural boy who had not even turned eighteen. As I listened, though, I was strangely oppressed by something. I felt a fear that questioned my existence, for something in the book connected to the fate of young people under the wartime system who were graduating from school only to be sent off to battle.

Having been born the son of a priest in a Zen temple in Shiga Prefecture and feeling proud that I would become an adult via the path of monkhood, I had been familiar with the title of the *Record* since my infancy. In fact, I had left for Kyoto after receiving my father's most treasured copy of the text. With this background I listened intently to the president's talks on the *Record*, expecting to be sent into combat. At that time I did not have sufficient presence of mind to realize that Japan was transgressing against Linji's homeland and taking the lives of his fellow Chinese. Whatever sophistry one might concoct, war violates the essence of Buddhism.

I spent days alone, juxtaposing with the *Record* a famous verse from the *Hagakure*: "The Way of the warrior (*bushidō*) is to discern the fact of death."[21] I have known no other way than to push issues to their final resolution, and in my wartime struggle I accomplished something worthwhile.

In 1942, the second year of students' departure for the front, I left school. For a year I lived in a mountain monastery, listening to further *teishō* on the *Record*. In accordance with the Non-Military Personnel Service Law I returned to school as a drafted student-worker, but after becoming ill I had to quit both school and work. At that point I started studying True Pure Land Buddhism (Jōdo-shinshū) at Otani University and became familiar with Shinran's *Kyōgyō-shinshō*. Eventually, Japan's surrender brought an end to the war. Though I managed to avoid the battlefield, I led days of post-war aimlessness amidst the chaos of Japanese society, suffering the widespread material and spiritual loss of self.

The preface of Hisamatsu's *Eastern Nothingness (Tōyōteki mu)* begins with the following passage:

> A so-called pure scholar is one who engages in scholarship for the sake of scholarship and in order to become a "scholar." Of course, this goes without saying. But I did not engage in scholarship with this intention. Scholarship was neither my ultimate goal nor my original interest, for I was staking my life on a problem.

When I joined the Gakudō-dōjō[22] after the war, what Hisamatsu wrote here became a crucial matter for me. Though at Rinzai Gakuin Senmon Gakkō I had heard about Hisamatsu and read his *Eastern Nothingness*, at that time his existence was distant from mine; despite the fact that I myself was being called into question by what he had written, I had failed to notice.

Soon after the war Hisamatsu brought up words or sections from the *Record* during discussions at the Gakudō-dōjō and in Zen talks during the organization's retreats. I was struck by how his talks differed from the *teishō* of sectarian Zen masters, and I soon plunged even deeper into the organization. Over the course of about ten years with Hisamatsu and Gakudō-dōjō I was gradually able to rid myself of aimlessness.

Around that time new approaches to the *Record* were emerging. The way of reading it along the lines of the *Hagakure* began drawing critical reflection. Nishida Kitarō is said to have stated that even if all of Japan were to burn, there would still be the *Record* and Shinran's *Tannishō*. I even heard statements to the effect that Zen masters who had pulled out from foreign territories were starting their religious life anew with the *Record*. New books on the text were being published, beginning with Suzuki Daisetsu's *The Fundamental Thought of the Record of Linji*[23] and Rikukawa Taiun's *Research on Linji and the Record of Linji*.[24] Both of these works delved into the *Record* in a way that diverged completely from traditional Dharma talks.

Simultaneously, at Kyoto University's Institute for Humanistic Studies (at that time the Institute for Asian Culture), Iriya Yoshitaka was working with experts in Chinese language, literature, and philosophy to analyze the *Record* from various new angles in an effort to correct mistakes in the Japanese reading and translation of the text. Simply put, they were seeking a new reading, and their efforts resulted in a revised Iwanami Bunko edition of the *Record*. Professor Iriya's work was not limited to the *Record*, however. Grappling with the *Chuanxin-fayao*,[25] the *Dunwu-yaomen*,[26] the version of the *Shenhui-lu*[27] edited by Hu Shi (1891–1962), the *Zutang-ji*,[28] and texts discovered at Dunhuang, he pursued pioneering research into original texts that spanned the range of Zen literature. With his concentration on the early texts and his interdisciplinary methodology, Iriya carved out an impressive niche in Zen studies. Continuing to this day are related research groups involving Iriya and me that have revolved around Ruth Sasaki's Kyoto branch of the First Zen Institute of America, Friday meetings at the Institute for Zen Studies,[29] and lectures at Hanazono University.

With the international goal of creating an English translation of the *Record*, authorities from such fields as Buddhist Studies, Philology, English Literature, and Chinese Literature worked together at Ruth Sasaki's institute. Collège de France professor Paul Demieville's French translation, which was published before the Sasaki translation, derived in part from our work as well.

Influenced by Hisamatsu's subjective reading of the text and by the Iriya group's new reading of early Zen literature, I have taken up the *Record* as my life text. This book is me. I have even thought that I was born in the world to read it.

In the fall of 1961, upon the urging of close acquaintances and Professor Iriya, I published *The Record of Linji with a Japanese Rendering and Annotations*.[30] I had immersed myself in this grand project, which far exceeded my ability, through the inducement of Mujaku Dōchū's *Dredging Commentary on the Record of Linji*.[31] What Mujaku wrote had no peers in the meager sectarian research on Zen texts, and it had moved me greatly. In fact, many sections of the English and French translations are based on Mujaku's commentary.

The first Iwanami Bunko edition of the *Record*, with Asahina Sōgen Rōshi's Japanese rendering and annotations, was published in 1937. After several reprintings, it was republished in 1967 with the inclusion of our criticisms and a new colloquial translation, but the publisher decided to leave in the traditional sectarian reading. The long-desired, thoroughly revised edition with Iriya's translation and annotations did not appear until 1990, over fifty years after the first Iwanami edition.

During that period there also appeared a translation of the *Record* by Seo-ong (J. Seio), chief abbot of the Cho-gye school in the Republic of Korea.[32] Seo-ong Rōshi trained at the Myōshinji monastery, and his approach to the text is indebted to Hisamatsu's talks. Research on the *Record* has generated other noteworthy results in recent years as well.

Whether one takes the standpoint of textual studies or relies on an internal, subjective method, how is one to understand "this seat" in the early line of the *Record*, "I ... have perforce yielded to customary etiquette and taken this seat"? Though Linji restricts himself in saying, "I, this mountain monk, having no choice in the matter," the ensuing discourse on the Dharma is based on "this seat." Linji also says, "If I were to demonstrate the Great Matter in strict keeping with the teaching of the Founders' School, I simply couldn't open my mouth," and he tells his listeners that there wouldn't be any place for them to find a foothold. It is certain that he has "yielded to customary etiquette" – literally, to human feelings – and has "taken this seat." The place where human feelings and the Great Matter of the Founders' School meet halfway is "this seat." All lectures referred to as "ascending the hall" are given from "this seat."

In a manner of speaking, "this seat" is an historical frame of reference, for it cannot be found apart from our global crisis. Yet this is not simply a matter of protecting Earth or thinking aloud how we might combat pollution. We must first discern that Linji is speaking from the frame of reference of his and our current history, a history that always swells with crises, a history in which life and death are notoriously uncertain.

Separate from any differences between the textual and subjective approaches, the nature of "this seat" is a problem of the text itself that we must not overlook. Linji's statement about taking "this seat" appears late in an early version of the *Record* found in the tenth volume of the *Tiansheng guangdeng-lu*,[33] and it was moved to the beginning of the *Record* during the Song Dynasty, as seen in the version of the text compiled in 1120. In the later text all of the "discourses" on the Dharma are from "this seat." The editor of the Xuanhe Gengzi version attaches great importance to Linji's words from the high seat, likening them to the Buddha's revelation of the fundamental aspiration behind his appearance in the world. The second chapter of the

Dharma-lotus Sutra, "Skillful Means," contains the line, "All the Awakened ones make their appearances in this world only for the one great matter." Indeed, all of the doctrinal teachings set forth by Chinese Buddhist sects are directed toward this great matter. In Zen records, the *Platform Sutra* of the Sixth Founding Teacher serves as a model for later texts.

From Zen discourses on the Dharma being referred to as "ascending the hall" we get the expression, "taking the high seat to address the assembly." Having been solicited by Counselor Wang the Prefectural Governor and his subordinate officials, Linji took that seat. Yet when he says, "Today ... having no choice in the matter," he is not bemoaning a heteronomous scenario, for he has made a decision in response to a tenacious request. His words, "having perforce yielded to customary etiquette and taken this seat," constitute a verbal response that backed up his unavoidable choice in that particular time and place. One might associate this utterance with the theory of True Suchness in the *Awakening of Mahāyāna Faith*, which includes the idea of True Suchness "following conditions" (J. *zuien*).[34] But as evidenced by Linji, with the once-and-for-all impact of talking to one, either "reversely" or "reciprocally," Zen texts diverge from sutras and commentaries. The *Awakening of Mahāyāna Faith* abstracts fundamental principles from relevant facts, whereas the *Record* captures in prose a once-and-for-all fact. The language in Zen records is something to be "committed to writing while there is light."[35] And as I wrote earlier, more than *what* is written, the *way* things are expressed takes first precedence.

The expression rendered "perforce" also means to "bend," "minutely," and "entrusting oneself to events," and it indicates thoughtful consideration for others. "Yielded" indicates submission, a situation in which there are no other options and one must act decisively. Shenxiu's last words in verse consist of three characters, *qu-qu-zhi* (J. *kutsu-kyoku-choku*),[36] meaning submitting, bent, and straight. Together the first two characters refer to skillful means, while the third refers to truth.

The characters rendered "customary etiquette" literally mean "human feelings." Mountain monks in Zen have traditionally advocated withdrawing from human feelings. In his *Zhengdao-ge*, Yongjia Xuanjue (675–713) writes, "The teaching of full and immediate attainment open to everyone [Ch. *yuandun*] is free from human feelings," and in his words Yongjia gives voice to the directness that permits no compromises, the directness that gives the teaching of immediacy its character. Human feelings or customary etiquette are a secular matter, divorced from the Buddha's awakened way of being. To perforce yield to customary etiquette thus is not something "in strict keeping with the Founder's School."

As I said earlier, Linji, pressed by Prefectual Governor Wang and his officials, is backed into a corner. Without undermining the Founders' School, Linji perforce yields and takes the high seat. He is compelled to yield to their request, yet he yields without discarding the Founders' School. "This seat" is opened up to the people listening right then and there before his eyes in solitary emancipation, to all the non-attached people of the Way. Linji is able to call his listener "this person" precisely because of "this seat," and "this seat" stands face-to-face with "this person."

The indicator "this" points to unique things with a specific form in an historical and geographical context. For the present speaker Linji, however, "this" indicates only that which has extinguished all forms, the whole to which no name can be affixed. Insofar as a person or a thing remains some sort of form, the indication provided by "this" will be unnecessary. The person in "this seat" ascertains "this person" and concretely expresses it in the way ascertained. Linji speaks to "this" listener who has, without a speck of doubt, been able to receive the indicated as "this I."

Only "this I" has been able to listen truly to the Dharma. For the listener, or the reader, there is no limitation more certain than this. This "I" that is not other than "this seat" is what causes Linji to yield perforce to customary etiquette, and it excludes no one.

In a certain sense, the "seat" is alive even now because of the demonstrative "this." If "this seat" were replaced by the pronominal phrase "this one" (Ch. *zhege*) or the adverb "here" (Ch. *zheli*), Linji's statement would shift from primary concreteness to a secondary expediency, and significant changes would emerge for the listener or reader. Because this is an oral record constituted by the demonstrative "this" in its concretely active use, the living movement of Linji's words, with their infinite elasticity, is directly transmitted. Words are not sounds, and letters are not things. Reading a Zen record is, from beginning to end, a matter of "this person." And the place where we can interpret "this person" as "this I," the place where this is possible and this interpretation is certified, is none other than "this seat."

"This person" names him- or herself Hisamatsu or Sasaki. That which lectures on the *Record*, translates it, or writes comments is, in all cases, "this person." This person himself or herself comments on "this person." These comments become lectures on the *Record* through the confirmation of "this seat." Linji's statement, "Don't accept what I state," offers the ultimate ground that makes it possible to comment on this *Record*.

For example, the "Discourses" section includes the statement, "Followers of the Way, grasp and use, but never name – this is called the 'mysterious principle'" (p. 11). Linji is speaking of "this person," but the structure of this sentence in the original violates grammar. Even though there is no grammatical subject or object, there already is something self-evident to the speaker and listener. This is a sentence sufficient for tasting the distinctiveness and attractiveness of Zen records. If one were to add the grammatical subject and object when translating the text into colloquial Japanese or a foreign language, the freshness of the original would get spoiled.

Further, this sentence superbly conveys the breathing of this person as well as the secret of this seat. And one might venture to say that because things determine themselves, "this seat" leaves the domain of historical and geographical events. This was not something the governor, his subordinates, and the mountain monk Linji intentionally determined. This is a one-time-only text that determined itself.

My discussion here has gotten into a somewhat narrow inquiry into single Chinese characters and phrases. Suffice it to say that sentences in Zen records have stripped away all useless words and reveal the wonder of a vigorous style. Withstanding a thousand years of wind and snow, these transmitted sentences have their own *raison d'être*. Each character and phrase has a source and a history. Convoluted exegesis is unacceptable, for what is needed is accurate penetration of the text. In this respect, close examination of "this seat" is the key to unlocking the *Record*, and this approach ties into all parts of the whole. This holds true for both textual and subjective understandings of the text.

Until now exegesis has been directed at the Zen records re-edited in the Song period, and it tends to be crudely dogmatic. Because Song re-editing was carried out under an authoritarian state, the "Ascending the Hall" and "Opening the Hall"[37] sections were turned into prayers for the benefit of the realm and for the acquisition of merit. In this process they ended up being no different from writings by Buddhist experts on scriptural teachings. At this point in time we need to dig down to the foundation of the "Ascending the Hall" and "Discourses" sections and deepen our critical understanding.

For example, scholars have regarded Prefectural Governor Wang Changshi (literally, mounted aide-de-camp to his majesty) as Wang

Jingchu, who practiced under the Zen figure Weishan Lingyou (771–853). But much of the relevant data and interpretations were appended to the historical record in later periods. Further research has revealed that Wang Jingchu lived in Xiangzhou, was never called the prefectural governor, and had no connection to the prefecture of Zhenzhou. The person who set Linji up in his monastery was a member of the Wang family who was serving as the "governor" of that region. Though referred to as a "governor," he was a commander stationed in that area with military duties and responsibility for civil and financial administration. Beneath him were various aides, who out of respect called him "governor."

At that time Zhenzhou was also called Zhenfu, and it was one of the three garrisoned prefectures in Hebei. From the mid-Tang these prefectures were granted substantial power by the central government with an eye toward defending against "northern barbarians." As central control weakened, the commanders could exercise power in that region as they wished.

The title "chief of mounted aides-de-camp to his majesty" is either what the prefectural commanders called themselves or a conciliatory gesture by the central government. From the beginning, there was little correspondence between name and reality. Interestingly, when Emperor Wu ordered the destruction of Buddhist images (842–45), these commanders did not comply. This is recorded with great detail in the diary of Japanese "Dharma-seeker" Ennin, who was travelling through this region on his way from Wutai to Changan.

The connection between Linji Yixuan and the "governor" of Zhenzhou is an important piece of data for ascertaining historically and geographically the "customary etiquette" of which Linji speaks. In returning to his home region of Zhenzhou and being pressed by "governor" Wang, Linji "yields to customary etiquette" and delivers the talks. Were it not for this "customary etiquette," there would be no *Record of Linji*.

According to the section of the *Transmission of the Lamp* (*Jingde chuandeng-lu*) about Linji (no. 12), he received permission to leave Huangbo and, after making a pilgrimage to the Chan Founder's Tower in Xionger, returned to his native village. There, upon the request of a person from what was called Zhao, he gave in and took up residence at the Linji (ford-facing) Chan Temple south of the capital of Zhenzhou. The reference in the *Zutang-ji*[38] is short, and the section in the *Song gaoseng-zhuan*[39] is the same as that in the *Transmission of the Lamp*. Linji was a native of Nanhua in the province of Cao, and this area of

Huabei was all part of Zhenzhou prefecture. The expression, "Zhaoren," a native of Zhao, is an old appellation for people of this area, and it is an appropriate way of referring to the Wang clan of Zhenzhou.

Under Emperor Wu's policy of destroying Buddhist images, Buddhism was crushed in many regions. Linji gave in to a Zhaoren's request and adopted a new Zen temple in Zhenzhou, whose images had been smashed, sutras burned, and monks driven away. From a place that was literally "no Buddha," "no Dharma," and "no Sangha," Linji's Buddha-Dharma was born. In reality, the true Buddha has no figure, the true Dharma has no form, and the true Way has no substance.

Eventually, during the civil war of the Five Dynasties period following the Tang, the Linji Chan Temple disappeared without a trace; it was a fleeting "town that was made to appear through a supernatural faculty [by a guide for encouraging his exhausted pilgrims on the way to their true destination]."[40] As a Dharma hall that was a temporary shack, it was appropriate for the mountain monk's "ascent of the hall."

In old versions of the *Record* one encounters the rare expression, "a blind shave-pate soldier" (rather than the more usual "blind shave-pates"), as well as the statement, "You can't tell good from bad, you old shave-pate soldier!" It seems that a shaved-headed person is improvising there. Judging from its location in the famous section of the *Record* on the fourfold relations between guest and host, the blind shave-pate soldier is something found more widely than only at the Linji Chan Temple. To that person, Linji calls out "Great Virtue" and expounds on his "Treasury of the True Dharma Eye." Linji also says, "You bald idiots, what's the frantic hurry to wrap yourselves in lion's skins while you're yapping like jackals?!" (p. 36). It is unfortunate that in later texts those words, "a blind shave-pate soldier," are edited out, for with those words Linji is expressing the awakened eyes of the Way as he cuts through all delusion.

In the "Critical Examinations" section of the *Record*, Governor Wang visits Linji and in front of the Monks Hall asks, "Do the monks of this hall read sutras or practice *zazen*?" He prompts Linji to make a remark to the effect that they neither read sutras nor practice *zazen* but become buddhas and founding teachers. In response Wang then criticises Linji, saying that even valuable gold-dust can be blinding in the eyes (p. 45). This criticism from Wang is a severe comment on Linji's Buddha-Dharma, and it is interesting that in later periods Linji is criticized as "an old shave-pate soldier of Jibei."

In the "Discourses" section Linji reflects on his past days of practice and tells the Followers of the Way, "If you want insight into Dharma as it is, just don't be taken in by others" (p. 25). He continues,

> Whatever you encounter, either within or without, slay it at once. On meeting a buddha, slay the buddha; on meeting a founding teacher, slay the founding teacher; on meeting an arhat, slay the arhat; on meeting your parents, slay your parents; on meeting your kin – slay your kin – only then do you attain emancipation. By not cleaving to things, you freely pass through.

The buddhas, founding teachers, and arhats are ideal renunciates, and proper etiquette toward parents and kinfolk is the foundation of Confucian ethics. Yet from Linji's perspective, the buddhas, founding teachers, arhats, parents, and kinfolk represent people who deceive you. All of the cultural values created by humankind can turn themselves into such delusion. The slaying of buddhas and founding teachers is not advocated because they lack or run contrary to values. Rather, because they have value they ensnare people. Linji views all of these objects of value as contrivances of the ancients, as useless devices, in short, as large-scale garbage. People refer to the crane device that the first Qin emperor used to build the Great Wall as a "Qin-period wheelworking drill," useful at the time but useless thereafter. Failing to grasp this point, people have made the buddhas and founding teachers into ostensibly valuable "things."

As I said above, because of Emperor Wu's persecution and a short-sighted civil war, temples and pagodas were burned and the Three Treasures – the Buddha, Dharma, and Sangha – were dealt a crushing blow. In all cases the things destroyed were Linji's "buddhas with form" (p. 32), the "methods of [spiritual] adornment" (p. 33), and the "aids to the Buddha's work" (p. 33). The Buddha-Dharma that has turned into a "thing" cannot reform itself through ordinary means. Though in most respects destruction is not something desirable, Linji rather welcomed the destruction of such things. As he said, to attain True Insight one must not be taken in by others, and this destruction is a perfect way to avoid entanglement. Of course, the motive for destroying images of buddhas was external to the perpetrators, and to that extent they could not transcend the destruction of images. Linji, on the other hand, transcends history and creates history.

The majority of religions have already turned into "things," and for this reason the meaning of Linji's "on meeting a buddha, slay the

buddha" is especially important. Masutani Fumio (1902–87) once commented that the one thing we must do is to break our attachment to
buddhas and founding teachers, and even if we cut them they will not
bleed.[41] This interpretation is the epitome of being taken in by others,
for he has set forth an outrageous misunderstanding. Linji is telling us
to slay the buddhas and founding teachers to which we are attached,
not to stop being attached to them. And he is not saying that the Five
Grave Sins – killing one's father, killing one's mother, injuring the
body of a buddha, killing an arhat, and causing disunity in the sangha
– are somehow expatiated and purified by Zen samadhi. Linji's thought
is totally different from religious traditions based on notions of salvific
figures functioning especially for evil people or saving people from
sinful karma. Of all the people who have ever offered interpretations of
the "Discourses" section, in all likelihood the only one who correctly
read it is Hisamatsu. Everyone else has lost sight of the *Record's* line of
thought, which cannot be replaced by or equated with the dogmas of
other historical religions.

At one point Linji exclaims, "Virtuous monks, generating the karma
of the Five Grave Sins, you attain emancipation" (p. 35). At one point
in the *Record* (pp. 35–6) Linji expounds on the Five Grave Sins and sets
forth an interpretation that diverges from others, such as the interpretation found in the *Laṅkāvatāra-sūtra*.[42] Hisamatsu states,

> All things are slain together when the Formless Self presents itself.
> Such is true, immediate Awakening, the Self-Awakening of the
> Formless Self. People who emphasize only negation teeter on the
> brink of utter darkness. And those who speak of affirmation in the
> usual sense are merely affirming things within and without. The
> true affirmation, on the other hand, is that which has thoroughly
> negated all things. It is the true insight into the Dharma as it is. It
> has eliminated all confusion caused by others and all perplexity
> about the Buddha.[43]

As his death approached, Professor Hisamatsu made much of the
expression, "Slay the buddha, slay the founding teacher." In a certain
sense, Hisamatsu's life was none other than his talks on the *Record*, and
these talks were formulated to culminate in "Slay the buddha, slay the
founding teacher."[44]

This reminds me of Senior Monk Fu of Taiyuan,[45] who at the last
moment of his life lectured on the *Mahāpārinirvāṇa-sūtra* in repayment
for his patron's kindnesses, ascended the platform, and entered

nirvana. As I unexpectedly stood beside Hisamatsu's deathbed, I saw that, as an external event which took place at a particular place and time, his "Talks on the *Record of Linji*" had ended long ago.

"I will not die." Professor Hisamatsu repeatedly said this, and, for people as dimwitted as I, he repeatedly lectured on the *Record*, even though he had already finished what he had to say about it. Toward the end of the war, in a small seminar on the *Shōji* (living-dying) fascicle of Dogen's *Shōbō-genzō*, Hisamatsu was already proclaiming *Mushōji*, no-living-dying.

When his talks on the *Record of Linji* began in 1962, he was already 73 and I was 40. As I now approach the age he was then, I think back fondly to all the favors and patronage I have received.

No-living-dying!
My teacher, Hisamatsu-Hōseki.

27 February 1992[46]

Notes

1. *The Record of Lin-chi*, tr. Ruth Fuller Sasaki (Kyoto: Institute for Zen Studies, 1975), p. 37; *Taishō shinshū daizōkyō* (hereafter *Taishō*), ed. by Takakusu Junjirō and Watanabe Kaigyoku (Tokyo: Taishō Issaikyō Kankōkai, 1924–1932), 47:502. Henceforth, all page numbers will refer to the Sasaki translation, portions of which have been adapted here.
2. At one point in the *Record*, Linji uses this expression in reference to Buddhist teachings, to the "worthless names" that the people in the assembly take to be real. *The Record of Lin-chi*, p. 21.
3. This expression appears in a commentary by Shandao (J. Zendō, 613–81), a Chinese Pure Land Buddhist, on the *Sutra on the Contemplation of Amitāyus* (see p. 154, n. 73).
4. For the FAS Society, see pp. xxi, n. 1.
5. This expression (Ch. *zhengfa-yanzang*, J. *shōbō-genzō*) appears first in a Chan record, the *Baolin-zhuan* (J. *Hōrinden*, compiled in 801 CE), which in one section describes how the Buddha, facing his death, turns to Mahākāśyapa, a disciple who has realized the "treasury of the true Dharma eye," and tells him that after the Buddha's death he should transmit this "treasury" to later generations. Cognate expressions in that text include the "true Dharma," "Dharma eye," "true Dharma-eye" "clean and pure Dharma-eye," "unsurpassed Dharma-eye," and the "treasury of the great Dharma-eye." The expression may be construed as connoting "awakened nirvana." It was adopted as the title of a collection of Chan/Zen koans by Dahui Zonggao (J. Daie Sōkō, 1089–1163), and it is the title of the magnum opus of Dōgen Kigen (1200–53).
6. *Tōyōteki mu* (Tokyo: Kōbundō Shobō, 1939).

7. *Zen to bijutsu* (Kyoto: Bokubisha, 1958); English translation by Tokiwa Gishin (Tokyo: Kodansha International, 1971).
8. This expression refers to the range of doctrinal teachings in Buddhism.
9. See p. 147, n. 39.
10. Ch. *dui-yi-shuo*, J. *tai-issetsu*. Cf. *Yunmen guang-lu, Taishō* 47:545c. Master Yunmen was renowned for his brief response to any questioner, and in the present case the three characters *dui-yi-shuo* seem to be the key to understanding him.
11. "Skillful means" used by a bodhisattva to lead sentient beings to Awakening.
12. Ch. *zong-tong* and *shuo-tong*; J. *shūtsū* and *settsū*. These expressions derive from the *Laṅkāvatāra-sūtra*.
13. Ch. *dao-yi-shuo*, J. *tō-issetsu*. Cf. *Yunmen guang-lu, Taishō* 47:550b.
14. The *Yunmen guang-lu* records the master's words in the following context:

   Questioner: "How can I realize the single path of the subtle function?"
   Master: "Thirty years later."
   Q: "The coffin [upon cremation] had both of the [Buddha's] insteps shown. What was this to express?"
   M: "[His] words."
   The questioner advanced and asked: "I wonder what you mean [by his words]?"
   M: "Tighten your sandal strings."
   Q: "What will it be when what I seek is neither a subtle function nor evidence?"
   M: "*Dao-yi-shuo*."

15. Ch. *Dasheng-qixin-lun*, J. *Daijō-kishin-ron*; though no longer extant in its Sanskrit original, the apparent Sanskrit title was *Mahāyāna-śraddhotpāda-śastra*.
16. An exposition of Huayan philosophy along the lines of the image of a gold lion; by Fazang (643–712).
17. The first major exposition in China of key Buddhist concepts; by Seng Zhao (384–414), a disciple of Kumārajīva.
18. A collection of passages on Pure Land Buddhist teaching, practice, faith, and realization; by Shinran (1173–1262).
19. See p. xv.
20. Now Hanazono University.
21. The *Hagakure* ("hidden under leaves"; 1716) is a compilation of talks on the warrior ethos.
22. See p. xxi, n. 1.
23. *Rinzairoku no kihon-shisō* (Tokyo: Chūōkōronsha, 1949).
24. *Rinzai to Rinzairoku no kenkyū* (Tokyo: Kikuya Shoten, 1949).
25. The aforementioned *Essentials of Transmitting the Mind-Dharma*.
26. J. *Tongo-yōmon*; by Dazhu Huihai (n. d.), a disciple of Mazu Daoyi.
27. J. *Jinne-roku*.
28. J. *Sodōshū*.
29. At Hanazono University.
30. *Kunchū Rinzairoku* (Kyoto: Kichūdō, 1961).
31. *Rinzairoku-soyaku*. Mujaku's dates are 1653–1745.
32. Edited by Lee Chong-ki and published by Aoyama Shoin in 1978.

33. J. *Tenshō kōtōroku* (compiled in 1036).
34. In *Dacheng-qixin-lun-yiji*, his commentary on the *Awakening of Mahāyāna Faith*, Fazang (643–712) explains the meaning of the "Rising-Perishing Division" as "following conditions," and he interprets it as "undergoing the beginningless perfuming of discrimination and becoming either contaminated or purified."
35. A line by Bashō (1644–94), recorded by Hattori Tohō, one of his disciples, in the *Kuro-zōshi*.
36. This appears only in the *Leng-ga-shi-zi-ji* (J. *Ryōga-shiji-ki*, "Record of the *Laṅkā* [-*avatāra-sūtra*] Teachers and Disciples"), compiled 713–16 by Jingjue (J. Jōkaku, 683–750?). According to this record, on 28 February 706, Master Shenxiu (J. Jinshū) died in the lotus posture without any signs of disease, leaving the three words as his will. Cf. Yanagida Seizan, *Shoki no Zenshi* (The Early History of Chan), *Zen no goroku*, vol. 1 (Kyoto: Chikuma Shobō, 1971), pp. 302 and 305.
37. *Kaitang* (J. *kaidō*), a ceremony in a Chan/Zen monastery in which a newly-appointed head priest "opens the lecture hall" for the purpose of giving talks on the Dharma.
38. J. *Sodōshū* (Kyoto: Chūbun, 1972), p. 362b.
39. J. *Sō kōsōden*, "Song Records of Eminent Buddhist Priests," vol. 12. *Taishō* 50: 779ab.
40. Skt. *ṛddhi-mayaṃ nagaram idaṃ vinirmitam*. This expression appears in the *Dharma-lotus Sutra*, chapter 7, verse 101d; *Taishō* 9:27a.
41. Masutani Fumio, *Bukkyō ni okeru Zen no ichi* (The Position Zen Occupies in Buddhism), *Kōza: Zen*, vol. I (Chikuma Shobō, 1967), pp. 72–3.
42. The *Laṅkāvatāra-sūtra*, ed. by Nanjio Bun'yū (Kyoto: Otani University Press, 1923), pp. 138–40. According to this Mahāyāna sutra, as conveyed in the recent translation by Tokiwa Gishin, who follows the Guṇabhadra Chinese version (*Taishō* 16:498b), those who have committed one of the five grave sins will have no way to escape the fruits of the transgression except when they come to realize ultimate truth through a good guide. Help will come to the transgressor who repents of the transgression – and, because of the repentance, cannot even move – if the person happens to meet an Awakened one or any "listener to the Dharma" (*śrāvaka*) or bodhisattva under the influence of an Awakened one. Then the person will realize the true way of reality and gain the confidence to face reality. This is what this text expounds about the "external five grave sins."

Just before this section, the sutra introduces the "internal five grave sins," the committing of which constitutes the attainment of ultimate Awakening: 1. Accompanied by joy and passion, desire, which leads one to rebirth, is active with motherhood; it is the mother of all beings. 2. Ignorance is active with fatherhood, in having a group of objects and faculties of perception arise as one's own. To sever completely the roots of both the mother and the father is to kill the mother and father. 3. Dormant passions resemble enemies (*ari*); they tend to cause violence like poisons caused by rat bites. Completely exterminating (*han*) them is the killing of the arhat (the "most worthy" among the sangha members). 4. The total being, which is made up of the five aggregates (*skandhas*), is not immune to being broken apart. The complete breaking apart of this being is called causing schism in the monastic order. 5. The seven discerning faculties or buddhas (eyes, ears, nose, tongue, body, consciousness, and ego) do not realize that what is external is nothing but one's own mind seen as such. When the seven buddhas are killed with an apparent wickedness that is actually free from passion, that is, with the threefold emancipating insight into voidness, formlessness, and wishlessness, blood is shed on the body of the *tathāgata* (the Thus Come, i.e., Buddha) with "wicked intent."

The concept of the internal five grave sins seems to have originated with the inception of the Māhāyana movement in India as something most characteristic of that movement. We know that in the eleventh chapter of the *Dharma-lotus Sutra* Śākyamuni announced that Devadatta taught him the Dharma-lotus truth in a former life. In the Theravāda tradition Devadatta had been blamed for transgression of the latter three of the five grave sins, and he had been regarded as having pushed Ajātaśatru toward committing patricide. Although this Māhāyana scripture remains silent about the contents of the Dharma-lotus truth, we can determine from various sources that what Devadatta is said to have taught in the former life was the internal five grave sins. (Cf. Tokiwa Gishin, "The Dharma-Lotus Truth Expounded by Devadatta," *Journal of Indian and Buddhist Studies*, 46/1 (December 1997), pp. 30–6.)

There is no doubt that when Linji and Hisamatsu used the expression, "slay the buddha and slay the founding teacher," both of them meant internal killing. They emphasized this to help people free themselves from not only worldliness but unworldliness as well.

43. See p. 54.
44. As his final words Dr. Hisamatsu left in handwriting, "Slay Buddha, slay God."
45. J., Taigen Fu-jōza, n.d., a disciple of Xuefeng Yicun (J. Seppō Gison, 822–908). Fu was a lecturer on the *Māhāyana Mahāpārinirvāna-sūtra* (*Nirvana Sutra*). While lecturing on the sutra, he was criticized by a Chan practitioner for being ignorant of what the *dharma-kāya* (i.e., nirvana that awakens to itself) really was, and as a result he devoted himself to *zazen* practice. While doing *zazen* he awakened, and at that point he went to Master Xuefeng. He kept practicing with the master and other brother disciples and never accepted any invitation to serve as a master himself. He remained there as an honored, senior-monk practitioner.

Later he left Master Xuefeng's monastery and returned to his native province of Yangzhou, where he stayed in Minister Zhen's household. The latter offered him respectful service, and one day Fu told the minister that the next day he would lecture on the whole text of the *Nirvana Sutra* so that he might repay the other's kindnesses.

The following day Minister Zhen prepared a special meal for the senior monk. After tea the senior monk ascended the high seat. He kept silent for a while, and then he swung down a ruler, saying, "Thus have I heard." He then called, "Minister."

The latter responded. The senior monk said, "At a time the Buddha," whereupon his life was gone. (*Liandeng huiyao* (J. *Rentō-eyō*), ch. 24, in *Zoku-zōkyō*, vol. 136 (Taipei: Xinwenfeng Press, 1977), p. 845a.) This story reveals that Senior Monk Fu's whole life was the *Nirvana Sutra*.

46. Professor Yanagida completed his manuscript on this day, the twelfth anniversary of Hisamatsu's death.

Zen Talks on the *Record of Linji*

1

I Simply Couldn't Open My Mouth

Today I will begin my talks on the *Record of Linji*. As you know, this record relates the sayings and actions of the Zen master Linji Yixuan[1] as compiled by his disciple Sansheng Huiran.[2] It has a long and well-established reputation for being quite impenetrable. We won't possibly be able to examine all of it during this retreat.

The meaning of the *Record of Linji* isn't something that ends with such outward expressions as words or actions. As Linji says at the beginning of the text,

> If I were to demonstrate the Great Matter in strict keeping with the teaching of the Founders' School, I simply couldn't open my mouth.[3]

Neither words nor actions can adequately express it. And yet, without my uttering a single word or making the slightest movement, it is now manifesting itself in all of its majesty, so it really doesn't matter whether I can cover all of the *Record* during this retreat or not. It is *immediately present truth*, beyond all words and actions. From this truth, Linji's record comes into being.

No matter how many words I use during these talks, if I rely only on verbal exposition, I will not truly lecture on Linji's record and you will not hear it. Only when our Original Face emerges and speaker and listener are one, does true speaking and listening take place. At that point, there is neither speaker nor listener. Linji often addresses his disciples as "You who are listening to the Dharma" (p. 7).[4] It can be said here that the *You* who is listening is the *I* who is uttering the words. This is not a question of a long, seven-day retreat: it is right here, right now. Linji then says, "I have unavoidably yielded to what people desire of me and have taken this seat for

3

preaching" (p. 1). This reveals his constant concern with going into the world for the benefit of others.

Linji's action is apt to be mistaken for mere expedient means – his descending to a secondary level to preach. But, in terms of the Original Face, the True Self, or what Linji calls the "True Person without Rank," all of Linji's words and actions are the great dynamic functioning[5] of the True Person. We must not think of them as mere expedients.

Moreover, all of Linji's words, without exception, are at the same time the words of "You who are listening." Viewing Linji's actions externally as *his* actions, or hearing his words as *his* words, is contrary to the way of being of "You who are listening." The listener and Linji are never two; none of Linji's statements or actions is other than the dynamic function of "You who are listening." Only when this oneness is achieved is the *Record of Linji* truly lectured on and truly heard.

When an authentic seeker of the Way reads or listens to Zen records, he or she doesn't get caught up in the written words or in the matter they relate. It is possible for us to grasp Linji's entire *Record*, in the fullest sense, by means of just one of its words or phrases. For example, he says, "I simply couldn't open my mouth." Right here, in this very utterance, Linji's True Person without Rank is manifesting itself. But, if we take this statement at face value, we miss the authentic sense in which it is uttered.

What does Linji mean when he says, "I simply couldn't open my mouth"? He doesn't only mean that the Dharma cannot be expressed in words. It is his True Face magnificently revealing itself right there. This "I couldn't open my mouth" is "You who listen," the True Person without Rank. Linji's great emancipatory functioning emerges from within this "I couldn't open my mouth," filling every page of the *Record* with great vitality and life. Yet I wouldn't want this activity to be taken as something eleven hundred years old. Linji is said to have died in 867.[6] If we regard his *Record* in the manner of historians, that is, as a document of the early period of Chinese Zen, it will be a mere record of the past, and not the words and actions of our living Self here and now. The way for us, as religious seekers, to respond truly to the *Record* is to seek it within ourselves. *Right now*, within us, where is it?

Throughout the *Record*, Linji stresses that we should not seek Buddha outside ourselves. That will only take us farther from it. The "Buddha" must be Linji himself, and this "Linji" mustn't be something we seek externally. Linji is within us – there is no Linji apart from our own Original Face. Only when this is realized does the *Record of Linji* reveal itself directly as our own words and actions. If we read it literally or merely copy Linji's behavior, we are doing nothing more than an empty impersonation. What we must do is extricate ourselves from the *Record* so that the words and actions of the living Linji emerge from us.

There is a Chinese master of the Song period named Songyuan Chongyue[7] who is an important figure for Japanese Rinzai Zen. He severely condemned the Linji Zen monks of his time for memorizing Zen records and imitating the actions described in them. He denounced such blind adherence to Zen texts and koans, saying it was worlds apart from authentic Zen. This critical spirit is important for us today as well. Many aspects of modern Japanese Zen deserve to be dealt one of Songyuan's crushing blows.

The only way to make the *Record* our own is for us to become the True Person without Rank and display its great awakened activity ourselves. We can't do this by imitating Linji. We must have a constant flow of new and spontaneous activity.

To study and practice Linji's Way means to free ourselves from him. His Original Face – the true Linji – must function as our own Original Face. Here, there can be no Linji, any more than there can be a Śākyamuni, Bodhidharma, or Sixth Founding Teacher. We must free ourselves from them all. Linji's well-known "Encountering a buddha, slay the buddha; encountering a founding teacher, slay the founding teacher" (p. 25) admonishes against having anything to do with buddhas or founding teachers. We must not be attached to them. They, of all things, are most apt to restrict us and entangle us in complications. Linji tells us to transcend them, and free ourselves from attachment to them.

It is easy for us to get caught up in what we revere. We have little trouble parting from what we despise; the difficulty is in parting from what we cherish. When we lecture on Linji's *Record*, we tend to look up to him. We feel drawn to him. But as long as he is outside us, he remains an *object* of our respect and devotion. That's not the way to venerate him. He wouldn't have hesitated a moment to give us a taste of his staff.

In the famous spisode known as "The fist strikes the old father," Linji delivers a blow to his teacher Huangbo Xiyun.[8] Such an action might seem extremely undutiful, but Linji himself knew that he had finally arrived at true filial piety. If Huangbo had merely been a teacher who existed as an external presence, Linji would never have been able to become his Dharma heir. This exemplifies what Zen means by the "transmission from Mind to Mind."

We sometimes hear the expression, "Nothing brought in through the gate is family treasure." No matter how exalted a Zen master might be, insofar as he exists outside of you, he isn't your own true family treasure. It is said that "gold dust is precious, but in the eye it blinds." If Huangbo were to have existed in any form within Linji's Original Face, within the True Person without Rank, he would have been nothing but a screen over Linji's eyes. Awakening to his Original Face, Linji became "solitarily emancipated" (p. 25) and "non-dependent" (p. 14), a man who relied on nothing. If any element of him remains in us, we are not solitarily emancipated or non-dependent, nor are we the True Self in "solitary freedom transcending all things" (p. 23) – the Self as itself. We all must realize Linji in ourselves and his *Record* as our own words and actions.

2
Who Is Pure and Direct in His Behavior?

Only two days are left in this retreat. I am extremely pleased to see how you have all been practicing earnestly day and night in this intense heat. I am sorry my health has kept me from participating with you more.

Since the text for this retreat is the *Record of Linji*, the lectures have special significance. We won't be able to cover all of the text in this one week. If possible, I would like to continue at a later date. What I want to do is to take some of the central ideas found in the *Record* and relate them to the present day. The points we take up, however, don't have to be those that have been considered important in the past. In lectures such as these, the most important thing is for you to grasp Linji firmly within yourself. Only then can you begin to talk. Now, with this in mind, let us penetrate to the center of Linji's *Record*.

As I said last time, the lecturer and the listener must be one. The lecturer is the listener, the listener the lecturer. That's how we lock eyebrows directly with Linji. He must be one with our True Self at this very moment. We have to inquire into his True Self. Who is Linji? To begin, let us examine the circumstances surrounding his decision to begin Zen practice and the events involved in his great Awakening.

We are told at the end of the *Record* that he displayed exceptional intelligence in his youth. As a Zen master, his style was razor-sharp. He has been compared to a general who is able to command three armies at once. To have all things right in the palm of one's hand, and to be able to use them at will, without any hindrance, requires an exceptional wisdom. You need eyes that have penetrated the whole. You must be able to function in extraordinary ways.

The characteristics of Linji's style, then, were already in evidence in his childhood. Later in his youth, he was tonsured and ordained as a

7

monk. The *Record* tells us that he "frequented lecture halls" (p. 62). This means he was studying scholastic Buddhism, the Buddhism Zen regards as "within the scriptures." He went to temples where Buddhist lectures were being given and devoted himself to mastering the Buddhist sutras, commentaries, and monastic guidelines.

After he had done this for a while, he realized the inadequacy of his approach. He called it a "medical prescription for saving the world" (p. 62). Now most people would not find fault with such a "prescription." They would take it to be Buddhism's proper role. But Linji was deeply dissatisfied with the kind of study he had been pursuing in the lecture halls.

Dissatisfaction with the approach to Buddhism prevailing at that time was one reason Zen flourished. Deshan, a contemporary of Linji, was a great student of the *Diamond Sutra*. But he, too, discovered that scholarly investigation was not the way to understand Buddhism, and that it could in no way help him bring about any fundamental change in himself. Even supposing we are able to lecture on the *Diamond Sutra* with great skill, if that can't help us transform our way of being, then we will end up like Deshan, unable to answer even the question of an old woman at the roadside.[9]

We can't transform our way of being through objective knowledge and ideas. True transformation is impossible unless we become our True Self completely. The *Diamond Sutra* says that "The past mind is unattainable, the present mind is unattainable, and the future mind is unattainable." As long as this statement is just words to us, its true meaning – that which is unattainable in any of the three divisions of time – does not emerge as our Self. This falls short of the true goal of Buddhism. We are merely reading about the virtues of the medicine; if we don't take it, we can't cure our illness.

When Deshan was stumped by the old woman's question, he realized that his labors up to that point had been for naught. For this reason, he set fire to his precious commentaries on the *Diamond Sutra*, which he had been carrying around with him everywhere. Of course, Deshan wasn't the only one who became disillusioned with scholastic Buddhism. Countless others have, too. Many have turned to Zen beyond the teaching of written words. The dissatisfaction of Linji, Deshan, and others like them was a necessary moment in Zen's development.

The awakening of the Sixth Founding Teacher[10] occurred when he happened to hear someone reciting a passage from the *Diamond Sutra*: "One should give rise to the Mind that abides nowhere." His awakening did not result from study of the literal meaning of the text – he directly realized in himself the Mind that arises without abiding anywhere. This is his basic significance as a person of Zen.

True Zen is not a matter of "gradual awakening," in which satori comes only after we practice for millions of eons. Buddhist emancipation is manifesting itself here and now. It isn't contingent upon time or place – it can only be "present manifestation." It must be an awakening suddenly attained; not something in the future, but actual existence, right now beyond past, present, and future. "Sudden" does not mean "in a short period of time." It means "as-it-is." "As-it-is" is the true *tathatā* (suchness). This is where Zen frees itself from the practice of gradual attainment.

The Buddhist monastic guidelines (*vinaya*) teach a gradual practice. Satori is said to open up through merits accumulated by observing certain rules of behavior. We must desist from evil and practice good, and we finally arrive at Buddhahood through the constant observance of the precepts. Good and evil in this sense, of course, are not limited to their usual ethical meaning. But even so, the precepts to be observed are endless, and it is only by observing all of them that we can become buddhas. As a result, Buddha comes to be posited in the beyond, or in the future. This is radically different from saying that Buddha is the "truly so" existing right here. It is not hard to understand why Linji came to harbor doubts about the precepts and scriptures, and concluded that they were only a prescription for saving humankind, not the truth apart from the scriptures.

Zen's extra-canonical tradition was already thriving in Linji's time, and it is unlikely that his decision to abandon scriptural Buddhism was reached without knowledge of that tradition. Since the Sixth Founding Teacher's time, this "transmission outside the teachings" had become increasingly known.

The lineage of the Sixth Founding Teacher includes Nanyue Huairang,[11] Mazu Daoyi,[12] Baizhang Huaihai,[13] and Huangbo Xiyun. Linji attained satori under Huangbo, which places him several generations away from the Sixth Founding Teacher. Zen in those days produced many masters of outstanding ability. It was truly a golden age. Linji's realization of the essential importance of the "teaching transmitted apart from the scriptures," and his decision to renounce his traditional Buddhist studies in order to concentrate on Zen, occurred within such a setting. We should take an example from this. Intellectual learning affects every area of life in the present world. Scholarship, in both Japan and the West, can be said to correspond to the study that took place in the Tang dynasty lecture halls. Modern

Buddhology, while taking in new Western ways of study, has tended to follow in the footsteps of traditional Chinese methods emphasizing the doctrinal study of the different schools. Practice has become an object of research. Living practice has been all but ignored.

The only tie most modern Buddhologists have to Buddhism is their objective research. They have become strangers to practice and, because of that, to satori itself. So long as they work in this way, that which they study cannot become the total functioning of their own True Self. They are unable to investigate *tathatā* or to interpret Buddhism from within the living *tathatā*. It is not possible for us to explain it, much less live it in everyday life, if we stand outside. It is essential, then, that Buddhist scholars – scholars in all fields, for that matter – ask themselves why Linji left the lecture halls. The question, ultimately, is What solves our most fundamental problem? What is the source from which that problem arises?

By the time Linji decided to leave the lecture halls, a great doubt had emerged in him. He went to Huangbo and devoted himself single-mindedly to Zen practice. The earnestness with which he applied himself is described in the "Record of Pilgrimages" section of the *Record*: "When Linji was one of the assembly of monks under Huangbo, he was pure and direct in his behaviour" (p. 50). "Pure and direct in his behaviour" describes the Linji who had resolved to grasp, at all costs, the true meaning of Zen's "transmission apart from the scriptures."

Linji had thrown everything aside to concentrate on a life of Zen practice. He could not have been anything but "pure and direct." He wasn't after a taste of Zen or a little knowledge. His sole objective was the investigation and elucidation of what Zen calls "one's own matter." This has nothing to do with anyone else. When one is investigating and elucidating oneself, one must be deadly serious. It is occasionally said that "to enter Zen, one must enter the realm of death," or that "you can't get a tiger cub without entering the tiger's lair." These sayings, like Linji's declaration that "the person who lives for the Dharma does not shrink from sacrificing life or limb" (p. 4), all emphasize that authentic exploration of the Way is not something to be undertaken in a half-hearted manner.

We are hindered, however, by various entanglements, which can constrict us until we are unable to function. They are what Buddhism calls "karma since the beginningless beginning." This karmic net must be cut away at one stroke. To sever these entanglements from within and cast them away – for the emancipated Self to emerge – is no easy matter. Many people think such liberation is impossible. This view gives rise to pessimism. We can't extricate ourselves from our situation in our normal way of being unless we have great resolve. To reach our goal, we must lay every other consideration aside. A resolute spirit is essential.

When we first go to a Zen monastery, it is extremely difficult to obtain permission to enter the *zendō*.[14] I was fortunate in having had a good teacher. "When you go to the *zendō*," he told me, "go as if your life is at stake. If you are going to go with the half-hearted intention of living through it and returning home, then you had better not go at all." There are three essentials for *sanzen*.[15] The first is Great Faith, so strong it won't allow us to leave our practice even for a moment; we go on even if it causes our death. The second is a Great Doubting Spirit – without it, satori is impossible. The third is Great Resolution.

When such a spirit of doubt arose in Linji, he turned away from the lecture masters. He had doubts about what he had been doing, and doubts about what lay in the future. He was unable to leave these uncertainties unsolved, and as a result Great Resolution arose in him. Those who lack this determination can't achieve anything. We need great resolve and considerable practice to awaken the Self and sever at a stroke the entanglements existing "since the beginningless beginning." Only then can our goal be realized. And yet, if we have this constantly in mind, it becomes a serious obstacle to satori.

One day, Nanyue walked to where Mazu was doing *zazen*. He picked up a tile and immediately became engrossed in polishing it. Mazu wondered about this and asked, "Master, why are you polishing a tile?" Nanyue replied, "I'm trying to make it into a mirror." What does he mean by this? If the notion of Great Doubt, Great Resolution, or Great Faith occupies our thoughts when we do *zazen*, we are not truly practicing. Nanyue asked Mazu, "When you make an ox pull a cart and the cart does not go ahead, which should you whip, the cart or the ox?" When we think that we must stake everything on our practice and this thought occupies our mind, we cannot do *zazen*. Though we can't practice without Great Faith, Great Resolution, and Great Doubt, they don't come to life and start working for us until they disappear from our minds. This is an element that is essential for authentic practice. Thinking that one must sit, and actually sitting, are two different things.

Linji achieved "practice-samadhi." With everything thrust away and forgotten, he was totally engrossed in his practice. In this "pure and direct" activity, Faith, Doubt, and Resolution were working with great intensity. The head monk said, "This fellow's still young, but he's not like the rest." Others, too, felt that there was something different about him, that he was no ordinary person. I regard this as only natural. This is how we must be when the resolve to practice the Way truly arises in us.

Linji kept on practicing singlemindedly, but he never went to Huangbo to ask about the Dharma. He just sat silently for three years, not once going to Huangbo with a question. Linji's way of practice at that time harbors extremely important issues that have to do with asking one's master for instruction, "entering the master's chamber," and *mondō*.[16]

The head monk went up to Linji and said, "How many years have you been here?" When Linji told him he had been there for three years, the head monk said, "Three years? Why don't you go to the Master and ask him about the Dharma?" Linji replied, "I don't know what to ask. What should I ask him?"

What about this? I'm sure we could think of any number of things to ask. To us, it seems inconceivable that someone engrossed for three whole years in practice-samadhi would have nothing to ask. But what is the ultimate question? Buddhism asks ultimate questions and gives ultimate answers. How about you? Right at this moment, what should you ask? How many people know *how* to ask? Do such people even exist? Can *you* ask a question, the answer to which, if received, will resolve your fundamental problem once and for all? If the question remains merely in our heads, it cannot become an ultimate question that will clarify for us the essence of the "special transmission apart from the scriptures." Here is where the significance of the Great Doubt Block comes into play. To ask the ultimate question – there is nothing else beyond that.

In the *Gateless Barrier*,[17] Wumen writes, "A million doubts become one doubt." If we deal with doubts one by one as they appear, our practice will go on endlessly, never achieving its true end. The precepts that Theravāda Buddhists observe are endless. The point is never reached where they can all be observed. In the end, the one fundamental question, which includes everything, never becomes known. Zen must pose this question. The Great Doubt Block, in which all doubts become one doubt, does not arise at the end of a line of objective or dualistic thought. All of me, all the world, all perception and cognition, and all sense objects must come together as one doubt. In terms of Buddhist doctrine, this total doubt corresponds to the eighth, or "store," consciousness. The eye, ear, nose, tongue, body, mind and all that they perceive must become one doubting mass. When that Doubt crumbles away, we attain satori, in which all our large and small awakenings become one Great Awakening. There is a time-honored saying: "Strike down with a sword into the field of the eighth consciousness." When we cut through the eighth consciousness and make it "turn over," the eighth consciousness turns into the four wisdoms. This is referred to as the "transformation of consciousness and the attainment of wisdom" – the wisdom of satori.

The fundamental question is not easy. It is understandable that Linji didn't know what to ask. We will never realize what he meant if we think the less of him for not knowing what to ask.

The head monk then said to Linji, "Quick! Go and ask him what the Buddha-Dharma[18] is all about."

Anyone, not only a practitioner of Zen, can ask about the awakened way of being, or the ultimate point of Buddhism. The truth of the awakened way of being, however, has nothing to do with what is referred to today when people speak of the "essence of Buddhism" or the "concept of Buddha."

The head monk is revealing his Original Face to Linji. He isn't simply telling him to ask about the essence of the awakened way of being. That essence is fulfilled beyond words in the head monk. Because it is, he has a way of questioning that can point Linji in the right direction. It is not the words – they could be said by anyone. To advise someone as earnest and determined as Linji to go and ask such a thing is not easy.

Linji was fortunate to have had an outstanding head monk. The way in which he guided Linji can be clearly seen, and the full extent of his kindness, the distinctive character of his Zen compassion, is realized when we have experienced such guidance ourselves.

Although the ultimate question is difficult to ask, when we Awaken, we realize there is nothing special. Awakening is *not* a matter of the future, or something apart from us; it is not an experience in time or space, but present existence right here and right now. It is the Formless Self which is beyond all temporal and spatial dimensions, constantly functioning while assuming forms freely and without hindrance.

Linji went to Huangbo as the head monk had advised. What happened there? What sort of Huangbo did Linji encounter? How did

Huangbo handle him? The living aspect of Founders' Zen is revealed in the way in which Huangbo dealt with Linji. In response to the ultimate question, an answer in terms of religious doctrine would, of course, be meaningless. What was the result of their first encounter? I would like to leave these matters for next time. In the meantime, I want all of you to become Linji and come up with that ultimate question.

3
There's Nothing Special in the Buddha-Dharma

Since the fall retreat, I have been lecturing on the *Record of Linji*. Today I want to take up the "Record of Pilgrimages" section of the text. To understand Linji and his record, we need to grasp what motivated him to begin his study of Zen, and what kind of satori he attained.

At first, Linji studied Buddhist scriptures, with a focus on Buddhist precepts. After a while, he realized that his approach was inadequate. He wanted above all to penetrate Buddhism's fundamental truth, so he went to Huangbo to begin his study of Zen. As one of the assembly of monks under Huangbo, he practiced *zazen* for three years with "pure and direct behavior." In Linji's third year there, the head monk said to him, "You've just been sitting. Why don't you enter Huangbo's chamber and question him?" Heeding this advice, Linji decided to go and have an interview with the master.

But Linji didn't know what – or how – to ask. When I say he had no idea how to question Huangbo, I don't simply mean he was ignorant of the kind of question he should have asked. He had practiced for three years in total earnestness, but he was filled with doubt. It was not ordinary doubt, but irresolvable doubt, so intense he couldn't even come up with a question.

Linji told the head monk he couldn't figure out what he should ask, so the head monk told him to ask what the Buddha-Dharma is all about. Provided with this means of inquiry, Linji went to Huangbo's chamber. Before he could finish asking his question, though, Huangbo struck him. Encouraged by the head monk, Linji went and questioned Huangbo a total of three times, and he was struck each time.

Why did Huangbo strike him? It seems that Linji was struck for no reason. But, the blows indicate that Linji wasn't acting in accordance with the awakened way of being. As the Zen master Deshan once said,

"Thirty blows if you can speak, thirty blows if you can't." When we realize the awakened way of being, there's no problem at all. If we have not yet realized it, however, we are dealt thirty blows of the staff whether we open our mouths or not.

Each of Huangbo's blows is the single-blow that immediately rejects all verbal and physical acts of those who have not realized awakening. The single-blow is both one blow and a million blows. It is the blow of absolute negation, which strikes once and strikes all. It can invite the intuition of non-arising, as the truth of reality.[19] With the single-blow, there is life in the midst of death; we secure new life in absolute death. So Huangbo wasn't dealing a blow to reprimand Linji or to negate one thing: his blow negates *everything*, and thereby brings about the absolute affirmation in which the total negation of all things is their total affirmation. Of course, this single-blow transcends our normal understanding. It cuts off speech and destroys the activity of the mind; it is beyond the four schemes of thought[20] and the hundred negations.

Linji could not awaken upon that life-in-death blow. Unable to open up satori after three years with Huangbo, he came to the conclusion that the time was not yet right for him, and he decided to take leave of Huangbo. He told the head monk that his karma must not be ripe, for he couldn't understand why Huangbo had struck him. The head monk expected much of Linji in the future, so when he heard this, he went and asked a special favor of Huangbo. He then told Linji to go and pay his respects to Huangbo, and to ask where he should go. When Linji did as instructed, Huangbo told him to go straight to a master named Dayu[21] in Gaoan. Following Huangbo's instructions, Linji set out.

Upon his arrival, Linji was asked by Dayu where he had come from, and he replied that he had come from Huangbo's place. Asked what Huangbo had said, Linji answered, "Three times I asked about the Buddha-Dharma, and three times I was struck. I don't know why I was struck, though." Linji's statement here is very crucial; he in effect said, "Huangbo struck me three times, but I don't know whether it was for some fault of mine. Was I in the wrong or not?" Now that might sound like an ordinary question, but for Linji it expressed the utmost possible doubt. He wasn't asking whether he had been scolded for some particular reason. Rather, that question expressed his fundamental doubt as to whether he had acted against satori, and if so, whether that was why he still hadn't attained it.

In response to Linji's question, Dayu said, "Huangbo is such a grandmother that he utterly exhausted himself with your troubles." He meant that there was no greater kindness than Huangbo's. Huangbo's blows can give life in the midst of death; he delivers the single-blow that can awaken others. His kindness, then, isn't verbal, as when one explains things with words. It is incomparable kindness and Linji abused it by showing up at Dayu's and asking whether he had been at fault or not. Upon hearing Dayu's words, Linji attained Great Awakening.

Huangbo's blows have nothing to do with being, or not being, at fault. They are blows to awaken us to the Self that negates all things and affirms them all. When Linji finally realized this, Huangbo's blows came alive in him and restored him to life. I don't mean that Linji simply understood why he was struck. Rather, he himself became the blows. Each blow was none other than Huangbo himself, and in receiving it, Linji became one with him; Linji became Huangbo, and Huangbo became Linji. This identity attests to the fact that Linji had attained Great Awakening. The single-blow is the Self that cuts off speech and destroys all mental activity, the Self that gives rise to the dynamic functioning that emancipates us from all things and brings us to life in them. The realization of that Self is Great Awakening.

When he achieved that awakening, Linji said to Dayu, "There really isn't much to Huangbo's Buddha-Dharma." He was in effect saying, "I had often wondered about the truth to which Huangbo had awakened. I had made it out to be something mysterious, something obscure and hard to realize. But, what?! It's only this!" We can see here that Linji had opened up a superb realization. When we awaken, we, too, realize there's nothing special or extraordinary about the awakened way of being of people like Huangbo. It is said that the True Dharma is in no way mysterious. Contrary to what people might think, *not* to awaken is strange, and when we do in fact awaken, we realize there's nothing mysterious involved. Our being awakened is most ordinary and matter-of-fact. Such ordinariness is the True Self. An awakened person finds it rather strange that he or she had ever been deluded, for to that person Awakening is ordinary and natural.

It has nothing to do with the distinction between awakening and not awakening. As the Sixth Founding Teacher said, "Originally, not-a-single-thing, so where is the dust to cling?" It's odd to complain about our passions, delusions, or inability to *really* do *zazen* and penetrate deep enough. Awakening is free from awakening and not awakening, and that fact is what is truly natural and self-evident.

Linji reached the point where he could say that there wasn't much to Huangbo's Buddha-Dharma. His statement is clearly different – or even opposite – from what he had been saying until then. He meant that there are neither passions nor delusions, awakening nor not awakening. Everything exists just as it is; the calm and constant mind is the Way. Linji wondered why he had ever been deluded, for that seemed quite strange to him. Only upon his Awakening could Linji have solved such problems of theodicy as "If reality is originally pure and free from discriminations, why does it give birth to mountains, rivers, and the earth?" or "Assuming God is the Creator, why are there evil people?" Linji faces no problem – to him, all of this is ordinary and matter of fact. Originally everything is pure and free from discrimination, so why do mountains, rivers, and the earth suddenly appear? This question is its own answer.[22] So rather than saying there isn't much to Huangbo's Buddha-Dharma, Linji might just as well have said that "There isn't much to the Buddha-Dharma – that is quite ordinary." A new Linji, unrecognizable at first glance, has emerged in his awakening.

Linji gave rise to the functioning of the single-blow when he said that there is nothing special in Huangbo's Dharma. With his words, he dealt one blow, or thirty blows, to Huangbo's Buddha-Dharma. Indeed, those words would never have been uttered if it hadn't been for the blow that gives life in the midst of death.

Dayu then grabbed Linji and cried out, "You bed-wetting little demon!" The demon is Linji, who had the audacity to show up one minute to ask whether he had done something wrong and then turned around in the next and say that there wasn't much to Huangbo's Buddha-Dharma. Dayu prodded Linji: "What kind of truth do you see? Right now, speak! Speak!" He pressed Linji for a response, in effect saying, "You talked big, but now try to say something about the ultimate point!"

By realizing Huangbo's blows in himself, Linji had changed from the initial Linji. Even if he wasn't approached in any way or didn't move a finger, his answer was already out before he was questioned. His being there was, in itself, proof of his Awakening. When pressed by Dayu, he immediately jabbed him three times in the ribs – he gave rise to dynamic functioning by answering Dayu's question with the blow that cuts off words and destroys all mental activity.

Being the great master he was, Dayu immediately let go of Linji and shoved him away. That shove is highly significant, for it indicates that he had accepted Linji's response and acknowledged him as an awakened man of Zen, rather than simply released his hold. Dayu's Zen functioning is expressed in that shove. With their jabs and shoves hammered together, the two men have become the most intimate of friends.

"Your teacher is Huangbo," continued Dayu, "so it's none of my business." He told Linji that he had better go back and study under

Huangbo. Huangbo was the one who had struck Linji, and his blows had now borne fruit. In saying that it was none of his business, Dayu praised Linji's ability and esteemed Huangbo's treatment of Linji.

Linji left Dayu and returned to Huangbo. When Huangbo saw him coming, he shouted out, "Here's that guy again! Coming and going, coming and going – when will it end?!" Linji retorted, "It's all due to your grandmotherly kindness!" Huangbo had struck Linji out of kindness, and that kindness had borne fruit. Linji made a customary greeting and took his place beside Huangbo, but the Linji who stood there was no longer the one who had asked about the nature of the Buddha-Dharma. What stood there was the true Linji, with the presence of a ten-thousand-foot cliff.

Curious as to what had happened at Dayu's place, Huangbo asked Linji where he had been. Linji told him that he had gone to Dayu as instructed, and when next asked what Dayu had said, he proceeded to give a vivid account of what had transpired. Hearing that account, Huangbo exclaimed, "I'll wait for that rascal to show up, and when he does, I'll give him a good taste of my staff!"

Without a moment's delay, Linji retorted, "Why say you'll wait! Eat it *now*!" and gave Huangbo a stinging slap across the face. With that immediate response, Linji's awakened activity revealed itself. By realizing Huangbo's functioning, in himself, Linji became Dayu and struck Huangbo.

Huangbo cried out, "You lunatic! Coming back here and stroking the tiger's whiskers!" Linji shouted back, "Kaah!" With that vivid functioning, Linji was acknowledged on the spot by Huangbo, who then said to another monk nearby, "Attendant, get this lunatic out of here. Take him to the meditation hall." And for the rest of his life, Linji made use of the True Self, the Original Face, to which he awakened at that time.

To Huangbo, it was worth sending Linji to Dayu. The awakened activity between Huangbo, Linji, and Dayu is set forth splendidly in this section of the *Record*. With the head monk's guidance, Linji had brought the ultimate question before the Master. For us as well, the one question we pose, and its answer, must be ultimate. Only from the question beyond all questions can there emerge the answer beyond all answers.

4
After Realizing the Great Block of Awakening

Linji went and questioned Huangbo three times, only to be struck three times. Unable to awaken through Huangbo's blows, Linji went to Dayu as instructed. It was there that he suddenly changed and awakened to the Linji who is the True Person of Zen.

Under Dayu, Linji acquired the extraordinary discernment that enabled him to say that "there isn't much to Huangbo's Buddha-Dharma." He achieved satori, the new life that follows the One Great Death. Awakening to the Formless Self, he realized its free and unhindered functioning.

Linji jabbed Dayu and slapped Huangbo – this is his dynamic functioning, the great vitality and life of the Formless Self. Without falling into the "pit of empty tranquility," emptiness expresses itself through Linji as totally unrestricted functioning. The True Person that gives free play to that functioning is the source of Linji's teaching. Since long ago, the encounter with Linji's way of awakening others has been characterized as hearing the "deafening thunder of the five grave sins," and Linji's Zen style has earned him the name, "General Linji." This reputation stems, of course, from the marvelous functioning of his Great Awakening.

That dynamic functioning appears through the events related in the *Record of Linji*. Yelling "Kaah!" and dealing blows, Linji's Zen mind gives it vivid expression. Only because his mind functions vigorously to awaken others can we speak of Linji as a person of Great Awakening. That mind is none other than his True Self, and it must be our True Self as well. Its functioning comes forth through a conversion of the self, from the sudden awakening in which our deluded self changes all at once into the True Self.

After experiencing that conversion, Linji stayed with Huangbo for a while and, to refine his awakened way of life, began the practice that follows satori. After satori, the awakened Self functions at all times and in all places. Encountering people and things in the world around us, the True Person brings itself into action in a wide range of situations. At certain times it awakens the unawakened, and at other times it mutually negotiates the Way with those who have already awakened. Fundamentally, it was this activity that created the *Record of Linji*. Linji's awakened way of being revealed itself in dynamic functioning, and the recounting of this constitutes his *Record*.

Linji's school of Zen developed into "koan Zen." The practitioner first opens up satori by means of an old-case koan. After that, he continues practice with many other koans, traditionally about seventeen hundred but not necessarily fixed at that number. Through those later prescribed koans, the practitioner refines and polishes his awakening.

The initial koan is referred to as the passage through the first barrier, and it is regarded as necessary for "seeing into one's Original Nature" (*kenshō*). Satori is opened up when one passes through the first koan, and one passes through the koan when satori opens up. In other words, to pass through the koan and to open up satori must be one and the same act. It is not right if the passing through of the koan takes place without the opening up of satori. It also falls short of the genuine practice of koan Zen if one does not pass the koan while opening up satori. Usually, though, satori is thought of as opening up because one first passes through the koan. This false view of satori is prevalent in present-day koan Zen – it is an abuse of koan Zen. Again, the opening up of satori and the passing through of the koan must be a single act.

Nowadays, Zhaozhou's *Mu* koan or Hakuin's "sound of one hand" is usually taken up in practice as the first barrier, the outer gate, through which one first enters Zen and sees into one's Original Nature. The practitioner, by passing through the koan, must become Linji's True Person without Rank, the Self as the "mind-dharma without form, pervading the ten directions." If he or she doesn't, that passage will be simply a lifeless occurrence, nothing more. In Linji's time, it wasn't by means of koans as found in present-day koan Zen that people saw into their Original Nature. They opened up satori through a variety of opportunities. As there were no fixed koans by which satori was uniformly achieved, neither were there special koans for the practice following satori. People practiced at all times and in all places – in each and every situation. The moment of satori was rather internal in those days, and, arising from within oneself, it was concrete and spontaneous. Since the formulation of koan Zen, though, that spontaneity has all but disappeared. The practitioner now receives koans from the

master and applies himself or herself to them. Regrettably, in this sort
of practice the moment of satori does not emerge spontaneously from
within.

In a certain sense, though, a koan received from another can be
internalized as something spontaneous by our entering so deeply into
koan-samadhi that the koan becomes a part of us. To arrive at koan-
samadhi is essential. The koan becomes the Great Doubt Block. In
Great Doubt there is no koan apart from the self and no self apart from
the koan. A million doubts become one doubt; they come together as
one all-encompassing doubt. That total doubt contains all particular
ones, but it isn't just a matter of our doubting the koans as objects of
investigation. The doubter and the doubted must be one; otherwise
our work with koans never becomes true practice.

The Great Doubt Block is discussed in the *Gateless Barrier*. As Great
Doubt deepens, there ceases to be a koan outside the self or any self
apart from the koan. The Doubt Block suddenly crumbles and turns
into Great Awakening, the Great Block of Satori. In that change, the
koan becomes a true koan, an "official letter of passage" with which
one can pass freely through the border checkpoint. The true koan is a
satori with objective validity and, like a public certificate, is never
something one alone considers authentic.

The first koan we pass through is ordinarily called the first barrier.
Only later, after passing through other prescribed koans, do we complete our investigation of the Great Matter. In koan Zen, to complete
that investigation is to finish studying all of Zen. Only then is our
practice brought to a conclusion.

So, there is satori of the first barrier and further practice after that.
The passage through the first barrier is called *kenshō*, and the practice
following that satori is termed "post-satori" practice. *Kenshō* is the
Awakening in which we penetrate the Self and awaken to it. It clarifies
Fundamental Wisdom and the Wisdom of Equality. The practice following satori lies in clarifying the Wisdom of Discrimination, which is
not ordinary discriminative knowledge but rather the Self's functioning in the field of discrimination. This is done through grappling with
prescribed koans. Such is the present state of practice in koan Zen.

In Linji's time, though, this wasn't the case. At all times and in all
places people of Zen refined and expressed their awakened state of
satori. To put it differently, the awakened state of satori manifested
itself in every situation. The central concern was how it manifests itself
on this occasion, how it functions in this situation. So, essentially,
being the functioning of Fundamental Wisdom, practice is not some-

thing leading to this wisdom. It is the true, awakened way of being of Zen. The functioning of satori is true action, true practice, and in it Zen's life is established.

Linji tells us that the True Person is the "master of all situations." True wisdom is always the master, the subject, and never is it otherwise. People sometimes speak of the loss of subjectivity or humanity, but the True Person is never lost. Losing something happens to that which is based on such discriminations as being and nonbeing or birth and death. Linji's True Person, however, is the pure Self without form. It is beyond all such discriminations as birth and death, appearance and disappearance, being and nonbeing, good and evil, affirmation and negation, and purity and defilement, so nothing is ever lost. Freed from all discriminations, the True Person is now revealing itself in all its grandeur. Neither lacking nor in excess, it fills all places, and that is why we hear such expressions as "master of all situations" and "without form, pervading the ten directions." Since the True Person has no fixed form, it is stable, grounded in absolute security from which it can never stumble. This point is clearly expressed through the living words and actions related in Linji's *Record*.

Linji pursued further practice after he opened up satori, and when he completed it, he was certified by his master. Huangbo certified him because he recognized the maturation and purity of his satori. In the "Record of Pilgrimages" section of the *Record*, it is related as an important event. This section, however, begins,

> Linji returned to Mt. Huangbo in the middle of the summer. Seeing Huangbo reading a sutra, he said, "I always thought you were a *person*. Now I see you're just a black-bean-eating old monk." (p. 56)

Linji went away and showed up again in the middle of summer. He arrived during the *ango*, which is a season of intensive practice. In traditional Zen, ninety-day *ango* retreats take place twice a year, once in the summer (the rain *ango*) and once in the winter (the snow *ango*). The monks stay on the mountain and practice intensively without going on any pilgrimages. Monks must participate in an *ango* from beginning to end, so coming or going in the middle is forbidden. In returning to Mt. Huangbo part-way through the summer retreat – around the first of June – Linji committed an infraction of the rules. We must ask ourselves why he did such a thing. Originally, he was very particular about precepts; he observed them to the letter and was said to be pure and direct in his behavior. Nevertheless, he violated the precepts by showing up late and thereby breaking the rules of the summer *ango*.

When Linji arrived, he saw Huangbo reading a sutra. He told him he had always considered him a Zen master of supreme ability but now realized he was just a "black-bean-eating old monk." Linji in effect said that he now knew Huangbo for what he really was: a bald-headed guy who just sat around "eating beans," that is, reading the words written in sutras. What did Linji really mean by that?

As you know, since long ago, the "motto" of Zen has been the expression, "Self-dependently transmitted apart from the scriptural teachings, not dependent on words or letters." From the Zen perspective, scriptures are nothing but scraps of paper for wiping up filth. To Linji, a Zen master is the living core of all buddhas' words as the root-source of sutras. The living core of all buddhas' words is independent of the words and letters of the scriptures, and it is transmitted apart from them. Since a Zen master is that very Mind, Linji never expected to find Huangbo reading a sutra. He is basically saying to Huangbo, "What sort of person are you, anyway? It seems I didn't see you for what you really are."

What Linji says to Huangbo reflects a discernment independent of words and transmitted apart from sutras. Vividly present is the Linji who has gone beyond scriptures and returned to their source. He is a practitioner who has penetrated to the core of Zen.

There's a problem, though. Linji discovers Huangbo reading a sutra. Their encounter falls within the scope of practice. Linji calls that sutra-reading Huangbo a "black-bean-eating old monk," but what about this? Is this an acceptable way of encountering Huangbo? This is the central problem of that episode. From the Zen perspective, Linji's statement is not mistaken. Nevertheless, Huangbo doesn't accept it. Why not? Their encounter is the deliberation of the Way that can only occur between two awakened people. Moreover, Huangbo has already acknowledged Linji as one who has attained Great Awakening, so what in Linji can't he accept? We must consider this question, but I'd like to leave it for my next talk.

5
Leaving after the Summer Retreat

When Linji returned in the middle of the summer retreat and found Huangbo reading a sutra, he said, "I always thought of you as a great teacher of the truth that is independent of words and letters and transmitted apart from the scriptural teachings. But now I see you're just a black-bean nibbler in monk's attire!" With these words, Linji displayed his extraordinary Zen insight to Huangbo.

We might expect him to say such a thing, for in the *Record* Linji negates our searching in sutras for the Buddha-Dharma. He says, "The mind-dharma is without form and pervades the ten directions; it functions right here." The Mind is briskly functioning before our very eyes. Linji speaks of us having a lack of faith, by which he means that we don't realize that the Buddha-Dharma is functioning here at this moment:

> Since people lack sufficient faith in this, they accept names and phrases, and try to speculate about the Buddha-Dharma from within words. They and Dharma, heaven and earth, are far apart. (p. 11)

It is a tremendous mistake to get oneself stuck in names and phrases by thinking the Buddha-Dharma is found in them. We shouldn't seek the Buddha-Dharma in words, for without form the true Buddha-Dharma is vigorously functioning right here.

Linji said to his disciples, "Followers of the Way, even though you could master a hundred sutras and commentaries, you're not as good as a monk who has no concerns." No matter how many writings we read and interpret, we can't measure up to a monk who has no concerns, the person Linji indicates when he says that "one who has no concerns is the noble person." Reading Buddhist writings will not enable us to awaken to the way of being of having no concerns. Nor

25

will it awaken us to the True Self. Linji admonishes his disciples against seeking the Buddha-Dharma in words, for it is not found where there are names and phrases.

One day, Counselor Wang, a disciple of Weishan,[23] called on Linji and asked him, "Do the monks of this monastery read the sutras?" (p. 45) Linji told him they did not. He then asked if they practiced Zen, and again the answer was negative. As far as Linji was concerned, the practice of Zen of which the Counselor spoke was not the true practice. Linji saw right through the Counselor and told him the monks didn't practice Zen. If we understand Linji's answer from a more awakened point of view, we see that Zen isn't something that has to be practiced. When Linji said that the monks didn't practice Zen, his true Dharma was openly and boldly manifesting itself. It is of no avail to think of Zen as something to be practiced.

Linji in effect told the Counselor that there was no Zen – no buddhas and no founding teachers – inside the borders of the great Tang empire. But the Counselor still didn't understand, so he questioned Linji again: "If they don't read sutras or practice Zen, what in the world do they do?" Linji replied, "All I do is have them become buddhas and founders." This statement communicates the essence of the matter: sutras aren't read and Zen isn't learned. Instead, Linji had his disciples become buddhas and founding teachers, and this was why the monks had gathered here. Once again, we can see Linji's great concern for our direct penetration of the True Self.

Linji saw Huangbo reading a sutra and reproached him for doing so. To Linji, what he said to Huangbo wasn't inappropriate: he was disclosing his true standpoint, a view crucial for us as well. Huangbo didn't accept it, though. What was it that he didn't acknowledge? Was it that Linji had a superficial understanding of Huangbo's way of being? Did Linji view the sutra-reading Huangbo, the sutra-reading way of being, so to speak, simply from the standpoint that awakened people aren't supposed to do that sort of thing? What was it that Huangbo didn't accept? Linji's statement obviously didn't sit well with him.

After staying around for a few days, Linji decided to leave. When he was about to go, Huangbo said to him, "You came in violation of the rules of the summer session, and now you are leaving before the end. Why don't you leave after it's over?" (p. 56) Huangbo wasn't speaking of finishing the session in the literal sense, but of something more profound. If we regard Huangbo as asking Linji to stay until the end of the retreat, or telling him that he violated the rules by coming and going as he did, we will miss the true significance of what he said. Linji took

Huangbo's statement lightly and said, "I came for a little while to pay my respects to you, Master." Huangbo liked this attitude of Linji even less. He yelled, "Get out!" and, striking Linji, chased him away.

There isn't any particular meaning to his chasing Linji out; all meaning is found in Huangbo's blow. When Huangbo struck Linji, he struck him hard. He tried to end the retreat for Linji by completing him then and there with that one blow.

Chased out, Linji left the temple and walked a few miles, but he still couldn't figure out why he was struck. Eventually, though, he turned around and went back to Huangbo and finished the summer retreat.

Some time later Linji again went to Huangbo to take his leave. Huangbo asked him where he was going, and he answered, "If I don't go to Henan, I'll return to Hebei." Linji is talking about heading north (*bei*) or south (*nan*) of the Yellow River, but he isn't just talking about the direction in which he'll go. He means he'll freely go anywhere he wants. He is expressing his free way of being, which has nothing to do with destinations. Manifest in what he says is the free, unhindered Awakening of "going when one wants to go, and sitting when one wants to sit."

Huangbo then struck Linji – a blow different from the previous one. This was a parting blow by which Huangbo says it is good for Linji to go wherever he pleases in order to awaken others. When he was struck, Linji once again expressed his dynamic functioning: he grabbed Huangbo and slapped him. Huangbo's blow and Linji's slap are the blow and slap of mutual acknowledgement.

Huangbo is now satisfied as Linji starts out on his own. It is as if a caged bird had taken flight:

> The bird caged for many years
> Today flies with the clouds.

Now it isn't that Linji has merely been freed from his cage by *kenshō* or Great Awakening; rather, he is setting out on a pilgrimage of compassion to encounter all people freely, and to have them become buddhas and founding teachers. Huangbo laughed heartily. He was truly satisfied, so he roared with laughter.

Huangbo then called an attendant and said, "Bring me the backrest and armrest that belonged to my late teacher Baizhang." Huangbo had awakened to the Dharma under Baizhang, who by this time was already dead. As a sign of the transmission of the Dharma, Huangbo had received the backrest and armrest Baizhang used when he did *zazen*. But when Huangbo called for these things, Linji again displayed the sharpness of his Zen functioning: he said he had no need for them.

Supposedly, Śākyamuni's robe and bowl were transmitted down through the ages to the Sixth Founding Teacher, at which point they were lost. Their loss is highly significant, for much harm results when people become overly concerned about such things. A famous Zen story relates that when the Sixth Founding Teacher fled south after receiving the bowl and robe from the Fifth Founding Teacher, Senior Monk Ming[24] pursued him and tried to take them away. Anything with a form thus becomes a hindrance. Sutras are hindrances, and even more so are backrests and armrests. What sort of proof are they? We don't need a paper certification of our Awakening: true Awakening fills heaven and earth.

Linji yelled out to Huangbo's attendant, "Bring me some fire. Burn them both!" We can readily perceive in these words Linji's way of being, which we, too, must master. Huangbo surely felt the same way, for Linji's utterance was a disclosure of the true way of being of one who has realized the Dharma. Huangbo acknowledged what Linji said: "Be that as it may, just take them with you. In the future you will sit on the tongue of every person on earth."

This is how it must have been when the Fifth Founding Teacher handed over the bowl and robe to the Sixth. Acknowledgement in Zen is different from receiving a diploma, which one might treat preciously. Monks sometimes receive a surplice or *nyoi*,[25] but that isn't something to get caught up in. When we get involved in these things, all sorts of problems arise.

Linji's asking the attendant to bring fire strikes a chord in us. In all respects, this is the way of being we must embody. This is what we realize in our attainment of the Dharma. You have all been applying yourselves diligently to your practice. There is one day left in this retreat, and I want all of you to complete this summer retreat in this true sense.

6
The One True Person without Rank

Today I will discuss the One True Person without Rank. This True Person is spoken of early on the *Record of Linji*:

> The Master took the high seat in the hall. He said, "On your lump of red flesh is One True Person without Rank who is always going in and out of the face of every one of you. Those of you who have not yet realized this, look, look!"
>
> Then a monk came forward and asked, "What about the One True Person without Rank?"
>
> The Master got down from his seat, seized the monk, and cried, "Speak, speak!" The monk faltered.
>
> Shoving him away, the Master said, "Your One True Person without Rank – what kind of dried turd is he!" Then he returned to his quarters. (p. 3)

Linji took the high seat in the hall. In other words, he ascended the Sumeru Platform to give a Dharma talk. Here in the Myōshinji compound there's a building called the Dharma Hall, and in it there's a Sumeru Platform. In most Buddhist temples a statue of the Buddha is set up and worshipped on a Sumeru Platform, but in a Zen temple, nothing is placed there. Instead, a living buddha or founding teacher gets up on the platform and gives a living Dharma talk. We rarely see this nowadays, though. On certain ceremonial occasions a master will give a talk from the platform, but usually it is unoccupied. For many years Chinese and Japanese masters "took the high seat in the hall," accounts of which appear frequently in Zen records. This testifies to the extent to which the Sumeru Platform was alive and functioning to awaken people. When used in this way, the Platform was full of life. As

29

a living Zen master, Linji ascended the Platform and said, "On your lump of red flesh is One True Person without Rank who is always going in and out of the face of every one of you. Those who have not yet realized this, look, look!"

Although opinions differ as to what this "lump of red flesh" means – it is variously explained as the mouth, the heart, the head, or the eyes – such interpretations aren't necessary: after all, the "lump of red flesh" refers to all of our body-mind. Linji means that the One True Person without Rank is *right here* in all of our body-mind, not that there is a True Person who vaguely exists "somewhere." Rather, that single, unique True Person without Rank is clearly found in each and every one of us.

What does it mean to be "without rank"? As far as "rank" is concerned, many examples come to mind. We can say we are ranked by honors bestowed on us, such as "senior grade, first court rank" or "senior grade, second court rank." It is a rank to be a student or teacher, merchant or civil servant, parent or child. Every body and mind involves ranks: to have eyes, ears, head, feet, and hands; to be sitting on or off the tatami; to be on the Sumeru Platform or before it; to be a buddha or a founding teacher, a sentient being or an ordinary person. Even truth and delusion, good and evil, are ranks. We may speak of being without rank, but all the same we come to abide in the place called being "without rank." Though not appearing to abide there, we come to do so when our not abiding occurs in fixed times and places. When we abide in it, even the ultimate stage of the Buddha-Dharma – nothingness, nirvana, *dharma-kāya*, satori – becomes a rank. In other words, anything in a fixed condition constitutes a rank, even the long passage of centuries or the vast reaches of outer space. Indeed, in our ordinary life it is quite rare for any of us to be truly without rank.

But Linji says there's a "True Person without Rank" who doesn't abide anywhere. He says there's One True Person, a unique True Person, and this Person is the true human being. Of course, if it were objectifiable, it would fall into a rank. If it were transcendent or immanent, or here in the present moment or at a midpoint in the ordinary sense, it would have a rank. There is a True Person, however, who is neither up nor down, left nor right, nor in the middle; it is neither past, nor present, nor future. It is the One, the unparalleled person. Since it exists in this way, it isn't a limited one: it is All and One, One and All. Though it is a One, it isn't determined as such. It is a One that cannot be called a "one." Linji tells us that such a human is the True Human.

When Linji speaks of it as a "true" person, there are no such ranks as true or false. It is the Truth without rank. If it were a truth that stands in opposition to falsehood, it wouldn't be without rank. That which is beyond all ranks is the Truth, or the Person of whom Linji speaks. This body-mind of ours is not the True Person without Rank. I have been speaking of the true human without rank, but if that human is other than our very self, we differ from the person to whom I am referring. Since the ordinary self isn't free of all ranks, it isn't the Self without Rank. What Linji is talking about is the Self beyond all forms – the true human being.

Linji, who is now up on the Sumeru Platform giving a Dharma talk, is none other than the One True Person. Only the True Person can ascend the platform; in fact, that very Person is the true Sumeru Platform. In Buddhism, the Sumeru Platform, like Mount Sumeru itself, represents the Buddhist cosmos. In Zen, though, Mount Sumeru and the Sumeru Platform must be a living mountain and a living platform, and the living Sumeru Platform must be the True Person without Rank. Linji is the Sumeru Platform, and the Sumeru Platform is Linji; they aren't separate entities. This is the true Linji and true Sumeru Platform.

In the *Record*, Linji says that the "mind-dharma[26] is without form and pervades the ten directions" (p. 11). This dharma isn't some kind of law, ideal, or idea; any mind-dharma that is other than the True Person isn't the ultimate one. Although it may differ in its verbal expression, Linji's mind-dharma is essentially no different from the Sumeru Platform. When he says that the mind-dharma pervades the ten directions, the "ten directions" do not signify a spatial expanse or infinite reaches of a temporal, boundless eternity. In fact, it is neither time nor space. We realize the ten directions only when we go beyond the four cardinal points and the four intermediary ones.

When Linji speaks of this Self without Rank, "without rank" means it is "without form." What he is speaking of is the Formless Self. It isn't merely without form, for it is the Self. And it isn't the ordinary self, but the Self with no form whatsoever. He calls this Formless Self the One True Person without Rank. Again, they are one, not two; otherwise we wouldn't be able to say it is "without rank."

The Formless Self is the Linji who has taken the high seat on the Sumeru Platform in the Dharma Hall. Linji addresses his disciples as "You who listen to this Dharma talk." Not only the person giving the talk, but every other person and thing is this Self, the True person that Linji says is "always going in and out of the face of every one of you." The One True Person without Rank – Linji – goes in and out of your faces. He breathes vigorously on your lump of red flesh. Linji cries out, "Those of you who have not yet realized this, look, look!" We must see it all *right here*. Nothing is hidden. There isn't any seeing or not seeing here. Disclosing itself in all its grandeur, the True Person actualizes itself in each and every one of us. Linji tells us to realize it clearly, to awaken to the One True Person without Rank. In this way, Linji is giving the ultimate Dharma talk.

We don't need to go back to the Linji of a thousand years ago. What is on each of your cushions right now is the One True Person without Rank. What isn't that way is not the True Person. Usually, we mistake what is not the True Person for the True Person. An old Zen saying relates how we lose ourselves and search for things, and in so doing take what is not the Self to be the Self. The True Self here upon every cushion is none other than the One True Person without Rank who sits on Mount Sumeru. Linji tells us to see this in its entirety. Of course, we can't see it with our eyes, touch it with our hands, or hear it with our ears. We can't think about it, feel it, or discriminate it in our minds. Such is the True Person without Rank. It cuts through all verbalization and destroys all mental activity. It goes beyond the four statements and the hundred negations. It isn't words: its true way of being has no rank, so it cuts through all speech and eradicates all activities of the mind. It is the truly unrestricted, eternal Self.

Since it is without rank, it never gets caught up in anything. It is free, emancipated, or, in more dynamic terms, a free and unhindered functioning. If we speak of a truly saved human, a religiously realized self, what we are referring to must be an ultimate religious person in this sense; anything ranked as a buddha apart from ordinary humans, or in a particular time or place, cannot be the True Person without Rank.

The True Person without Rank is the only Person who can be the true Buddha. Since the true Buddha is beyond all images and idols, nothing with form can be the true Buddha. We often think of a buddha as holding a high, exalted position, as something unapproachable and cut off from us in a completely different realm. The "One True Person without Rank" is a more concrete way of expressing the same thing as "buddha," and so it feels closer to us. It is our True Self, the Formless Self that is manifesting itself here and now, and whose demonstration *zazen* ultimately is.

As we start our seven-day retreat, I wish to remind you of our primary goal: to realize this One True Person without Rank right here upon our cushions, to awaken to the Formless Self. People say it is difficult because the Self is far from us, but actually there is no distance at all. Just as you are, there isn't a trace of separation. People speak of being one with Buddha, but there is no Buddha apart from the Self, and no Self apart from the Buddha. Nor is it a matter of coming in contact with Buddha or not – there is no distance involved. Hence, "The Self-Buddha is True Buddha"; "It is at once mind and Buddha"; "What is mind is Buddha"; "It is neither mind nor Buddha" – all of these are expressions of the dynamic presence of the True Person without Rank.

Now, as I mentioned before, Linji said, "Those of you who have not yet realized this, look, look!" In koan practice these days, much emphasis is placed on this "look, look!" If "look, look!" isn't the dynamic presence of the One True Person without Rank, however, it will be a mere pattern or form, or will simply end in some fixed form of action. We face the danger that the koan of the True Person as now practiced will fail to bring about the realization of the True Person in us. It is possible to realize clearly the dynamic presence of the One True Person through that very "presencing," but if we don't advance to that point, the koan won't do us any good even if we pass through it. I want all of you to realize this One True Person without Rank, which involves neither becoming nor not becoming.

According to the *Record*, a monk came forward and asked, "What about the One True Person without Rank?" Such a question shows how caught we can get in ranks. Even though Linji's talk allows no room for questioning, the monk steps forth with a question. When Linji speaks of the One True Person without Rank, it is already dynamically presenting itself. Thus the monk's question is wide of the mark. What a way of stalling for time!

Linji says there is One True Person without Rank who is always going in and out of the face of every one of you. The True Person is immediately present. The question, "What about the One True Person without Rank?" has meaning for the first time when Linji himself poses it. What about this One True Person without Rank?

7
Speak, Speak!

There is One True Person without Rank who is always going in
and out of the face of every one of you. Those of you who
have not yet realized this, look, look! (p. 3)

When Linji proclaimed this in a talk from the high seat in the Dharma
Hall, a monk came forward and asked, "What about this One True
Person without Rank?" If the monk had already realized the One True
Person when he asked this question, he wouldn't have been just any
ordinary questioner. If it is the True Person who has come forth and
asked about the One True Person without Rank, then Linji must have it
out with him on equal terms. Though Linji said that it's "always going
in and out of the face of every one of you," the monk looked outside
himself and asked a question; he was already wide of the mark. It is of
no avail to seek the True Person outside yourself.

The monk wants Linji to give an explanation of the True Person. A
mondō in Founding Teachers' Zen is not something like that. It
involves our direct demonstration of that True Person. If all we do is
turn to someone and ask about the True Person, we won't ever be able
to demonstrate it. As we read in the *Record of Linji*, Yajñadatta thought
he had lost his head somewhere, so he ran around looking for it.[27] But,
of course, that which goes around looking is the head itself. However
long we search, we can't find what we are looking for, for there's no
"head" outside us – it's right here, close at hand, in the very searcher
himself. Though we know better than to seek the Buddha elsewhere,
we tend to act like Yajñadatta. Linji is saying that the True Person is
right here; but, oblivious to that fact, the monk turns to Linji and tries
to get him to talk about it. Such an approach isn't the Zen that is apart
from the scriptural teachings, but rather Zen within such teachings, a

form of doctrinal instruction. Again, Linji's act of taking the high seat aims at having us directly demonstrate the True Person.

Many years ago, when I was doing koan practice under a teacher, a new monk started practicing in the monastery. He was given the *Mu* koan. He thought the answer was written down somewhere, so he went around looking for books on Zen and Buddhism. He couldn't find the answer in anything he read, so he started asking various people. That didn't help either. Once he felt he had come across the answer somehow, so he went to the roshi to present it to him, but the roshi told him that it wasn't that sort of thing. He then asked me, "Where the heck is it written? Where can I find it?" Maybe this is how it is for all of us in the beginning of our practice. Even if we search all over the world and read all of the Buddhist scriptures, we can't find the True Person anywhere. The True Person without Rank is right at hand as we search. Linji says that it is "always going in and out of the face of every one of you." Functioning right here with great briskness and vitality, it is none other than our True Self, the True Self that cannot be found outside ourselves. In the FAS Society, that Self is called the Formless Self, the Self with no form whatsoever.

Even though he is addressing the great Linji, when the monk starts looking outside of himself and asks about the True Person without Rank, he is heading in the wrong direction. That's why Linji gets down from his seat, seizes him and says, "Speak, speak!" This is how the functioning of the True Person must be. Linji is trying to make the questioning monk answer. Linji doesn't answer – he makes the monk do it. The grabber Linji and the grabbed monk are one, not two, so Linji's functioning is none other than the monk's True Person without Rank.

"The monk faltered." "Faltered" here means that the monk tried to answer but couldn't. He was so flustered that he couldn't do anything. When told to speak, he had no idea what to say. This is a very important point. If everything he had possessed up to that point had been snatched away by Linji's functioning, he would have become the Great Doubt Block. He would have become no-minded and thereby forgotten himself. This is totally different from being stupefied. If the monk had been but a hair's breadth from the True Person's ranklessness, he probably would have attained Great Awakening when Linji grabbed him and shouted "Speak, speak!" But, instead, the monk was totally surprised.

Linji shoved the monk away and said, "Your True Person without Rank – what kind of dried turd is he!" This reminds me of the famous koan in which a monk asks, "What is the Buddha?" and Yunmen[28] answers "A dried turd!"[29] Now one might wonder whether this monk had questioned Linji only after becoming one with the True Person, but that isn't the case here. Linji criticizes the monk's "True Person without Rank," or rather the monk himself, as being no different from a dried turd. Moreover, when the monk looks outside himself and regards the True Person as something to be revered, he gets totally entangled in that approach. To never get entangled is to be without rank. The monk gets caught up in seeking the True Person outside himself, and that's why Linji says, "Your True Person without Rank – what kind of dried turd is he!" With these words he snatches away the True Person conceptualized by the monk, and returns immediately to his chamber.

Here again, the True Person without Rank is revealing itself to the monk with great vitality. Yet the monk still doesn't catch on. When Linji yelled at him and returned immediately to his chamber, he was working to have others cross the sea of life and death. These living methods were used one after another on the monk, but in the end he couldn't witness Linji's True Person.

When we pose a question such as the monk's, we distance ourselves from the dynamic "presencing" of things just as they are. In the words of the Sixth Founding Teacher, "Zen is the realization of the supreme vehicle." These words refer to the way of Founding Teachers' Zen exemplified by Linji. He demonstrates the essence, the marrow, and the ultimate source of the whole Buddhist canon; he comes from and returns to the "mother of all buddhas," the "root-source of all things."

The One True Person without Rank goes in and out of everyone's face. It functions freely and self-abidingly. In the terminology of Pure Land Buddhism, it goes to and returns from nirvana freely; going out at times and returning at others, it is not attached to either, since it neither comes nor goes. In terms of the Five Ranks,[30] it functions freely in the rank of the straight and freely in the rank of the leaning, but never gets caught up in either. Anything that gets caught up cannot be spoken of as the True Person. A similar expression of this is found in the *Diamond Sutra*: "One should arouse the Mind that abides nowhere." The *Vimalakīrti-nirdeśa-sūtra* speaks of creating all things from the place of non-abidingness; one creates without abiding in the creation, and this non-abidingness is based upon ranklessness. It does not indicate simply flowing without abiding anywhere. It is the place of abiding while not abiding, which is none other than nirvana. Zen also speaks of "creating all things without attaining even one of them." This and all of the other expressions indicate the One True Person without Rank.

Linji isn't separated from us. The Linji who is the One True Person isn't even an inch away. In the realm of the True Person, the Linji of a thousand years ago is no different from us. Only when there is no temporal or spatial separation can we speak of the True Person without Rank. There is a koan about Daitō Kokushi (d. 1337), the founder of Daitokuji, being the reincarnation of Yunmen. Yunmen taught around the same time as Linji, which means he lived over three centuries before Daitō was born. Where was Yunmen during those three hundred years? An intriguing question. If we actually penetrate the One True Person without Rank, though, it makes no difference whether the period involved is 500, 1000, or 2500 years, and the question of where Yunmen was poses no problem whatsoever. For that reason, I want all of you to awaken to, or self-realize, the One True Person without Rank. I want you to have the True Person in you awaken to itself, for that is the alpha and omega of doing *zazen* here. I am not lecturing on Linji or his record: I'm lecturing on our True Self. There is no need to depend on Linji or to regard him as an authority. The authority is here in us, hence Linji's expressions: "Solitarily emancipated" and "nondependent." If we become attached to Linji, we disobey him. Be the follower of the Way who isn't dependent on founding teachers or buddhas, who is solitarily emancipated and unattached – that is the true way of being.

Time is passing quickly. Today is the midpoint of our retreat. Our singleminded application is for nothing other than realizing the True Person in us. In Linji Zen, or in Zen in general, one does not try to awaken by observing precepts. All precepts are contained in the True Person. Precepts apart from the True Person are not true ones; they are defiled precepts. Zen speaks of the "formless, single-mind precept," in which the myriad precepts return to the one precept at the source of all precepts. This formless precept, which brings all precepts to culmination, is the single-mind precept of Zen. We need not take care to polish it all the time:

> Originally, not-a-single-thing,
> so where is the dust to cling?

I'd like to stop here for today.

8
The Mind-Dharma is without Form and Pervades the Ten Directions

In my last talk I discussed the One True Person without Rank. Today I want to examine Linji's discourse entitled "The mind-dharma is without form and pervades the ten directions":

> The Master addressed the assembly, saying,
>
> "Followers of the Way, it is urgently necessary that you endeavor to acquire true insight and stride boldly in the world without letting yourselves be deceived by delusive fox spirits. One who has no concerns is the noble person. Simply don't strive – just be ordinary. Yet you go and run hither and thither outside yourselves and make inquiries, looking for some helper. You're all wrong!
>
> "You only try to seek Buddha, but Buddha is merely a name. Don't you know what it is that runs around seeking? The buddhas and founding teachers of the three periods and the ten directions appear only in order to seek the Dharma. You followers of the Way who are the students of today, you, too, have only to seek the Dharma. Attain the Dharma and you're all done. Until then, you'll go on transmigrating through the five paths of existence just as you have been.
>
> "What is the Dharma? The Dharma is the mind-dharma. The mind-dharma is without form; it pervades the ten directions and is functioning right before your eyes. Since people lack sufficient faith they accept names and phrases, and try to speculate about Buddha-Dharma from written words. They and the Dharma are as far apart as heaven and earth." (pp. 10–11)[31]

Linji tells the assembly what they must do. They must "endeavour to acquire true insight." Steer clear of all mistaken, hindering views and "acquire true insight." This insight is no mere orthodox interpretation

38

or a true understanding. It is none other than satori, the self-awakening of Buddha-nature, which is not found apart from our True Self. "Acquire," then, means to awaken to the True Self.

Linji tells the monks to "stride boldly in the world." "Stride boldly" can mean to go as one pleases. Here it means to walk through the land, to "strut" under heaven – freely and without hindrance. We must act, live on; otherwise we will be deceived by delusive fox spirits and tricked by evil mountain and river spirits. One might take such spirits as external, but countless internal things deceive us as well. Free yourself from all internal and external deception. Otherwise, you can neither maintain true subjectivity nor live genuinely in the world. If you acquire Linji's "True Insight," you can stride free and unhindered, without being deceived by anything. But if you do not, the evil spirits of mountains and rivers, and the buddhas and founding teachers you usually revere, will ultimately confuse you. If buddhas and founding teachers stand outside us, they lead us astray; if self and other are two, we are deluded. "Sentient beings and Buddha are not two, Buddha and ordinary humans are one." If buddhas and founding teachers exist apart from us, they are neither true buddhas nor true founding teachers. The importance Zen places on this is evident in Linji's most incisive utterance:

> Meeting a buddha, slay the buddha;
> meeting a founding teacher, slay the founding teacher.

All buddhas and founding teachers divorced from the self cause confusion, so they must be destroyed and cast aside. A "sentient being" is one who is confused about Buddha and considers it a transcendent "other." But Zen does not do this, for it clearly recognizes that in the true Buddha, sentient beings and Buddha are one, not two.

In such writings as the *Essentials of Transmitting the Mind-Dharma*, we run across expressions like "The *sambhoga-kāya* is not the true Buddha" and "The *nirmāṇa-kāya* is not the true Buddha." People are apt to take the manifested forms of the Buddha for the true Buddha. Zen strongly rejects this. Zen, and Buddhism in general, regard the Buddha as the *dharma-kāya*, and the other two forms as its functioning. A *dharma-kāya* seen as estranged from the other two bodies is not the true Buddha, though. The *Diamond Sutra* and other scriptures drive home the point that any Buddha we can see with our eyes, hear with our ears, or touch with our hands is not the true Buddha: the Tathāgata is beyond the functioning of consciousness.[32] Our realization of this true Buddha constitutes true insight. With this insight, we are never confused, even if a buddha or founding teacher should appear before us. It is the wisdom with which we can distinguish truth from falsehood and right from wrong. This discerning insight must come alive in us with great vigor, and this is why Linji repeatedly admonishes the assembly to acquire "true insight."

Linji says that "he who has no concerns is the noble person." This oft-quoted statement appears in the calligraphy of Zen figures and others, like the Shingon priest Jiun Sonja (1718–1804). Many people take this expression in a passive sense. It appeals to those who yearn for a life with no troubles, emancipated from worldly matters, to those who live with their noses to the grindstone, tossed about by worldly affairs. Others wish they could experience such a feeling, if even for a moment. Were we to display these words on a busy street corner, people would surely become enthralled by them, but only passively.

Of course, this "noble person who has no concerns" does not refer to a temporary peace of mind or composure. Nor does it indicate apathy or an attitude of peace-at-any-price. Only when we free ourselves from all entanglements and stride boldly do we have no concerns. Then, as the True Person who has no concerns, we can face adverse circumstances and yet remain unencumbered by them. Only this way of being is the truly noble person. Of course, this Person is beyond all distinctions of class or race, and in it there is no difference between buddhas and ordinary humans. That is why if buddhas and founding teachers exist outside me, I am not this Person who has no concerns. The word "noble," then, is not the antonym of "ignoble" or "poor." Rather, it indicates a higher dimension of nobility beyond high and low. As this noble person, we do not refrain from acting – we have no concerns while engaging ourselves in all sorts of complex situations. "In concerns, have no mind; in mind, have no concerns" is a famous statement by Deshan. It was a favorite of Nishida Kitarō, who often wrote it in his calligraphy. Bodhidharma tells us, "Getting free from the thought of the externality of all beings, stilling all hankerings in the mind, making the mind like pieces of wood or pebbles – one should thus enter the Way."[33] Both of these remarkable statements get to the heart of having "no concerns."

"Simply don't strive." Don't scheme this way or that, make discriminations between things, or search outside yourself for the Way or the Buddha. When we have no concerns, we never strive. Striving means to have concerns. Not striving means to be no-minded, to have no concerns.

Linji continues. All you have to do is "just be ordinary. Yet you go and run hither and thither outside." The monks look for the Self outside themselves. The admonition, "Just be ordinary," comes from Nanquan's[34] statement, "The calm and constant ordinary mind is the Way." This was his response when he was asked, "What is the Way?" It was the occasion whereby Zhaozhou encountered the living Dharma and opened up satori. Nanquan's reply is thus often quoted. But do *you* know what this calm and constant mind is? If your mind does not get beyond distinctions of past and present, or east and west, it falls far short of the truly calm and constant mind. So does an unsettled, transmigrating mind.

The calm and constant mind is everywhere, in every time and place. Nowhere is it lacking. It pervades all things. Unless it permeates one's body and mind, it cannot be considered the calm and constant mind. Only when this mind is our own do we have nothing to do and confront life-and-death and good-and-evil without becoming bewildered. In Zen we have an expression: "Being born and dying, coming and going, is the true subjectivity." This true human subjectivity is the calm and constant mind. This Self dies and lives without becoming confused in the midst of the manifold complications of human life. Any "mind" standing in distinction to body as consciousness or psyche differs from the calm and constant mind, which Zen refers to in the expression, "the transmission from Mind to Mind." This true Mind is anything but the normal mind, which never stays calm and constant.

Linji scolds his students: "Just be ordinary. Yet you go and run hither and thither outside and make inquiries." "Hither and thither" is a translation of two Chinese characters that literally mean a family or house other than one's own. We look outside ourselves and run around searching for something to help us, ignorant of the fact that our true "helper" is here close at hand. It is one's own affair – the True Self. We usually look for the True Self outside. But when we do, we are heading in the wrong direction, like when Yajñadatta searched for his head. Looking hither and thither is a great mistake.

"You're all wrong. You only try to seek Buddha, but Buddha is merely a name." Linji chides us for seeking Buddha outside ourselves. Buddha is then merely a name, a phrase, like any other of our discriminations. No matter how finely we distinguish something as Buddha, it will always fall short of the True Buddha. The sought Buddha is never the true one.

Nanquan said that "the calm and constant mind is the Way." With these words, he provided an opportunity for Zhaozhou to encounter the living Dharma. He also added, "If you try to seek it, you immediately turn against it." Ordinary Mind isn't found where we search. Now you might wonder how you can practice without seeking, but there isn't any room to doubt what Nanquan says. Whenever we search for Buddha and satori, we go against them. From the perspective of the Self, what we seek are mere names and phrases. Truth itself has nothing to do with language.

Linji asks his disciples, "Don't you know what it is that is running around seeking?" Everyone seeks Buddha, the Way, or the Self, but what is it that is scurrying about looking? You must turn your light in upon yourselves. That is to say, you must step back, not forward, and return to your source, to your center in the Dharma-nature. Then you return to the Self that is prior to the birth of *all* things, not just "prior to your birth from your parents." Whenever we forget the source from which all our discriminations arise, we turn to things apart from us. But that source is not other than us – it has to be the absolute Self, functioning right here. It is the calm and constant way of being, the One True Person without Rank. We must return to this True Self from which all discriminations emerge.

And yet we continue to search outside ourselves. However long we search, we cannot find our heads, for the searcher is the head itself. That is why Linji asks, "Don't you know what it is that is running around seeking?" We are all seeking. But what are we after? With this question, Linji guides people across the sea of life-and-death.

Linji continues. "The buddhas and founding teachers of the three periods and the ten directions appear only in order to seek the Dharma." To seek the Dharma is to realize what runs around searching. "You followers of the Way who are the students of today" – you who are assembled and endeavoring here – "you, too, have only to seek the Dharma." There is nothing else to do. All followers of the Way should just wholeheartedly seek the Dharma, with no distracting thoughts about other things. This, of course, is extremely difficult. It's one thing to be deluded about buddhas and founding teachers, but yet another to be hindered by external disturbances and internal delusions. If we are hindered by them, we can't seek the Dharma singlemindedly, and if we don't seek it singlemindedly, nothing is brought to fulfillment. Buddhas and founding teachers, on the other hand, *come only to seek the Dharma.*

Śākyamuni said, "Concentrating one's mind on a single matter, nothing is left unrealized." In discussing *dhyāna*, Buddhism stresses concentrating one's mind in one place. True *dhyāna* isn't merely a matter of controlling the mind, but it does have such an aspect. If our mind fails to become composed and settled, our practice will not reach completion. If we don't truly turn inward and concentrate the mind, our attention will drift outward as we try to ascertain what it is that seeks. In this unsettled condition, "our mind is constantly running around like a horse," "scrambling about like a monkey." If we stop at the point where our legs and shoulders hurt, we will never concentrate the mind and realize that which seeks. If we focus the mind, all inner and outer disturbances resolve themselves naturally. When we try to resolve them, they only become more tenacious. But if we sit and concentrate our minds on one thing – on that which seeks, the source of our seeking – our minds will naturally stop being distracted, even if we don't intend not to worry about our legs hurting or our attention drifting.

There is a Zen saying, "*Kenshō* comes first." This expresses the "one-mind" precept. We don't open satori by observing the precepts to the letter. When we do open up satori, all precepts are contained in it. The "formless one-mind precept" appears in the *Platform Sutra of the Sixth Founding Teacher* and Daitō Kokushi mentions it in one of his expositions on the Dharma. Those who think they can't achieve satori because of their sensual desires are told not to worry: if you achieve *kenshō*, such concern will disappear of itself, whether you try to resolve it or not. Even if you observe one, five, ten, three-hundred, or eighteen-hundred precepts, you will never achieve *kenshō*. *Kenshō* is immediate – there's no reason why it should be hard to attain. When we suddenly awaken to the Self, we see into our Original Nature. Of course, there is no need for us to become awakened – we already are.

"You, too, have only to seek the Dharma. Until then, you'll go on transmigrating through the five paths of existence." When one achieves *kenshō*, all transmigration is "turned over" and transformed into Dynamic Functioning. We transmigrate through the five paths or realms – hell, the land of hungry spirits, the animal kingdom, the human world, and heaven – tossed about by temporal and spatial matters. But we don't need to extricate ourselves from this. A line in one of Hanshan's[35] poems reads, "Ah! Round and round I go in the three worlds." This is not ordinary transmigration, but transmigration in which we stride boldly through the world. Ordinary transmigration has turned into free and unhindered activity.

Linji asks the assembly "What is the Dharma?" He has discussed our searching for the Dharma, and now he asks about the Dharma itself.[36] What sort of thing is the Dharma? What do *you* make it out to be? According to Linji, "The Dharma is the dharma of mind." The word "mind" is crucial here. Linji doesn't mean "mind" in the usual sense.

When he says the Dharma is the dharma of "mind," his words would have no impact if he himself were not this very mind-dharma; they would become mere terms and phrases. But he himself is this mind-dharma, and that which is genuine in his discourses is springing forth here with great vitality.

"The mind is without form; it pervades the ten directions and is functioning right before your eyes." These aren't written words – the mind-dharma is boldly presenting itself and Linji is asking his disciples if they can see it. He is in effect saying, "Without form, it's pervading the ten directions and manifesting itself right here before us. Do you see? What runs around doing the seeking is none other than it. It is revealing itself right here, right before your eyes. But you can't see it with your eyes. Even so, it's manifesting itself and functioning right in front of you."

Linji goes on to say that "people lack sufficient faith in this." We don't understand that which is functioning right before us. Our lack of faith stems from not noticing it and not becoming it, from its not *being present as us*. In this respect Linji is not talking about ordinary faith or devotion. It is not a matter of believing or not believing, knowing or not knowing, or even experiencing or not experiencing in the usual sense. Linji isn't pointing to a lack of belief or the negative consequences arising from it. Since we haven't awakened to the Self, we "accept names and phrases" and get caught up in mere words.

The assembly is told that they "try to speculate about the Buddha-Dharma from written words." "Written words" are not simply something on paper, but anything distinguished; not only scriptures and the records of founding teachers, but all discriminated things, discriminated nothingness included. We turn to them and from them try to speculate. In making precise distinctions and comparing various possibilities, we end up speculating about the Buddha-Dharma, in the sense of gauging and conjecturing. This is no different from a lack of faith, for it separates us from the mind-dharma that is the true Buddha-Dharma. In such speculation, the person and the Dharma drift as far apart as heaven and earth. It's like going east when you want to go west, or down when you want to go up. You're heading in the wrong direction, barking up the wrong tree.

"The mind-dharma is without form; it pervades the ten directions and is functioning right before your eyes." Isn't this the absolutely formless Self? I think that's enough for today.

9

You, the Follower of the Way Right Now before My Eyes Listening to the Dharma

In my talks until now, I have discussed the True Buddha. I have stressed its formlessness. Today I will continue that theme with an examination of the following discourse in the *Record:*

> Followers of the Way, the true Buddha has no shape, the true Dharma has no form. All you are doing is fashioning models and creating patterns out of illusory transformations. Anything you may find through seeking will be only a wild fox spirit; it certainly won't be true Buddha. It will be the understanding of a heretic.
>
> The true student of the Way has nothing to do with buddhas, nothing to do with bodhisattvas or arhats. Nor has he anything to do with what is held to be excellent in the three realms. Having transcended these, in solitary freedom, he is not bound by things. Even if heaven and earth were to turn upside down, I wouldn't have a doubt; even if all the buddhas of the ten directions were to manifest themselves before me, I wouldn't have any joy; even if the three hells were suddenly to yawn open at my feet, I would be fearless. Why is this so? Because, as I see it, all *dharmas* [things] are empty forms; when transformation takes place they are existent, when transformation does not take place, they are non-existent. The three realms are mind-only, the ten thousand *dharmas* are consciousness only. Hence:
>
> Illusory dreams, flowers in the sky – why trouble to grasp at them!
>
> Only *you*, the follower of the Way right now before my eyes listening to the Dharma, only you enter fire and are not burned, enter water and are not drowned, enter the three hells as if strolling through a pleasure garden, enter the realms of the hungry ghosts

and the beasts without suffering their fate. How can this be? There
are no *dharmas* to be disliked.

If you love the sacred and hate the secular, you'll float and sink in
the life-and-death sea. The passions exist dependent on mind: have
no-mind, and how can they bind you? Without troubling to discriminate or cling to forms, you'll attain the Way self-effectively in a
moment of time.

But if you try to get understanding by hurrying along this byway
and that, after three *asaṃkhyeya kalpas* you'll still end up in the
round of life-and-death. Better take your ease sitting crosslegged on
the corner of a bench in a monastery. (pp. 22–3)

All you followers of the Way. All of you studying and practicing Zen.
The True Buddha has no shape. The True Dharma no form. The True
Buddha is what Linji calls the "True Person," the "dharma of mind."
Our true way of being, the way of being truly human, has no shape. It
is beyond all shapes. It has no form whatsoever. When we use special
terms, like Buddha, nirvana, or *tathatā*, we tend to think of it as something apart from or transcendent of us. Here, "True Self" is so immediate and close at hand we can't even say it is "close." Inasmuch as such
words as Buddha and Dharma are apt to delude us, they are in this
respect hindrances.

Linji indicates our true way of being in such direct expressions as
"True Person" and "True Self." It is independent of words or letters,
and transmitted apart from scriptural teaching. Buddhism doesn't
really need scriptures. It is just our direct awakening to Self – here we
find the source of the Buddha-Dharma. Linji points to this when he
declares that there is no Buddha and no Dharma apart from "you, the
person who is listening" to the Dharma here at this moment. This
person has no shape, no form, no root, no source, and no abode, and
yet it is functioning here with great vitality in all circumstances.

Responding actively to all possible circumstances, the True Person
functions in a place that is no-place. Although we speak of the place of
the True Person's functioning, even that *place* does not exist. Again, it
is no-place. Hence Linji warns, "When you look for it, it retreats farther
and farther. When you seek it, it turns more and more the other way.
This is called the 'Mystery'." The Sixth Founding Teacher said that "the
Mystery is right where you are." To search for an external Mystery
outside oneself is far wide of the mark. It isn't something separate from
us. It is not found apart from the freely functioning, shapeless and
formless Self.

This mystery is never hidden. Linji, borrowing a Confucian expression, says, "I hide nothing from you." He means there is no mystery apart from the "person who is listening to the Dharma," the Person manifesting itself right before our eyes. Nevertheless, basing ourselves on false things, we grope about in the dark. Even if we should find something, it will be only a "wild fox spirit," an unreal apparition. Neither "Buddha" nor "Dharma" is the True Self, so if we should find either of them outside ourselves, it will be nothing but the spirit of the wild fox. In taking it to be the Buddha or Dharma, we will be followers of "wild fox" Zen. Linji tells his disciples that it "won't be the true Buddha," for it will be the understanding of a heretic, meaning that which is something different from truth.

"The true student of the Way has nothing to do with Buddhas." When we truly study and practice the Way, we don't seek or attach to any clay, wooden, metal, or conceptualised buddhas external to our True Self. Nor has the true student anything to do with bodhisattvas or arhats, or what is "held to be excellent in the three realms." There are countless excellent things in the three realms of desire, form, and formlessness. The true seeker has nothing to do with them. They are mere apparitions. Even if the brilliant gold figure of a buddha suddenly appeared, the seeker would know it for what it is, a wild fox spirit, and would not be deluded by it.

"Loftily emancipated from these, in solitary freedom, he is not bound by things." "Loftily emancipated" means to be liberated from all restrictions. This is how the true Buddha with no shape, the true Dharma with no form, is formless, empty, and dependent on nothing. And this itself is true existence. Since such a person is solitarily emancipated and non-dependent, he neither becomes attached to things nor reveres anything external to himself. This is the meaning of "without holiness" in Bodhidharma's celebrated answer to Emperor Wu's question about sacred truth: "Vastly open without holiness." In contrast, the "sacred truth" in the Emperor's question is a transcendent holiness, belonging to the dichotomy of the mundane and the holy. True holiness involves no distinction between the mundane and the holy, or between ordinary, unawakened humans and Buddha, the awakened one. True holiness is formless and solitarily emancipated, never bound by things.

"Even if heaven and earth were to turn upside down, I wouldn't have a doubt." I am the self that doesn't even begin to doubt when the world is turned upside down. This does not refer to doubting something objectively – my very Self is doubtless. It might best be called "the doubtless." Here there is neither doubting nor even not doubting, so I am totally free from doubt, no matter what happens.

Even if all the buddhas of the ten directions were to manifest themselves right before Linji, he says he would "have no joy." Such manifestations are no cause for rejoicing. Whoever experiences joy over such things has neither seen nor awakened to the formless True Buddha. Of course, we are apt to be deluded by the mysterious appearance of those manifestations. But the Formless Self is not bewildered. It doesn't mistake them for the True Buddha. Only in this total emancipation does the True Buddha appear.

When we penetrate the Formless Self, we experience no joy and no grief. For this very reason we can speak of total, eternal, true joy. Only in the "formless joy" is true joy found. It bears no resemblance to joy in the usual sense. We open up satori and exult, yet it is foolish to view such exultation as the mark of satori, for to be without joy or grief is the true state of awakening.

"Even if the three worlds were suddenly to yawn open at my feet, I would be fearless." If the three hells of covetousness, anger, and ignorance were to appear suddenly before Linji, he wouldn't feel a bit afraid. There is no room for fear to enter him. He neither fears nor does not fear. Again, this lack of fear does not indicate not fearing at certain times as opposed to fearing at others. The way of being in which one neither fears nor does not fear is the true "fearlessness," the true state of "having-no-fears" that is mentioned in the *Heart Sutra*. If we fail to attain such fearlessness, we cannot speak of being truly without fear.

Fear does not disappear through our eliminating individual fears one by one. Having no fear is simply a way of being, an aspect of the true Buddha or true human being. It is essential to realize that neither our lack of fear nor our lack of joy constitutes the true Buddha. True formlessness does not come from negating something in ourselves. Since our True Self is formless, all things are negated and affirmed once – through the presence of the Formless Self. Zen uses the term "sudden" for this, meaning that all things are negated and affirmed simultaneously, not little by little as in gradual practice and gradual satori.

This total negation-affirmation does not take place in the future or apart from us, for it is the true present. This is critical in our practice. We tend to search outside ourselves or within ourselves, but if inside and outside are themselves not the Self, they remain outside us. Linji stresses this point and lifts up the Self with his words, "you who are listening to the Dharma."

Why is this so? Why is there no thought of joy, grief, or fear? "Because as I see it," Linji says, "all *dharmas* are empty forms; when transformation takes place, they are existent, and when transformation does not take place, they are non-existent." When we awaken to emptiness as the characteristic of all that exists, we realize that all things are empty (Skt. *śūnya*) of self-nature. This emptiness is the true way of being of the Formless Self, for the characteristic of emptiness is to be formless. Linji tells his disciples that "when transformation takes place, they [*dharmas*] are existent, and when transformation does not take place, they are nonexistent." We usually think that whatever doesn't change exists, and whatever changes doesn't exist. But from the standpoint of emptiness, nothingness that is neither existent nor non-existent – in other words, that which is formless – is eternal. Being or existence, on the other hand, is that which is subject to change. True Being, however, is not this kind of being, nor is True Nothingness this kind of nothingness. The emptiness of all things means that when nothingness changes, it is being, and when being changes, it is nothingness. In terms of true emptiness, there is freedom from being and nothingness: not caught up in either, the True Self engages in total functioning through both being and nothingness. Accordingly, there is no reason to grieve if one is nothingness or rejoice if one is being.

"The three realms are mind-only, the ten thousand *dharmas* are consciousness-only." Now if we take this "mind-only" and "consciousness-only" to be that of the usual Buddhist theories of mind-only and consciousness-only, we will fail to grasp what is actually expressed. "Mind-only" must be the True Self. The same goes for "consciousness-only." The three worlds and the myriad *dharmas* arise from the True Self. Unless we awaken to the formless mind-only, we live amid the three worlds and myriad things that arise and disappear in endless transformation. This point is extremely important. From our perspective, Linji's statement, "the three worlds are mind-only, the ten thousand *dharmas* are consciousness-only," expresses the true Dharma-world. This is a world that is free of thoughts of joy or fear and freely manifests itself in accordance with all things. Since mind and consciousness usually are not seen in this way, they cannot be anything but the world of birth–death transmigration, the discriminated world of form. We must "turn over" the mind and consciousness so they may become the mind-only and consciousness-only that is the source of actuality. We have to turn over the eight consciousnesses, die to our usual mind and consciousness. Only then do we attain the true mind and true consciousness, the mind and consciousness of the True

Person. In this attainment, the eight consciousnesses, which are but wild fox spirits, turn over and become the four wisdoms.[37] The four wisdoms are the true world of actuality.

We face the constant danger of viewing the eight consciousnesses as the true mind or true consciousness. Zen has always made much of Zhaozhou's statement, "Cut down with a sword into the field of the eight consciousnesses."[38] The "field" or foundation called the eight consciousnesses – including ordinary consciousness and the unconscious – is our "mind field." From this mind-field arise all our discriminations. We must rid ourselves of this field by striking down into it.

The Chinese priest Yuanwu says, "There is nothing much to my functioning."[39] There really isn't anything special about the functioning of the True Zen Person. We annihilate the eight consciousnesses with one stroke of the sword. This is immediate awakening. The eight consciousnesses "turn over" and become the four wisdoms, and the nest of binding passions and delusions is destroyed.

"Hence, these illusory dreams, flowers in the sky – why trouble to grasp at them?" They are all negated with ease. And when needed, they are used freely. When we gain new life through death, illusory dreams and flowers in the sky change into the true form of reality.

"Only *you*, the follower of the Way right now before my eyes listening to the Dharma" – this person is right here. Nothing is hidden. This listener has no form. It is the Formless Self, the person of the Way who is solitarily emancipated and non-dependent.

"Only you enter fire and are not burned, enter water and are not drowned, enter the three hells as if strolling through a pleasure garden." In Buddhist terminology, "pleasure garden" usually refers to a place of holy seers. It is not necessarily akin to the realm of hermits, though – it is the true world. The person of the Way disports himself in this true world without joy or despair. He or she goes freely through heaven and hell.

Linji tells us that this follower of the Way "enters the realms of the hungry ghosts and the beasts without suffering their fate." He wanders among beasts without descending to their level, totally unaffected by them. He is emancipated from all adverse circumstances and goes in and out of them at will. Emancipation and affirmation are realized by only one agent: this *you* who is listening to the Dharma talk. What is this listener?

In addressing his disciples, Linji often says such things as "How can this be? There are no *dharmas* to be disliked." We find similar expressions in the *Xinxin-ming*:[40] "Just avoid picking and choosing" and

"When the mind does not arise, the ten thousand dharmas have no fault." There are no things to be disliked. This has nothing to do with liking or disliking something. Nor is it a matter of loathing ordinary humans and seeking the holy, or of detesting hell and searching for heaven. To dislike one thing and search for another is the very source of birth-death transmigration and sinful karma. What is confused in this way about the Buddha and searches about for it is a sentient being. What has awakened to the Buddha is a buddha, an awakened one. Birth-death transmigration arises from our confusion about the Buddha. Because we have not grasped the true way of being of the Buddha, anything we take as the Buddha only becomes an obstruction to practice, a hindrance to our realization of the true Buddha. We need to cut away and discard our attachment to the Buddha and the Dharma. Not to be caught up in the Buddha or the Dharma is the true stance to have in practice, and the consequent non-arising of mind is our True Self. Therefore, "if you love the sacred and hate the secular" you will give rise to birth-death transmigration and forever fail to find your way out of it.

"The passions exist dependent on mind: have no-mind and how can they bind you?" Passions arise in any mind that picks and chooses. Without such a selective mind, how can passions bind you? Actually, then our very passions are awakening, for they turn over and become awakening, so there is no reason to hate passions and no need to seek awakening. When you realize this, you will discover true Awakening.

"Without troubling to discriminate or cling to forms, you'll attain the Way self-effectively in a moment of time." If we neither like nor dislike things, if we are not caught up in this, the Way will be realized of itself without a moment's delay. Of course, it is not that we attain it – it is unattainable. The Way is presencing itself right now. This is its true way of being. If you wait a moment to grasp it, you will be too late. The Way is the self-effecting Dharma. It is not made to be as it is by something else – it is as it is from within by its very nature. Actually, there is nothing that makes it so and nothing that is so. This is the true self-effecting Dharma, and precisely this is the True Self. Without seeking anything, the True Self is present here as the manifestation of absolute truth.

Linji continues: "But if you try to get understanding by hurrying along this byway and that, after three *asaṃkhyeya kalpas* you'll still end up in the round of birth–death transmigration." We cannot part from the world of birth–death transmigration and attain the Way by running all over the place. Since we often mistake the source of birth–death transmigration for the True Self, we cannot extricate ourselves from that world. The birth-death transmigration we "end up in" is not birth and death alone in a literal sense. It is the world with existent things and non-existent things, things with value and things without value. We cannot readily extricate ourselves from that world.

Therefore, you had "better take your ease sitting cross-legged on the corner of a bed in a monastery." "Take your ease" is like Linji's "noble person who *has no concerns*." This is the realm of one who has gone beyond birth–death transmigration, who has "gone back home and sits calmly," who has returned to the True Self. I don't mean to imply that this is some sort of existent realm – it is no-thing. This no-thing, this having "no concerns," isn't a passive approach to life, either. Rather, it is true, unrestricted functioning. Acting without restriction and yet not acting; involved in many things, yet having no concerns; having no concerns yet engaging oneself in many things: such is the "no concerns" spoken of here. It isn't something passive, as in the command to "stop fretting and sit down." On the contrary, it is the ultimate realm of awakening.

The "monastery" Linji speaks of is actually the world. "Sitting cross-legged" must be the sitting (J. *za*) of the walking, standing, sitting, and lying indicated by the expression, "Walking, too, is Zen; lying, too is Zen." Otherwise it is not yet truly having no concerns. Linji tells his disciples to reach the true realm of having no concerns. Actually, you don't have to arrive at that realm – it is *you* just as you are.

10
Independent of All Things

In the *Record*, Linji addresses the assembly as follows:

> Followers of the Way, if you want insight into the Dharma as is, just
> don't be deluded by others. Whatever you encounter, either within
> or without, slay it at once. On meeting a buddha, slay the buddha;
> on meeting a founding teacher, slay the founding teacher; on
> meeting an arhat, slay the arhat; on meeting your parents, slay your
> parents; on meeting your kin, slay your kin – only then do you
> attain emancipation. By not cleaving to things, you freely pass
> through. (p. 25)

He tells them, "Followers of the Way, if you want insight into the
Dharma as is, just don't be deluded by others." This insight is the "true
insight" mentioned earlier in the *Record*. It is beyond our discriminat-
ing mind. Should you desire to realize this insight and penetrate the
True Buddha, the True Dharma, and the Formless Self, you mustn't get
confused by anything outside yourself. Not only people but also things
separate from the Self are delusive, and you can't let them confuse you.
You must awaken to the Self that is never deluded by others.

Linji drives this point home: "Whatever you encounter, either
within or without, slay it at once!" Each and every thing you come
upon must be dealt a blow of that stuff and a loud "*kaah!*" The word
"within" refers to all the mental phenomena that arise in our minds;
"without" indicates the countless external things in the world. We
mustn't get confused by any of them. Since they prevent the true,
formless Self from awakening, Linji tells us to "slay" them all, to
negate each and every one of them. This killing must be absolute.
Destroying things or depriving a body of life falls short of what Linji

describes. So does mere mental or logical negation. In his negating, all things disappear together. As indicated by such expressions as "Originally, not-a-single-thing" and "like empty space," nothing is there, not even a speck of dust. This is what Linji means by slaying. If you think you have slain by taking life, that thought will have to be slain, too.

"Whatever you encounter, either within or without," you must destroy completely. Sparing nothing, you obliterate everything, and only then do you find tranquility. But if you should get attached to the slaying, you will mistake it for true insight and end up seeing only the slaying. If that happens, the slaying will never be anything positive or active. This is an extremely important point.

All things are slain together when the Formless Self presents itself. Such is true, immediate Awakening, the self-awakening of the Formless Self. People who emphasize only negation teeter on the brink of utter darkness. And those who speak of affirmation in the usual sense are merely affirming things within or without. The true affirmation, on the other hand, is that which has thoroughly negated all things. It is the true insight into the Dharma as it is. It has eliminated all confusion caused by others and all perplexity about the Buddha. In fact, in this true insight, delusion can't even begin to arise.

With this in mind, Linji says, "On meeting a buddha, slay the buddha." In Buddhism, nothing is more revered than a buddha. Yet quite often a so-called "buddha" must be slain, for we can get confused about it. In other words, whenever a buddha is something apart from us, we become perplexed about it. Hence we must slay it – if we don't, the true Buddha will never appear. And when you meet a founding teacher, "slay the founding teacher," too. Bodhidharma, Linji, Dōgen – none of them is anything true. But since we consider them true, we get caught up in their acts and words, and so doing, lose sight of the True Self. Kill the founding teachers, too! If you merely pay homage to such disciples of the Buddha as the sixteen or five-hundred arhats, you'll never attain true insight.

Linji goes even further: "On meeting your parents, slay your parents." As far as our physical bodies are concerned, our gratitude finds no greater object than our mother and father. But if we regard them as sacrosanct, they, too, will delude us. This is true for other close relatives as well, so Linji says, "On meeting your kin, slay your kin." Only by slaying all those people do you attain emancipation. "Emancipation" is our shaking free from all of them, even buddhas. This is the only way we can become totally free.

Except for the true insight – the True Self – there is nothing sacred. Even so, the True Self isn't to be discriminated as sacred. Apart from the True Self just as it is, the solitarily emancipated, non-dependent Self, the Original Face which is not-a-single-thing, there is no true Buddha. Anything other than this True Self is delusive. So if you don't penetrate the Self, you will never attain emancipation.

Linji refers to sutras, commentaries, and precepts – the so-called twelvefold division of teachings in the Three Vehicles – as "just so much paper to wipe off privy filth." Ordinarily, people would consider it sacrilegious to speak of them in that way. But from what standpoint do we judge Linji's statement to be sacrilegious? Very few of us have realized the true holiness of these teachings from their source. We tend to regard them as holy because they are said to be holy, or because they are the teachings of Śākyamuni, Vasubandhu, Dharmākara,[41] or other prominent Buddhists of the past. But have we actually realized their holiness in the depths of our hearts? If we haven't, our reverence is but deluded belief, a simple adherence to dogma. At the base of our being we can realize that such teachings are deserving of reverence. But if we don't penetrate to that depth, taking something as holy will be delusive – Dharma delusion, as it were – hence anything but sacred.

Emancipation, then, is neither a feeling nor a temporary experience: it is the very way of being of the Formless Self. Accordingly, for Zen, *kenshō* is crucial. To see the Self, to bring about the self-awakening of the True Self, is our primary concern, for if we fail to awaken, everything is delusion, and we become inextricably caught up in our binding passions. Accordingly, such occurrences in Zen *mondō* as abrupt hitting with staffs and the yelling of "kaah!" should not be interpreted in our ordinary way of thinking. If all internal and external things are truly slain upon the blow of the staff, the staff itself is holy and deserving of gratitude. But it is not the staff that has done the slaying – nothing is given by the staff, nothing at all. What happens is that the Self awakens to itself. If we mistake our ordinary self for the True Self, any attempt to awaken by means of it will be like looking for fish up in a tree. People often speak of self-power and other-power, with Zen supposedly corresponding to the former. Ordinary self-power, however, cannot become true self-power if it doesn't disappear. Self-power is true self-power only when the "self" involved is the Formless Self. This Formless Self awakens only through itself; more accurately put, the Formless Self self-awakens.

I speak of awakening to the Formless Self. It is important to note that we do not have someone else awaken us, for we can awaken only by ourselves. Linji tells his disciples that in attaining emancipation, one does not cleave to things. As the Formless Self, we don't cling to anything internal. In this way we never get stuck, not even in ourselves. So if what we take to be the Formless Self gets stuck, it is anything but the true Formless Self I speak of here.

Awakened, "you pass freely through." Since we adhere to nothing, we are free. There are no obstructions; we are unhindered and self-abiding. This is quantitatively and qualitatively different from being free in the usual sense. In passing freely, we don't get attached to things. But, if we get caught up in this non-attachment, it becomes a mere condition or state of mind. More than our not being attached, the lack of any attachment whatsoever is true existence. There is no need for support from others.

In the *Record*, Linji also says,

> Among all the students from every quarter who are followers of the Way, none have come before me without being dependent on something. Here I hit them right from the start. If they come forth using their hands, I hit their hands; if they come forth using their mouths, I hit their mouths; if they come forth using their eyes, I hit their eyes. Not one has come before me in solitary freedom. All are clambering after worthless contrivances of men of old. As for myself, I haven't a single *dharma* to give to people. All I can do is cure illness and unloosen bonds. You followers of the Way from every quarter, come before me without being dependent upon things. Then I will confer with you. (p. 25)

"Among all the students from every quarter who are followers of the Way, none have come before me without being dependent on something." I want to focus on this statement, for it is central to today's talk. Linji tells the assembly that no one has come forward without being attached. He urges his disciples to come forth without being dependent on anything. Whoever can do so is beyond attachment to any internal or external thing. But what is it that comes forth in this way?

Our mutual investigation and negotiation of the Way must emerge without our being dependent on anything. If we find in this mutual investigation that we are attached, we must slay all things, no matter what they are. Wherever you are, come forth without being dependent on anything!

Linji continues his talk, saying, "Here this mountain monk hits them right from the start." The mountain monk is Linji, and he is letting us know that he strikes anyone who comes forth dependent on something. He doesn't let them open their mouths. Such severity is found throughout Zen. Hearing this, some people might consider Zen unapproachable. Having difficulty entering into Zen, they might complain that it is distant and unrelated to them. Yet as long as it seems distant, we can't possibly come forth without being dependent on anything.

To strike, strike, and strike again; to be struck, struck, and struck again. Meeting a buddha, slay the buddha; meeting a founding teacher, slay the founding teacher. The more something seems holy, the more you must kill it. Whatever we are attached to is likely to appear sacred, and this is the greatest source of confusion.

Linji tells us, "Here I hit them right from the start. If they come forth using their hands, I hit their hands." If people show up doing something with their hands, Linji strikes them there right away. In Zen, we find many instances of people bowing with their hands pressed together, slapping others on the cheek, and doing various things with staffs. It is clear from Zen records that no other teaching expresses itself to this extent through the hands as opposed to speech. Assuming this is true, it is highly significant.

But, by generating assorted forms and postures with such hand movements, people have imitated Zen expressions. Linji tells his disciples that he strikes without hesitation whenever the use of the hands is mere imitation or the result of someone scheming this or that. Whether the person comes with a palm, hand, fist, arm, or grasped object, Linji strikes it. Such is the sharpness of his functioning. It approves nothing. People might ask why nothing is acceptable. Why isn't anything acceptable? Things aren't acceptable because they aren't. This is a truth. There isn't even any need to say, "Because they are unacceptable they are not acceptable."

"If they come forth using their mouths, I hit their mouths." If someone steps forth saying something, Linji will hit the person on the mouth. People utter various words and phrases, but Linji doesn't accept any of them. The mouth he speaks of here is that which gives reasons, speaks in a loud or soft voice, or is silent. No matter how the mouth is used, whoever comes forth relying on it is immediately struck by him.

"If they come forth using their eyes, I hit their eyes." If people step before him doing something with their eyes, Linji will immediately poke them. Eyes do many things: they open, close, blink, stare, glance to the side, and look at things. Zen often uses the expression, "raising the eyebrows and blinking the eyes." To raise the eyebrows or blink the eyes is, in truth, a living technique, a vivid act of Awakening. And yet the eyes tend to be used in ways which call for a blow.

As a group, these actions of the hands, mouth, and eyes correspond to the body, mouth, and mind: the deeds, words, and thought referred to in Buddhism as the three categories of karmic actions. These actions are not limited to the hands, mouth, or eyes, though. No matter what part of the body is relied upon when a person comes forth, Linji will strike it. "Body" here indicates any part of the body or the body as a whole. Whenever people come forth using the body, they are struck. If you come forth using the mouth, you will be struck in the mouth. No matter what you say or what sounds you make, Linji will hit you immediately. If you come forth using the eyes, he'll hit your eyes. Though he doesn't discuss them individually, Linji is referring to the six consciousnesses – the five sense organs and what we usually call consciousness. He doesn't specifically mention the mind in the *Record*, but fundamentally he is dealing with the body, mouth, and mind as the three loci of action, and the eye, ear, nose, tongue, body, and mind as the six consciousnesses.

"Not one has come before me in solitary freedom." This is the same as his statement, "None have come before me without being dependent on something." "Something" here doesn't indicate matter or an entity with a three-dimensional form. In "solitary freedom," one is not dependent on *any* sort of "thing" in any way at all. To Linji, no one has come forth in solitary freedom – everyone has shown up dependent on something.

"All are clambering after worthless contrivances of men of old." The prominent Zen figures preceding Linji said and did various things that have become occasions for the Awakening of others. If we merely imitate them, our behavior will fall short of living action. In modern Zen, the use of old-case koans often amounts to nothing more than a "clambering after worthless contrivances of men of old." Although *living* koans are most important in Zen, koans tend to become mere forms, or are seen as pertaining to men in times gone by. Koans often are mere imitations and emasculations of living Zen, and thus lack vitality. At present this is one danger with koans, an evil they have universally fallen into. Even in his day Linji cautioned against this. Of course, at that time there were no koans as we presently know them, but many people turned to the occasions of the awakening of past Zen masters and came forth trying to make use of them.

When truly alive people make use of something in all of its vitality, they do not get caught up in distinctions between old and new.

Usually, though, the old is mere dregs or remnants and the new is an imitation or fabrication. In light of this danger, we must come forth in solitary freedom, independent of all things. We don't need to rely on ancient masters. Right now, truth is presenting itself – it is immediately present. This is the true insight. No immediately-present truth is found apart from the True Buddha, the True Dharma, or the Formless Self.

So Linji says, "As for myself, I haven't a single *dharma* to give to them." All is originally possessed by each and every one of you. By everyone, with no exceptions: *you* are that truth. Sometimes, when people hear what Linji says here, the True Self immediately awakens. Indeed, you have everything you need just as you are this very moment. "Just as you are" – there are no truer words than these.

When people hear the expression, "Just as you are," they wonder if it only refers to their present condition. In the Tang dynasty, Huiming, one of the disciples of the Fifth Founding Teacher, ran after the Sixth Founding Teacher, whom Huiming assumed had gone away with the transmission of Zen from the Fifth Founding Teacher. Hoping to get the transmission, Huiming overtook the Sixth Founding Teacher, who said to him, "Think not of good, think not of evil. At that very moment, let me see your original face." Told in effect, "Isn't it you, just as you are right now?" Huiming immediately opened up Great Awakening. Therefore, *not* being just as you are is false, a sort of lie, as it were. If we penetrate the statement that we are fulfilled just as we are, our investigation will arrive at the manifestation of the true Original Face, the immediately present truth.

People often ask questions about the nature of Zen, the Buddha, or the Dharma, but their questions cannot be answered by those who are questioned. The answer is in the questioner. There's no need to ask. Linji's "I haven't got a single *dharma* to give" means the same thing as a well-known statement by Deshan, the master who burned his commentaries on the *Diamond Sutra*: "In my teaching, there are no utterances to make." There is nothing that ought to be discussed in Zen. This is quite reasonable and matter of fact. That's why both men, and other masters, make such statements.

Musō the National Teacher, founder of Tenryūji in Kyoto, practiced under a master named Yishan Yining.[42] Musō is not regarded as Yishan's Dharma-heir, but he received the benefit of Yishan's instruction and has much in common with him. For example, Musō's calligraphy originated in Yishan's works, and this is evident in the strong stylistic resemblance. Early in his training, Musō went to Yishan and said to him, "The very matter of my true Self is still unclear." The elucidation of our True Self is none other than Zen practice. Musō was asking for instruction so as to clarify his Self, like many people had done. In response, Yishan said, "In my teaching, there are no utterances to make. I haven't a single truth to give to people." Deshan and Linji had already said this, so it might seem that Yishan was trying to improvise with borrowed expressions. But his were not words of empty imitation. What he said came from deep within his being; his statement was an expression of the True Self. Were he not expressing the True Self by uttering such ultimate words, he would be lapping up the dregs left over by others before him. In Linji's terms, he would be "clambering after the worthless contrivances of men of old." If Yishan were an imitator, he would have to be told to kill all the founding teachers he met.

Though it varies slightly depending on the speaker, the expression, "I haven't a single truth to give to others," comes forth from the True Self. It stresses that there is nothing to teach or to be taught, and that a mind that desires to be taught deviates from the truth. We should not think of having others teach us about satori or give it to us: what counts is the investigation and elucidation of one's own matter.

The statement that there is nothing to give is highly significant. Awakening isn't something that can be given to another. Linji tells his disciples that all he can do is "cure illnesses and unloosen bonds." He can only remove obstacles. That from which obstacles are removed is unmistakably the Self. It would be completely wrong, though, to think that curing diseases and removing obstacles is all there is to awakening to the Self. If having someone cure our illnesses and unloosen our bonds were enough, such a self would be totally empty. The view that such a removal is enough results from worthless emphasis on emancipation and negation. As stated by the Sixth Founding Teacher, fundamentally we have no illnesses or bonds: "Originally, not-a-single-thing, so where is the dust to cling?" Bonds and illnesses cannot exist in the Self.

"You followers of the Way from every quarter," all of you seekers pursuing the Way, "try coming before me without being dependent on things." Linji said earlier that no one had come before him without being dependent on something. Now he asks his disciples to actually come forth without relying on anything. He asks them to step forth so he can meet their True Self and negotiate the Way with them. This is the true encounter. No other way of encounter comes close – it is the consummation of a Zen *mondō*. As we saw before, a *mondō* is never a matter of the hands, mouth, or eyes, nor of movements, vocalizations, or thoughts: it hinges upon that which comes forth without being dependent on anything – the true agent of *mondō*, the host and the guest.

Linji further states,

> Five years, nay ten years, have passed, but as yet not one person has appeared. All have been ghosts dependent on grasses or attached to leaves, souls of bamboos and trees, wild fox spirits. They recklessly gnaw on all kinds of dung clods. Blind fools! Wastefully squandering the alms given them by believers everywhere and saying, "I am a renouncer of home!" all the while holding such views as these.
>
> I say to you there is no Buddha, no Dharma, nothing to practice, nothing to realize. Just what are you seeking thus in the highways and byways? How blind! You're putting a head on top of the one you already have. What do you yourself lack? (p. 25)

"Five years, nay ten years, have passed, but as yet not one *person* has appeared," says Linji. No one has come forth as the *you* who is listening to the Dharma. Linji's statement makes it hard for us to talk lightly about satori or koans. He in effect says to his disciples, "What are you if you haven't penetrated that great matter?" Koans that are passed through one by one are mere contrivances of men of old. We mustn't fall into such delusion concerning our koan practice. Zen has declared that it never descends to the level of sutras, commentaries, or precepts, yet it has fallen into these contrivances of men of old. It has gotten itself chained to old-case koans. Zen is of no use if it fails to be an immediate manifestation of truth.[43]

Those who fail to attain this are all ghosts "dependent on grasses or attached to leaves, souls of bamboos and trees." Though we might not be attached to grasses and leaves, we, too, can be spirits caught up in all sorts of internal and external things.

Solitarily emancipated and non-dependent, we are what we truly are. Otherwise, we aren't worthy of mutual investigation with Linji. But when we are what we truly are, the mutual investigation is over even before it begins.

"They recklessly gnaw on all kinds of dung clods." How revolting! Yet everyone acts that way. The blind fools without true insight waste the alms given by the faithful. All they do is collect alms and dissipate them on clothing, food, and shelter. They go about "wastefully squandering the alms given them by believers everywhere, saying, 'I am a renouncer of home!'" They profess themselves monks or renouncers of the world, but contradict such self-designations with their actions.

Wearing purple garments and robes of gold brocade, seated as guests of honor in parishioners' homes, they self-complacently pronounce themselves monks. "All the while," they are "holding such views as these." Linji comes down hard on them. He asks his disciples if monks who are no different from maggots burrowing in dung qualify as true renouncers of home. His critical power is in a class of its own.

Back then, there were problems like those Linji points out. What about now? Over a thousand years have passed since Linji's death. Those long years must surely have had a maturing effect. Contrary to what you might expect, though, with the passage of time, Zen has begun to dote. It is now gasping for life.

"I say to you there is no Buddha, no Dharma, nothing to practice, nothing to realize. Just what are you seeking in the highways and byways?" People search outside for the Buddha or the Dharma that is majestically present in themselves. They practice *zazen*, and try to open up satori. Linji asks them what it is they are searching for external to themselves. He asks them, in effect, "Why don't you look inside yourself? What are you going to seek outside? Isn't it your Original Face that you are searching for?"

Linji continues, "How blind! You're putting a head on top of the one you already have." It's like putting a roof over the one already on the house, or holding a bamboo hat over the one already on your head. You have it right now! Zen literature offers many statements about searching. A section in Hakuin's *Zazen wasan* (Hymn in Praise of Zazen) reads, "It's no different from someone being born a child in the house of a rich man, yet getting lost in an impoverished village." The *Record of Linji* tells of how Yajñadatta "lost his head." The commentary on *Ten Pictures of an Ox* tells of a person who thinks he has lost his ox, even though it has never been lost. Not knowing where to look, he wanders around vacantly, searching in mountains and fields. Finally, he realizes that what he has been seeking all along is the searcher himself. Well aware of what can happen to someone in that situation, Linji addresses those who come to him as "*you* who are listening to the Dharma."

"What do you yourself lack?" Through what deficiency are you searching? That which knows sufficiency is itself complete. Everything is provided. There is an infinite treasury in the midst of not-a-single-thing. Nothing is lacking. As I've mentioned before, only by realizing in yourself the true words spoken by Linji can you read and listen to his *Record*.

11
Not at all Thus

As I discussed in my last talk, Linji asks his disciples to come forth without being dependent on anything. This is described in the section of the *Record* entitled "Critical Examinations," which refers to mutual examination of the depth of one another's way of being. Ordinarily a seeker of the Way engages in a *mondō* with a master. The master probes the student, and the student probes the master. This mutual investigation of the Way unfolds vigorously in the interaction between Linji and Puhua:[44]

> Puhua was always going around the streets ringing a little bell and calling out:
>> If you come as brightness, I hit the brightness;
>> Come as darkness, I hit the darkness;
>> Come from the four quarters and eight directions, I hit like a whirlwind;
>> Come from empty sky, I lash like a flail.
>
> The Master told his attendant to go and, the moment he heard Puhua say these words, to grab him and ask, "If coming is not at all thus, what then?"
> The attendant went off and did as he was instructed.
> Puhua pushed the attendant away, saying, "There'll be a feast tomorrow at Dabei-yuan [Great Compassion Temple]."
> The attendant returned and told this to the Master. The Master said, "I've always wondered about that fellow." (p. 42)

Puhua lived in Zhenzhou from before Linji established the Dharma there on the bank of the Hutuo River. His teacher was Panshan Baoji,[45] an outstanding Zen master. The occasions and opportunities Panshan provided to help others awaken to the Dharma are now used as koans. He once said in a talk, "The three realms [of desire, form, and formlessness] are without any characteristics, so in what place do you seek your Self?" This parallels the question the old woman asked Deshan on his pilgrimage: "If the past self is unattainable, the present self unattainable, and the future self unattainable, what self do you intend to refresh?" Zen records abound with such questions.

Now this Panshan was a disciple and Dharma-heir of Mazu Daoyi, which makes Puhua a grand-disciple of Mazu. Historical data on Puhua is lacking, so it is not known where or when he was born. From all indications, he was quite eccentric. And yet he wasn't a nobody, or a mere off-beat monk. Rather, he was a highly capable master, whose conduct happened to be out of the ordinary.

This does not pertain directly to the subject at hand, but, as you might know, in Japan those who play the bamboo flute as a form of Zen practice are referred to as the Fuke School. This school is named after Puhua (J. Fuke), and the monks regard him as their founding teacher. They have an organization called Meian Kyōkai, the Association for the Teaching of Brightness–Darkness, whose members – itinerant Fuke priests – carry dark begging bags with the white characters *mei-an* (brightness–darkness).

Near where Linji lived, Puhua went around the streets ringing a bell. As he walked, he announced, "If you come as brightness, I hit the brightness." "Brightness" refers to discriminations, things which are clear and totally manifested. As a thousand differences and ten thousand distinctions, countless things are presenting themselves in brightness. In terms of Dongshan's system of the Five Ranks,[46] this is the rank of the leaning, of a part or a distinct entity, and it is represented by a white circle. Whenever this brightness comes, Puhua hits it; when the part shows up, he deals it a blow.

Puhua says more: "Come as darkness, I hit the darkness." In opposition to brightness, "darkness" refers to that which is without discrimination. In total darkness, we can't see anything, so distinct objects can't even begin to appear. In terms of the Five Ranks, this is the straight, the place of non-discrimination and equality. It is depicted by a totally blackened circle. The condition of knowing nothing while in total darkness isn't ignorance in the usual sense, for in Dongshan's view, the straight and the leaning, or equality and discrimination, are an inseparable pair like brightness and darkness; they are "the straight with the leaning inside, and the leaning with the straight inside."

As I said in my last talk, the true Buddha is without form, and the true Dharma without shape. This formless, shapeless Original Face is expressed by the black circle. It is totally different from ordinary ignorance, for ignorance (Skt. *avidyā*) has been broken through and has become true knowledge (Skt. *vidyā* or *prajñā*). The black circle thus stands for the unique, formless True Self of equality and non-discrimination. To regard it as ignorance is to confuse heaven and earth. In Buddhist terminology, darkness refers to nirvana, nirvana as Emptiness or Nothingness. Brightness is its functioning, the discriminations that appear as the expressions of Nothingness, and hence it is anything but discriminations in the ordinary sense.

This, then, is the darkness that is none other than brightness, and the brightness that is none other than darkness. Neither is effected alone, for it is only when they are one that they can be, respectively, brightness and darkness. First Puhua talks about brightness: when brightness comes along, he hits it. Next he tells us that when darkness shows up, he strikes that, too. Neither brightness nor darkness is acceptable, so Puhua announces that he hits them both.

This is not the first place in the history of Zen where we encounter "brightness and darkness." They appear before Puhua's time both as individual terms and in such expressions as "brightness and darkness as an inseparable pair." It is Puhua, however, who first darts about the streets, ringing a bell and telling everyone that "If you come as brightness, I hit the brightness; come as darkness, I hit the darkness." The activity that takes up brightness and darkness, that very way of being, is widely known as Puhua's unique Zen functioning. So, whenever we hear the words, "Come as brightness, I hit the brightness," we are immediately reminded of him. In fact, the expression is so unique to him that it seems to be tied up with his very being.

Since Puhua walks the streets talking about how he hits brightness and darkness, other pedestrians see him as deranged, and wonder what he's talking about. He wanders around ringing a bell, and indeed, to perform a Buddhist mass while playing a tune of brightness and darkness is a fine model for itinerant monks: "Come as brightness, I hit the brightness; come as darkness, I hit the darkness. I strike them both down."

"Come from the four quarters and the eight directions, I hit like a whirlwind." Puhua lets everyone know that when people come from any of the many possible directions with no gaps between them, considering or calling themselves "something," he whirls about and strikes them down. Many things show up from the four quarters and eight directions: sometimes enemies and at other times buddhas and bodhisattvas. Even if all of them were to show up together from every direction, Puhua would knock them all down.

When you "come from empty sky, I lash like a flail." In more common parlance, "empty sky" is space. Space has no form, so even if you come without form, Puhua will "lash like a flail." The flail spoken of here is a tool for threshing rice, millet, and other grains. Nowadays there are advanced machines for doing such work, but in the past grains were threshed by an assortment of tools. Some were T-shaped instruments, and others were staffs. The flail of which Puhua speaks is a pole with short rods fastened to the end, so with a single movement the tool strikes the grain in several places at once. In any case, should empty sky appear, Puhua will lash at it again and again without a moment's delay. No matter what comes, regardless of the direction, be it brightness or darkness, and even if it should be "without form," Puhua will strike it down. This he lets everyone know, as he walks down the street ringing a bell.

Seen from an ordinary perspective, Puhua takes negation to an extreme. He sweeps everything away. He says he negates each and every thing that comes along. This is the total negation expressed by the words, "Meeting a buddha, slay the buddha; meeting a founding teacher, slay the founding teacher." It spares nothing. Were but a single grain of millet to remain, his action would fall short of true negation, the Original Face of not-a-single-thing. He must strike both being and non-being, "is" and "is not." His Awakening is so penetrating that he accepts nothing. If he didn't take negation to this extreme, it would fall short of true negation, and would never result in the way of being of not-a-single-thing. He is the one who comes forth completely independent. In a sense, he walks around challenging people to "come forth without being dependent on anything."

Given their shared way of being in the mode of "not-a-single-thing," we must regard Puhua and Linji as intimate friends. Although he was a disciple of Panshan, Puhua helped Linji in his teaching in Zhenzhou. He is highly praised by Linji himself, and hence occupies an important position in the *Record*. In the episode in question, Linji hears that Puhua is hanging around the streets. Eager to investigate him, he devises a scheme to find out how Puhua handles things and where he stands (Ch. *jiaoxia*, J. *kyakka*) in his Awakening. He tells his attendant to go to Puhua, and the moment he hears him utter his unique words, to grab him and say, "If coming is not-at-all-thus, what then?" Linji thus sends an attendant to check Puhua out.

The attendant is said to be Luopu.[47] Although he is not mentioned by name in the *Record* or in any of the commentaries on the text, apparently he was staying at Linji's place, serving the master as an assistant. Since Luopu, too, is a man of ability, Linji chooses him to test Puhua. He tells him that if he sees Puhua walking around ringing a bell and saying, "Come as brightness, I hit the brightness," he should grab him and ask, "If coming is not-at-all-thus, what then?" "Thus" here means "in such a manner," and the negative is best expressed directly as "not like that," "not in such a manner," or "not-at-all-thus."

When someone comes not-at-all-thus, what then? Linji in effect says to Luopu, "Go ask Puhua about when someone comes not as brightness or darkness, nor from the four quarters and eight directions, nor from empty sky." Come forth not-at-all-thus. Certainly this is a complete negation, just as with Puhua's functioning before. With it, Linji tests whether Puhua's negation is total or not, whether it knocks down brightness and darkness, the four quarters and eight directions, the empty sky, and everything else.

To come forth not-at-all-thus, and to come forth without being dependent on anything – as problems posed to Puhua, these are the same. Such is the approach in our practice: if coming is not-at-all-thus, then what? In this episode, we can see the keenness of the *mondō* between Linji and Puhua, the sharpness of their awakened functioning. How will Puhua receive the way of being that is thrust at him by Linji, the way of being in which one is not-a-single-thing? The way he "receives" Linji is truly a marvel. How does he receive Linji's awakened functioning? Linji is quite ill-natured, but Puhua is no ordinary man.

Luopu goes to Puhua and asks him, "Of coming is not-at-all-thus, what then?" Puhua pushes him away, saying, "There'll be a feast tomorrow at Dabei-yuan." The brilliance of Puhua's living strategies to awaken others is quite evident in the shove. He receives Linji's awakened Zen functioning by saying that a feast will be offered to beggars the following day at Dabei-yuan. What is he really saying here? Is he giving an evasive answer? Far from it.

In his response Puhua exhibits his activity which is "not-at-all-thus." He hits brightness when people come as brightness, and hits darkness when people come as darkness. And when someone comes not-at-all-thus, he hits "not-at-all-thus." This "not-at-all-thus" evident in his response has nothing to do with thinking this or that, utilizing forms or patterns, or probing in various ways. Such approaches don't even come close.

Puhua tells Luopu that a feast will be offered at Dabei-yuan the following day. This Dabei-yuan corresponds to the so-called Hiden-in that existed in Japan around the time of Kōbō Daishi (774–835), which was a place for the free dispensation of medicine and food to the poor. Puhua was essentially living like a beggar. He would approach people who crossed his path, draw up close, and ring his bell in their ears. As the person turned away, Puhua would reach out his hand and say, "Give me a coin." It was not an easy life. He taught by walking around as a beggar, sticking out his hand and asking for money. Like Hanshan and Shide,[48] his behavior is quite bizarre, and it distinguishes him as one of the many eccentrics in the history of Chinese Zen. On the surface, his statement about the feast might strike you as merely eccentric, but if that were all there is to it, he wouldn't have truly received Linji's awakened functioning. What is he really saying? This is the central point of their mutual examination.

Hearing Puhua's response, Luopu goes back to Linji and tells him what happened. Linji exclaims, "I've always wondered about that fellow." He always thought Puhua might be special, but now he is sure. His statement that he "always wondered" about Puhua does not express doubt, but, on the contrary, praise. At one level Linji is saying that he wondered what Puhua was all about and that he now knows how crazy he is; and at another level, he is praising Puhua and his marvellous response. That is why one commentator attached the words:

> Deep in the night,
> They watch together:
> On a thousand rocks, snow.

In this episode, centering around the question, "If coming is not at all thus, what then?" both men express their functioning in full accordance with the other. This is truly an encounter between two people who come forth without being dependent on anything. It is an outstanding mutual examination of the depth of one another's Awakening, and reveals a main aspect of Zen *mondō*. Interacting as they do, they are like an arrow and a dagger holding each other up.

The essence of what transpires between them lies in coming forth without being dependent on anything, in the non-dependent practitioner of the Way. Two more days are left in this retreat. When Linji tells you to come forth independent of all things, how will you come forth? I want all of you to apply yourselves to this question without being dependent on anything.

12
I Do Not Pay Homage to the Buddha or the Founding Teacher

In one episode of the *Record of Linji*, Linji visits a temple named Dinglin-si to pay his respects at a stone erected in memory of Bodhidharma.

> Linji arrived at Bodhidharma's memorial tower. The master of the tower said to him, "Venerable sir, will you pay homage first to Buddha or to the Founding Teacher?"
> "I don't pay homage to either Buddha or Bodhidharma," said Linji.
> "Venerable sir, why are Buddha and the Founding Teacher your enemies?" asked the master of the tower.
> Linji swung his sleeves and left. (p. 57)

Although people have advanced divergent arguments about the year of Bodhidharma's death, the date most commonly agreed upon is October 5th, 536, the second year in the reign of Emperor Wu of Liang. On December 28th of that year, Bodhidharma was buried on Bear Ear Mountain, whose twin peaks resemble a bear's ears.[49] For many centuries, October 5th has been the day traditionally set aside in Zen temples for a memorial service for Bodhidharma.

When the monk assigned to watch over the memorial sees Linji approaching, he greets him with the words, "Venerable sir, will you pay homage first to Buddha or the Founder?" The monk is surely a man of ability, and his greeting is no easy question. Are you going to pay homage first to the pioneer of Buddhism, or to the founder of Zen? The monk's question is not simply about the order of reverencing. He asks not only which will be reverenced first, but also whether the two figures will be reverenced simultaneously. How about you? What would you do in response to the monk's question? Pay homage first to the Buddha and then to the Founding Teacher? Or would you start with the Founder?

The crucial issue, then, is how one pays homage, not the order in which homage is to be paid. If Linji doesn't truly pay homage, his taking the trouble to visit Bodhidharma's tower is meaningless. How do we truly revere the Buddha and the Founder?

Linji responds to the monk's question by saying, "I don't pay homage to either Buddha or Bodhidharma." Here he has come all the way to Bear Ear Mountain and yet he won't pay homage to either one. What about this? What does he mean by saying he isn't going to revere Śākyamuni or Bodhidharma? Does he mean that he won't revere them in the usual sense? Or has he come *precisely because he will not pay homage*?

Linji says he won't pay homage to either, so it isn't a matter of starting with one and then going to the other, or even of paying homage to both at the same time. He says he won't revere either. What could he mean by this? What we must do is pay the "homage of no-homage." Otherwise we can't even begin to revere someone in the true sense.

As I have stressed repeatedly in these talks on the *Record of Linji*, in Zen we do not seek the Buddha and the Founder outside ourselves. Reverence of a figure apart from ourselves falls short of our ultimate way of being, for no external Buddha or Founder is true. The Buddha and the Founder are the Self; and the Self is the Buddha and the Founder. Only in awakening to this do we realize the true way of being of the Buddha and the Founder, which is the true way of being of the Self. This Awakening is true homage. Herein we discover the true meaning of reverence in Zen.

Paying homage at a grave or worshipping at a Buddhist statue – engaging in idol worship, as it were – does not constitute true homage. Even if you turn yourself wholly to the Buddha and Founder and stake your mind and body on taking refuge in them, your action will still fall short of true homage. In ordinary homage, one reveres the Buddha. Such is the case with the *nenbutsu*. This form of reverence usually involves more than the verbal act of chanting the name of the Buddha, for there are also physical and mental ways of practicing *nenbutsu*. Ordinary homage thus can draw on the body, mouth, and mind as the three loci of action.

Yet none of these three ways of practicing the *nenbutsu* or paying reverence amounts to true homage. Revering Buddha in your heart or staking your life on taking refuge in Buddha is a type of mental homage, and this falls short of the ultimate form of reverence. It is only in our inner depths, in the foundation of normal homage, that we realize true homage. Ultimate homage is thus prior to the three types of action. In it the Self and the Buddha or Founder are one.

Since this differs from homage in the usual sense, Linji says he will pay no homage to either. This "no-homage" is worlds apart from the homage spoken of by the master of the tower. Linji is demonstrating his distinctive strategy for awakening others, a strategy of compassion, and remarkable compassion at that. His formidable Zen functioning deals the monk a painful blow of the staff; it strikes the monk's homage. That is to say, as the compassion at work here, Linji's response presents the true mode of homage to the monk with his half-baked notion of reverence. This true homage is not mere words. Nor ideas, of course. In saying, "I do not pay homage," Linji pays the homage of no-homage.

Linji is the One True Person without Rank. He is the Formless Self, which is presenting itself here. The monk creates an occasion for this to happen when he asks Linji which he will pay homage to first. In response, the True Self freely and naturally presents itself. Unless we express such true homage, we can't avoid eating Linji's blow. If asked such a question by the master of the tower, many of us would pay only the type of homage that deserves a blow from the staff of pain. Linji's homage, though, cannot be paid through words or the three types of action. His homage emerges only upon Awakening to the True, Formless Self. In Awakening, we pay homage to all the buddhas of the ten directions. It is up to all of us to master the true mode of homage.

I went to a meeting of the Buddhist Youth Organization of Ehime University the other day as an invited speaker. Nearby in Matsuyama stands a temple on the spot where Ippen Shōnin was born. The temple houses a famous national treasure: a wooden statue of Ippen. I had seen the beautiful work once before, on a trip to Ehime Prefecture right after the war. The other day I went and paid my respects once again.

For a long time I have held high regard for Ippen's *nenbutsu*. As you might know, it is said that Ippen went to Hottō Kokushi, founder of the Zen temple Kōkoku-ji in Yura in Kishū,[50] and achieved a penetrating insight into the true *nenbutsu*. One of the many accounts of what happened is included in the record of Ippen's sayings and actions.

According to that version, in response to the question, "What sort of thing is the true *nenbutsu*?" Ippen answered, "When the *nenbutsu* is chanted, neither Buddha nor I – just the voice, *Namu Amida Butsu*." He thus expressed his understanding, but Hottō didn't accept it. Ippen seems correct in saying that there is no Buddha and no self but only *Namu Amida Butsu*. And yet Hottō wasn't satisfied with what he said. Why wouldn't he accept it? Since Ippen was clearly expressing the oft-written idea that, so to speak, God and the human are one, his remark may be viewed as deserving no criticism. And yet it is still no good. Ippen kept working at it, though. He next said, "When the *nenbutsu* is chanted, neither Buddha nor I – *Namu Amida Butsu, Namu Amida Butsu!*" Hottō accepted this answer, exclaiming, "Right, just as you say!"

Ippen's second response diverges markedly from the first, for the understanding it expresses is quite different. The *nenbutsu* must present itself. Explanations are no good. "Just the voice: *Namu Amida Butsu*" and "*Namu Amida Butsu, Namu Amida Butsu!*" are totally different responses. We all tend to explain things, though, as Ippen at first does. It is fine to explain truth when it presents itself, but we are apt to think that the explanation alone is truth. It is thus not acceptable to stop short of what is true. A Zen *mondō* or koan gets at what is true. If we do not directly express that which is most real, we haven't gotten at the truth. In this regard, Ippen's second response is virtually identical with Zen. How should we pay homage to Ippen? Perhaps his *nenbutsu* is the truest form of homage to him: *Namu Amida Butsu, Namu Amida Butsu!*

And yet even his second response is a verbal *nenbutsu*. In contrast, there is a truly free *nenbutsu* that transcends the three types of action. It goes beyond chanting the *nenbutsu*, thinking it, or physically paying homage. Hence any *nenbutsu* that ends in one's voice, body, or mind isn't ultimate, and cannot be viewed as the true *nenbutsu*. This holds for homage as well.

So from our vantage point, we can, or rather must, penetrate through Ippen's response. What sort of penetration is it? It is the discernment compelled by the statement, "When the *nenbutsu* is chanted, neither Buddha nor I – *Namu Amida Butsu, Namu Amida Butsu!*" That is to say, we must discern whether Ippen's response is something true. The "*Namu Amida Butsu, Namu Amida Butsu*" that comes from an even deeper source is no mere chanted or verbal *nenbutsu*. It freely expresses itself as verbal, physical, and mental actions. Usually the *nenbutsu* ends in so-called "voice samadhi" or "body samadhi," the samadhi of bodily action, in which the mind becomes one with the action. With koans, we must be very careful of this. The passing through of a koan must be *kenshō* (seeing into one's Original Nature). Passing through a koan without seeing into one's nature is of no avail. It is a mere event or fact. So what is *kenshō?* It must be self-extrication from the three types of action, and then free expression of Awakening as physical, verbal, and mental acts. We must penetrate the Formless Self – otherwise *kenshō* is impossible. Therefore, from our perspective, though Ippen's *nenbutsu* appears to be *nenbutsu* samadhi, it still hasn't freed itself from the shackles of verbal action.

We are bound not only by the shackles of such verbal action, but by a variety of shackles. Even the Buddha and the Founder turn out to be shackles. They are the final entanglement we experience, and as such they are the fundamental demon. Though demons assume a variety of forms, the Buddha-shackle and Dharma-shackle discussed here are the ultimate demon. And if we awaken to the True Self and simply dwell there, we will get bound up by the shackle of Self. Caught up in such shackles, we won't gain freedom unless we push on to the place from which Linji says he doesn't pay homage to the Buddha or the Founder. Indeed, in vigorously displaying his homage, Linji is free of such shackles.

The master of the tower responds to Linji, "Venerable sir, why are the Buddha and the Founder your enemies?" The monk clearly doesn't understand the true way of paying homage, even when it is revealed right before his eyes. Hearing Linji's statement, you might think, "Oh, I see," but the monk asks Linji what sort of hostility or grudge he bears against the Buddha and the Founder. Perhaps this is what most people would do. Had Linji held his hands flat together before his chest and bowed to the tower, the monk would certainly have been pleased and said something like, "You have worshipped well." But he knows nothing about paying true homage. Nowadays it isn't rare for such people to be head priests in temples.

Asked if he had a grudge against the Buddha and the Founder, Linji "swung his sleeves and left." This strategy adds further luster to the brilliance Linji has already displayed. He swings his sleeves. Some people interpret this as sweeping away the dust called the Buddha and the Founder. But such a lifeless interpretation is wide of the mark. The swinging of the sleeves more likely refers to the quickness of Linji's exit.

Bodhidharma was once summoned by Emperor Wu of Liang. In their meeting, the Emperor asked Bodhidharma about the essence of Zen, and Bodhidharma answered, "Vast emptiness, nothing noble." The Emperor next asked Bodhidharma who he was. Bodhidharma replied, "I don't know." The Emperor didn't understand either response. Bodhidharma quickly departed. He supposedly went to Shaolin-si in Wei and spent nine years gazing at the wall.[51] Someone later wrote,

"Not even if the whole country had chased him would he have returned."[52] As this verse indicates, even if all the people in the world had followed him, he wouldn't have looked back.

Likewise, though with less of an aftermath, "Linji swung his sleeves and left," for he had finished his homage and had no more business there. The monk needs to comprehend this. He most likely feels that Linji left without paying homage. Actually, though, Linji's way of paying homage at Bodhidharma's memorial stone is magnificent, and it has made a significant impact.

We have gathered here today for the last retreat of the year. The twentieth anniversary of our organization is fast approaching. Though this is an organization in form, it must also be fulfilled in content. Otherwise it will be of no use. There must be rich content, from which the organization takes its form. The crucial line of development is not form preceding content, but content fulfilling itself and hereby giving rise to form. As we approach the twenty-year mark, we must realize that such fulfillment lies first and foremost in truly awakening to the Formless Self. Let us create the type of content which brings everyone to full life.

13
True Insight

In the "Discourses" section of his *Record*, Linji discusses what the study of the Buddha-Dharma must be.

> The Master said: "Nowadays one who studies Buddha-Dharma must seek true insight. Gaining this insight, you are not affected by birth-and-death, but freely go or stay. You need not seek that which is excellent – that which is excellent will come of itself.
>
> "Followers of the Way, the eminent predecessors we have had from of old all had their own ways of saving people. As for me, what I want to point out to you is that you must not be deluded by others. If you want to act, then act. Don't hesitate.
>
> "Students today cannot get anywhere: what ails you? Lack of faith in yourself is what ails you. If you lack faith in yourself, you'll keep tumbling along, bewilderedly following after all kinds of circumstances, be taken by these myriad circumstances through transformation after transformation, and never be yourself.
>
> "Bring to rest the thoughts of the ceaselessly seeking mind, and you'll not differ from the Founder and Buddha. Do you want to know the Founder and Buddha? He is none other than *you* who listen to this discourse." (p. 7)

Linji says that those who study the Buddha-Dharma must seek true and genuine insight. In so-called Buddhology, the Buddha-Dharma is studied as an object of knowledge. The student investigates it from various angles and explains what it is. Through such study, one obtains knowledge of the Buddha-Dharma. Of course, scholarship must be objective and exact, but the study Linji speaks of diverges radically from the academic study of Buddhism with its various methodologies, for he says that, in studying the Buddha-Dharma, we must seek true insight.

People are apt to view Linji's "True Insight" as a particular interpretation or understanding of the Buddha-Dharma. But Linji is not talking about our having a specific intellectual insight into the Buddha-Dharma, however correct and objective the insight might be. The true insight isn't an objective and exact understanding of the Buddha-Dharma, or a grasp of its theoretical and philosophical principles. Linji is not concerned about knowing or experiencing the Buddha-Dharma in this way. Rather, true insight must be the living Buddha-Dharma. That is to say, it is the Buddha-Dharma that he calls true insight.

Prior to Linji in the history of Zen, people gave this true insight various verbal expressions, such as the Original Face, Mind, the True Self, Buddha, and the Founding Teacher. Linji terms it the "formless mind-dharma" in saying that "the mind-dharma is without form." Here in our organization we call it the Formless Self. In any event, true insight is never something we seek as an object outside ourselves. It is immediately presenting itself. It is alive, and expressing itself in all its vitality. The crux of seeking true insight is to realize this fact.

If we get hung up on the word "seek," we are liable to think of true insight as something apart from ourselves. This is why Linji constantly stresses that it is never something to be sought externally. In Linji's words, it is *you* who are listening to the discourse. It lies here in the very seeker, in this listener to the Dharma. Should we seek it externally, it will immediately drift farther and farther away. Therefore, when Linji tells us we should seek true insight, the true way of seeking is not to seek. The lack of any seeking is true seeking. The true meaning of "seek true insight" is our directly becoming the Formless Self here and now.

"Gaining true insight, one is not affected by living-and-dying." To gain true insight is to awaken to our Original Face or the True Self. When we do so, there is no longer any life or death. Since we have extricated and liberated ourselves from living-dying, we aren't plagued or entangled by it.

Living-dying includes all things, and hence doesn't refer just to the limited events of living and dying. Should we think of the living-dying "one is affected by" as limited to living and dying in the usual sense of the terms, our understanding will be extremely narrow. When we extricate ourselves from living-dying, we are extricated from all things, and when we extricate ourselves from all things, we are extricated from living-dying. Insofar as we have form, there is living-dying, so it is only when we are formless that there is no living-dying. Thus, in becoming formless, we free ourselves from living-dying.

In conjunction with living-dying, we often encounter the expression, "binding passions." The extrication of oneself from living-dying is referred to as nirvana, and extrication from so-called binding passions is called *bodhi*. Living-dying and the binding passions are one and the same thing. Likewise, nirvana and *bodhi* are identical. In this sense, our not being affected by living-dying is, so to speak, the Self of nirvana. That is to say, the Self is nirvana, or *bodhi*.

Not affected by living-dying, one "freely goes or stays." Living is equivalent to staying and dying is equivalent to going, so the one who "freely goes or stays" is free in living-dying. Without getting entangled in living-dying, we freely live and die in its midst. We endlessly transform ourselves, never becoming entangled in the ongoing transformation. In the midst of impermanence, we constantly change without getting caught up in it. Only then do we find freedom.

Since we are the Formless Self, we are free. This ultimate or absolute freedom is hence different from the relative freedom standing in opposition to non-freedom. Ultimate freedom of itself accompanies true insight. In this sense we can call it the merit of true insight. And true insight is not gained by trying to extricate ourselves from living-dying or by trying to become free. When we penetrate true insight, living-dying automatically ceases and we are free. This is why Zen stresses that "*kenshō* comes first."

We do not reach true insight by accumulating merit through the practice of various precepts. No one reaches satori by collecting merit. That is why we speak of abrupt awakening. From the Zen perspective, the attainment of Buddhahood is not realized in the infinite future. Without any change of time or place, true insight is vigorously presenting itself – right now and right here. To realize this is to gain true insight. Hence the expression, "In a single leap one directly enters the Tathāgata stage."[53]

Linji thus tells everyone that "you need not seek that which is excellent." We often seek excellence, supreme states of mind, supranormal powers, and liberation. But we try to seek such "branch" attainments without realizing their "root": the attainment of true insight. Such excellences will come to us on their own in our attainment of true insight. But if we seek them we will never attain true insight. True insight is attained right here. Hence, a mind that longs to open up satori and strives to do so is far removed from satori. In fact, satori emerges where that mind has been brought to rest. True insight is *you* who are listening to the Dharma. Should you look farther and farther outside yourself, satori will become all the more distant. This is expressed by such statements as "Yajñadatta used his head to seek his head," and "Born in a wealthy home yet lost in an impoverished village." The crux of the matter is that "If you seek it, you go against it." You might wonder how you can arrive at what is excellent if you don't seek it, but if you look for it, you will only go against it. That which is excellent will arrive in and of itself.

Once true insight is attained, various merits emerge naturally from it. That which is excellent will be provided, without any seeking on our part. All precepts are inherent in *kenshō*, and this is called the "Zen precept." *Kenshō* includes all merits, but the basis of the merits is no-merit.

Emperor Wu of Liang had performed a variety of good deeds before he summoned Bodhidharma: he had built temples, fed and clothed monks, sponsored the carving of sculptures and the translation of Buddhist writings, and done other meritorious acts. When he met Bodhidharma, he asked him what sort of merit he had accrued by doing such things, and Bodhidharma answered, "No-merit." What is this "no-merit"? It doesn't mean there is no merit whatsoever. The idea of no-merit is later found in the talks of the Sixth Founding Teacher, who spoke of "the way of being of not-a-single-thing." This not-a-single-thing encompasses all merits. As indicated by another expression, "Inexhaustible is the capacity of not-a-single-thing,"[54] that which is excellent will come to us in and of itself.

"Followers of the Way, the eminent predecessors we have had from of old all had their ways of saving people." All the Zen founding teachers have had ways of getting people to attain true insight. Linji might also be referring to himself, for he, too, uses living strategies to awaken others. Deshan once said, "There are no words or phrases in my teaching; I haven't a single thing to give to people."[55] This approach is not limited to him. In *The Treatise on the Essentials of Abrupt Awakening and Entering the Way*,[56] Dazhu makes the same statement: "I haven't a single thing to give to people." There is nothing to give. True insight simply *is*. It isn't something we can have others teach us or give us. "That which comes in through the gate is not the family treasure."[57] The true riches of a home do not come from the outside. The True Insight is *the Self*, the Formless True Self, which isn't something we gain from the outside. Unless this Self opens up and awakens, there is no way to save people.

"As for me, what I want to point out to you is that you must not be deluded by others." What Linji means by "point out" is conveyed by the

Zen expression, "Pointing directly to the human mind, having one see one's nature and attain Buddhahood."[58] He is indicating the True Self of the person. He is pointing directly to your True Self, and thereby having you yourself see into your original nature and awaken to the Self.

The "others" Linji sees as deluding us can be interpreted as being masters or guides who are mistaken in various ways. But when he says that "you must not be deluded by others," he isn't referring just to them. He is concerned about delusion in the more general sense of the entire range of human actions. We mustn't get confused by individual acts, including utterances. Even the principle called Dharma – and even a true master – is delusive if it remains something external to us. Such delusion is so subtle that Linji had to say, "Slay the buddhas and slay the founding teachers." In other words, depending on how we treat them, even founding teachers can cause delusion.

But the Self can't be deluded by others, and true insight never gets bewildered by things. This is not because the Self or true insight tries to avoid delusion. Rather, when you arrive at the Self of true insight, there is no way you can be deluded by others.

"If you want to act, then act. Don't hesitate." To arrive at true insight right here, don't wobble. Linji is pointing directly to your Mind, to have you see into your original nature and attain Buddhahood. His pointing is anything but roundabout. When he says that it is presenting itself, he is pointing directly. There is no other way to open satori than by realizing, or awakening to, oneself. Therefore, "If you want to act, just act. Don't hesitate." Don't waver!

"Students today can't get anywhere" – you students fail to arrive at true insight – "What ails you?" What in the world is the source of this illness? "Lack of faith in yourself is what ails you." Linji does not use the term "faith" in the sense of ordinary faith in an object external to us. Nor is he saying that we should have faith in the Self. The lack of faith is your failure to awaken to the Self that is presenting itself here and now.

In searching outside ourselves, we tend to think of the Buddha as something transcendent. When we are told to seek Buddha within rather than without, we can understand this admonition to mean that there is no Buddha apart from the Self. We must awaken to this. We must realize that, as expressed in the statement, "All beings have the Buddha-nature," the Buddha is no "other," no transcendent entity to be sought externally. Rather, the Buddha is the true "I." The True Self is the Buddha, and there is no Buddha-nature apart from our True Self. Therefore, we must believe in the Self that is the Buddha.

Since seeking outside ourselves in a transcendent direction is a mistake, it is correct to say that the True Self itself *is* the Buddha. But Linji does not intend to have us just believe that the Buddha-nature is inside us. If we take Linji's statement to mean that we should have faith in the fact that the Self is Buddha, we will fail to discern the depths of what he says. By "faith in yourself," he means our realization that we are the Self right now, our immediate awakening to the Self that is the Buddha or the awakened one. Accordingly, the ultimate illness is our not being awakened to the Self.

"If you lack faith in yourself," if you have not awakened to the Self, "you'll keep tumbling along." You will be tossed about by all sorts of things. You will be restricted by things, chased about by them, and lose all freedom and subjectivity. You won't ever "become master of all situations." But this "tumbling along" can turn over and become freedom in each moment. You can reach the point where "the Calm Self in ordinary life is the Way awakened to Itself,"[59] and "every day is a good day."[60] Otherwise you won't be able to "disport yourself in the forest of living-dying," for you will be tossed around by things and lose yourself in the process.

But if you attain to true insight, your entanglement will turn around and you will be able, as Zhaozhou says, to "make free use of the twelve hours."[61] You will use things rather than be used by them. You will become the master, the protagonist. We sometimes encounter the expression, "The mind turns in accordance with a myriad of circumstances, and the place of turning is truly profound."[62] This "accordance" is nothing passive. Rather, it is freedom in the midst of all conceivable situations. And the mind here is True Insight, the True Self. The mind moves everywhere, and yet leaves no traces. There is no place of stopping.

"Taken by these myriad circumstances through transformation after transformation," you will "never be yourself." If you lack faith in yourself, you will be knocked around by myriad circumstances. You will get tossed about by all situations, and hence will never realize freedom. Nor will you realize that the place of turning and transformation is profound. Therefore, all day you tumble along, devoid of subjectivity. You have no composure. Only when ultimate composure is true insight do you truly become composed, for usual composure is nothing more than a state of consciousness in a particular situation and as such totally lacks any eternality. It is a composure in which one is not really composed. It is the same as tumbling along in living-dying: where is there any true composure? If you think of composure as people usually do, that is, as a kind of silence, you won't get at the composure about which I am speaking.

In the statement, "The Mind turns in accordance with a myriad of circumstances, and the place of turning is truly profound," the profundity is the consummation of composure. Accordingly, the composure mentioned in the Vow of Humankind[63] must be eternal composure, not the composure of a certain moment or a state of consciousness. Herein arises the necessity of attaining True Insight. When you arrive at True Insight, you become composed even if you don't try to do so. Consciously trying to become composed is of no avail. Composure is not a state of consciousness, nor a physical state. We first gain composure in the dropping off of body and mind. And the attainment of this composure is the ultimate event in the world of living-dying.

"Bring to rest the thoughts of the ceaselessly seeking mind, and you'll not differ from the Founder and Buddha." Though we speak of True Insight, if there is a mind that seeks it, we will never arrive at it. There isn't any ever-seeking mind in True Insight. No seeking at all. We renounce the seeking mind altogether. To renounce it is to negate it. Though Linji speaks of bringing it to rest, it will come to rest by itself when the true insight is gained. And when the ever-seeking mind comes to rest, we realize freedom. At that point, "you'll not differ from the Founder and Buddha." Our very way of being itself is the Founder, the Buddha.

Linji calls out to the assembly, "Do you want to know the Founder and Buddha?" Do you want to become identical with the Founder and Buddha? *You* listening to the Dharma! Linji turns directly to the assembly and points to the Founder and Buddha. What is it that is listening?! What is listening to the Dharma? There is no Founder or Buddha apart from what is listening to Dharma. I want you to penetrate this, Linji says to us.

True Insight and study of the Buddha-Dharma must be like this. It is just as Linji says.

14

The Meaning of the Founder's Coming from the West

One episode in the Discourse section of the *Record of Linji* revolves around the "meaning[64] of the Founder's coming from the west." I want to discuss this today.

> Someone asked: "What is the meaning of the Founder's coming from the west?"
>
> The Master said: "If he had had a meaning, he couldn't have saved even himself."
>
> The person continued: "Since he had no meaning, how did the Second Founding Teacher attain the Dharma?"
>
> The Master responded: "'To attain' is to not attain."
>
> The person said: "If it is 'to not attain,' what is the meaning of 'to not attain'?"
>
> The Master said: "It is because you cannot stop your mind which runs on seeking everywhere that a Founding Teacher said, 'Bah, superior people! Searching for your heads with your heads!' When at these words you turn your own light in upon yourselves and never seek elsewhere, then you'll know that your body and mind are not different from those of the founding teachers and buddhas and on the instant have nothing to do – this is called 'attaining the Dharma.'" (p. 33)

A monk asks here about the "meaning of the Founder's coming from the west," about why Bodhidharma went to China from India. This question first appeared in Zen circles long before Linji's time – in fact, from the beginning of Zen – and over the years people have asked it on countless occasions. Of course, Zen originated in Bodhidharma, so it is

82

only natural for us to inquire into the fundamental meaning of his taking the trouble to journey from India to China.

Although this question asks about the meaning or purpose of Bodhidharma's going to China, it isn't concerned merely with the particular issue of why he did so. That is to say, in asking about the meaning of Bodhidharma's arrival from India, the monk is trying to get at the root-source of Zen. From the Zen perspective, though, the question asks not about Zen as a particular sect, but about Zen as the essence of Buddhism. And as I have said, Zen isn't simply the essence of a specific religion called Buddhism, but the essence of humanity, of the True Self. Hence this question about the meaning of Bodhidharma's going to China from India can be restated, "What is our True Self?" We might also ask, "What is the cardinal principle of the Buddha-Dharma?" Of course, this is the question Linji asked Huangbo three times, the question for which he received three blows.

Linji answers the monk, "If he had had a meaning he couldn't have saved even himself." If we try to grasp conceptually the "meaning" or "purpose" for which Bodhidharma came from India, we won't understand why he came. Nothing like that is involved, says Linji, as he snatches away all meaning from the monk's way of questioning, and thereby gives direct expression to the "meaning of the Founder's coming from the west." From his perspective, in true meaning there is no meaning at all.

The questioning monk fails to understand Linji's disclosure of the "meaning of the Founder's coming from the west," so he pursues the idea that there isn't any meaning, and asks another question: "If he had no meaning, how did the Second Founding Teacher attain the Dharma?" From the ordinary perspective, this is a reasonable question, for Zen is the tradition of transmitting and attaining the Dharma, the "transmission from Self to Self." Hearing that the Second Founding Teacher, Huike, attained the Dharma from Bodhidharma, we are apt to assume that there must be a thing called Dharma involved, and that this Dharma is the "meaning" in question. We might ask how, if there is no meaning, we can speak of attaining the Dharma. But this question derives from objectifying the Dharma, from seeing the "meaning" objectively. And the monk isn't only objectifying the meaning – he can't even fathom what it is. He thinks the Dharma is a fixed thing, a limited entity. He isn't alone, though, for people usually think the "transmission of the Dharma" indicates some special thing called "Dharma," which is transmitted.

As Linji always says, "The mind-dharma[65] is without form and pervades the ten directions." The dharma of mind is formless. It has no
form, so there is no attainment or non-attainment of it. Since we can
attain something only if it is "some thing," that which isn't any thing
at all is unattainable. We are originally equipped with the Dharma, in
which all means of verbal expression are cut off and all activities of the
mind have ceased. So how can we speak of attaining or not attaining
it? How can we speak of transmitting or not transmitting it? Though
people talk about transmitting or not transmitting the Dharma, they
aren't getting at the reality itself. They have objectified the "meaning"
or "Dharma" as some sort of thing. And when they conceive of it in
that objectified way, it ceases to be the Dharma itself or its meaning.
All along, Linji has been disclosing the Dharma, the basis from which
he gives his discourse. This is a superb aspect of Zen *mondō* – Linji is
speaking by means of the true "meaning."

But the monk doesn't understand. Tangled up in language, he can't
delve into the heart of the matter. He asks about there being "no
meaning." Meaning is no meaning, and this "meaning of no meaning"
is precisely the meaning of Bodhidharma's coming from the west. But if
"no meaning" were a lack of meaning or purpose in the ordinary sense,
it would be a mere negation. From Linji's perspective, "no meaning"
indicates the very reality in question: "This is it!" "If he had had a
meaning he couldn't have saved even himself." It is just as Linji says.

We see this expressed by the Second Founding Teacher, who is said
to have received the Dharma from Bodhidharma. He declared, "When I
seek my Self, I can't attain it." This statement directly expresses the
transmission of the Dharma to him from Bodhidharma. Yet when
people hear the words, "transmission from Self to Self," they think
there is something transmitted, even though the transmitting Self is
unattainable. In ultimate truth, however, "the Self is unattainable."
Speaking of truth, let me mention here that truth, too, tends to be seen
as some sort of "meaning." In any case, the Second Founding Teacher
attains peace of mind when he realizes that the Self is unattainable.
That is to say, he receives the transmission of the Dharma from
Bodhidharma when he realizes that nothing is transmitted. Here, too,
people misconstrue words by taking this "unattainability" and "no
transmission" to mean that there is no Dharma involved. Such is the
limitation of a mere verbal understanding.

In response to the monk's question, Linji says, "'To attain' is to not
attain." True attaining is non-attainment. In a sense, to *not* attain is to

attain. If you should attain something, you aren't engaging in true attainment. Linji is kind enough to answer this way, but this may still fall short of a direct expression of the truth, for even now the monk doesn't understand.

The monk next asks, "If it is 'to not attain,' what is the meaning of 'to not attain'?" He is going around in circles. No matter how many times he asks a question, he fails to comprehend what Linji is really saying. People tend to get this way. In doctrinal Buddhism, one approach repeatedly negates everything, arguing that Dharma is not this, not that, and not even "not that." Nothing like that at all. Not, not, not. Yet no matter how long you continue to negate things, you won't ever encounter what is real. Even if you were to pile negation upon negation for thousands of years, you wouldn't arrive at truth. Therefore, you must "go beyond a hundred negations." The true Dharma lies beyond even a hundred negations. It isn't this, or that, or anything. But it isn't a sheer negation. The "thing" is there. It is that which isn't anything whatsoever. That is why it is neither this nor that.

The "meaning of the Founder's coming from the west" is that which has no form – the Self. Precisely this is what is meant by "unattainable." And yet, as we have seen, the monk goes on to ask about the meaning of "to not attain." Knowing that this questioning will be forever repeated to no avail, Linji flips things around and says, "It is because you can't stop your mind that a Founding Teacher said, 'Bah, superior people! Seeking for your heads with your heads!'" Linji is telling us that if we stopped the mind that searches everywhere, we would comprehend the meaning of Bodhidharma's coming from the west. No matter how much we seek it outside ourselves, we will only become eternally busy. The meaning of the Founder's coming from the West is found where the seeking mind has stopped. And it isn't found outside us, but inside. Though we look all around outside ourselves, we are endowed with "it" all along. It is our Original Face. Apart from our Original Face, there is no meaning in the Founder's coming from the west.

Now, about this "inside." This term often appears in the *Record* and other Zen texts, where we are told not to look outside ourselves. But if we should search internally, "inside" will be external to us as well. Linji isn't discussing "inside" and "outside" in the usual sense. Rather, "inside" is *right here*. The "thing" itself, the Self itself, is the "inside." It is an inside without inside or outside, hence the expression about our Awakened nature: "It is neither inside, nor outside, nor in the middle."

Inside, outside, and the middle are all external. And that which does not have an inside, outside, or middle, the place that is neither inside, nor outside, nor in the middle – that is the true "inside." That is what is meant by the expression, "Do not look outside for your true way of being." What tells us this is the Self; from its perspective, everything that is "something" is external. Thus Linji in effect admonishes us: "Stop the mind that searches everywhere."

The seeking mind looks everywhere – inside, outside, and in the middle – and hence diverges from the Self. It is said, "When you seek it you turn against it."[66] Because you haven't brought your seeking mind to rest, you go around in circles. Linji scolds us: "Bah!" He admonishes us against seeking far and wide. Stop! Stop that seeking mind! When you do, you will discover the true meaning of Bodhidharma's coming from the west.

"Seeking your heads with your heads!" You can't seek the Buddha with the Buddha. It's like trying to find your self with your self. This expression, "Seeking your head with your head," appears in the *Record of Linji* and several other Zen texts. It originates in the story of Yajñadatta, a handsome Indian man who always enjoyed looking at himself in the mirror. One day, however, his face was not reflected there. He was shocked. Wondering where his face had gone, he started to search all around for it. As you can gather from this story, "to look for one's face with one's face" means that even though the sought is the very seeker, we seek it externally. Though you may search for a hundred or even a thousand days, you won't find what you are looking for. This idea is also expressed in Hakuin's *Zazen wasan:* "Born in a wealthy home, yet lost in an impoverished village."[67]

We speak of the Self, the ultimate True Self. That which is objective or particular can be sought externally, but the Self, which is a self and yet a formless self, cannot be objectified or sought outside of us. It can't be other than itself. The realization of this is crucial in Zen practice. Though we constantly seek outside ourselves for Zen, it is none other than the Self. This is why Linji admonishes us to stop the seeking mind. Be careful, though – he isn't telling us not to seek. If we lose our bearings here we will fall into error. Though we might search for ten thousand eons, we won't ever reach our goal. In truth, the Self is not even a hair's breadth apart from us; it is right here where we stand. It is close at hand, closer to us than anything at all. The Self is the Self – nothing is closer. If you search externally for this closest thing, you won't ever find it. Linji says here, "Bah, superior people! Always seeking your heads with your heads!" He warns us that it is a mistake for the head to go around looking for itself.

Linji tells you to "turn your own light in upon yourselves and never seek elsewhere." Again, he is telling you not to seek your head with your head – the sought-after head is in the seeker, and hence it is right here.

This morning I didn't know where my handkerchief was, and though I looked for it, I couldn't find it anywhere. I searched unsuccessfully around the room, but I finally found it in the "pocket" of my kimono sleeve. This sort of thing happens to us from time to time, so we are told to turn the light in upon ourselves, to stop seeking elsewhere. This admonition comes from the true way of being of the Self, where there is no "seeking" and no "not seeking," either. Ordinarily we fail to realize this, so we have no choice but to make all-out efforts to find what has been lost. We seek Awakening, try to become the Buddha, or have faith in and worship the Buddha, all the while taking Awakening or the Buddha to be something apart from us. Buddha-nature isn't above or below us, inside or outside of us, or in the middle. That which is presenting itself here and now is Buddha-nature. When we fail to realize this, we seek Buddha-nature inside ourselves. So doing, "whenever we seek, we turn against it." But when this seeking mind is stopped, we first discover Buddha-nature. The *Heart Sutra* says,

No eyes, ears, nose, tongue, body, or mind;
No color, sound, smell, taste, touch, or thought-object.

Why was this written? What does this mean? These words indicate the way of being of the Self that cannot be sought externally. The True Self isn't something we can seek after with our minds. It is found where the activity of the mind has ceased.

"You'll know that your body and mind are not different from those of the Founder and Buddha." To realize that your body-mind doesn't differ from the Founder and Buddha, you must stop seeking externally and "drop off body and mind." Dropping off body and mind – no eyes, ears, nose, tongue, body, or mind, no color, sound, smell, taste, touch, or thought-object – there are no buddhas or founding teachers apart from you. The Self as buddhas and founding teachers isn't apart from us, and in grasping this we discover the meaning of Bodhidharma's journey from India, the "cardinal principle of the Buddha-Dharma."

When we realize we aren't different from the founding teachers and buddhas, we will, "in that instant, have no concerns." Right here and right now, we have no concerns, for the seeking has come to a halt. The meaning of the Founder's coming from the west now presents itself, *right here*. And yet we often seek satori far away. We take it to be something distant, something ordinary people can't reach. But such is not the case. There is nothing easier, nothing more simple. It is the easiest action to perform. It is beyond difficult and easy – it is just as it is, which is the same as saying it is right here.

For the person who has realized this, there is nothing to do. We read in the *Record*, "The one who has no concerns is the noble person." This expression often appears in calligraphy, such as the beautiful piece by Jiun Sonja.[68] Only when we have nothing to do are we the noble person. Of course, "noble" here doesn't refer to one pole of the dichotomy between nobility and commoners. To be noble is to have no concerns. Hence, "The one who has no concerns is the noble person."

"On the instant we have no concerns – this is called 'attaining the Dharma.'" Linji says that having no concerns – precisely that – is the attaining of the Dharma. Nothing is attained. If you speak of having attained something, you are mistaken. "There is no Dharma to be attained," "no Dharma to be given." We sometimes encounter the saying, "Descending to save sentient beings." In "descending to save," there is no Dharma to be given, so you can have others attain the Dharma. Because the Dharma isn't apart from the Self, it can't be obtained from the outside. "That which comes in through the gate is not the family treasure." If our way of attaining the Dharma leads us to value our certification paper, it will have less worth than toilet paper. True certification[69] occurs only when we realize that the Dharma goes beyond attainment, that we are the True Self. But we tend to get caught up in things, forgetting that the Dharma isn't something we receive from others. Ask yourself: who certifies whom? The Self does it to the Self. There is no other type of certification. Nevertheless, certification tends to get off the track and become fixed as something apart from us. The transmission of the Dharma becomes a mere form, which prevents the Dharma from being transmitted in the true sense. Contemporary Zen people need to think seriously about this. For each of you the Dharma is truly unattainable. You must realize the attainment of the unattainable. You must confirm yourselves.

15
The Three Vehicles' Twelve
Divisions of Teachings

Recently I have been giving talks on passages of the *Record of Linji* that I find especially interesting. I will continue doing so throughout this retreat, and today I'd like to focus on an early section of the text, in which a lecture-master asks Linji about the Three Vehicles' twelve divisions of teachings. Let me start by reading their dialogue.

> A lecture-master asked, "The Three Vehicles' twelve divisions of teachings reveal Buddha-nature, do they not?"
>
> "This weed patch has never been spaded," responded Linji.
>
> "Surely the Buddha would not have deceived people!" said the lecture-master.
>
> "Where is Buddha?" asked Linji.
>
> The lecture-master had no reply.
>
> "You thought you'd make a fool of me in front of the Counselor," Linji chided.
>
> "Get out, get out! You're keeping the others from asking questions."
>
> Linji went on to say, "Today's Dharma-assembly is concerned with the Great Matter. Does anyone else have a question? If so, ask it now! But the instant you open your mouth you are already way off. Why is this so? Don't you know? Venerable Śākyamuni said, 'Dharma is independent of words, because it is neither subject to causation nor dependent upon conditions.'" (pp. 1–2)

A lecture-master is a person who studies scriptures in an attempt to elucidate doctrinal Buddhism as opposed to Zen, the direct awakening to Buddha-nature as the source of scriptures. Monks who engage in such study are referred to as "scholars of the various facets of Buddhist teaching," and the head of a group of these monks is called a lecture-master. In any case, a lecture-master steps forth and asks the kind of question one would expect from a scholar of doctrine. In effect, he is asking, "Even the Three Vehicles' twelve divisions of teaching elucidate Buddha-nature, do they not? Such elucidation isn't done only by Zen, right?"

The Three Vehicles are the vehicle of the Śrāvakas, the vehicle of the Pratyekas, and the vehicle of the Bodhisattvas.[70] They include both Theravāda and Mahāyāna teachings. The twelve divisions of teachings constitute an older way of classifying the Buddha's teachings. Hence the expression "Three Vehicles' twelve divisions of teachings" refers to all Buddhist teachings conveyed in words, to the entire Buddhist canon.

In Zen, however, we don't rely on the Three Vehicles' twelve divisions of teachings. The goal of Zen is a direct awakening to the source of those writings, to the essence expressed therein, to the basis of the 84,000 Dharma-gates,[71] or to what Zen calls the "Self,"[72] "Buddha-nature," "Self-nature," and "Original Face." This direct awakening finds expression in a Zen saying:

Not relying on words or letters,
An independent transmission apart from doctrinal teachings;
A direct pointing to humanity's True Self,
Having one see one's nature and attain Awakening (Buddhahood).

The "doctrinal teachings" are the Three Vehicles' twelve divisions of teachings. Their source, however, does not rely on words or letters, and it exists "apart from doctrinal teachings." Without depending on the words and statements of Theravāda or Mahāyāna Buddhism, we awaken directly to their source, to the "Self" that is independent of doctrine.

Because this way of transmission diverges from the type of Buddhism that has been conveyed by scriptures and doctrinal teachings, it generates such expressions as "not relying on words or letters" and "an independent transmission apart from doctrinal teachings." Further, because the Self is directly transmitted from Self to Self, we also encounter the expression "transmission from Self to Self." This "Self" is our Original Self, our Self-nature, which is none other than the Awakened One (Buddha). Zen points directly to the Self and has us see into our Self-nature to attain Buddhahood. It is a "direct pointing to humanity's True Self," through which we see our original nature and attain

Awakening. Humanity's True Self is the original Self common to us all, the Self prior to scriptural expressions. In ordinary Buddhist parlance, it is "Buddha-nature." People might think that "Buddha-nature" refers to some sort of transcendent essence of the Buddha separate from us, but along with the expression "Humanity's True Self," it connotes the true nature of original humanity.

Some people are apt to see Buddha-nature as an immanent potential for becoming a buddha, but it's no such thing. It doesn't exist internally, externally, or in the middle. Here and now – this is Buddha-nature's true way of being. In other words, right in this time and place we humans are Buddha-nature. There is no special need to depend on scriptures. Though you may seek the true Buddha in scriptures, it isn't found there. At this very moment, in this place, we awaken directly to our true way of being, or, you might say, we have one awaken to it. This manner of awakening is the direct pointing to humanity's True Self. But to see into our original nature and become a buddha is not to see our Self-nature objectively with our eyes, or to know it objectively with our ordinary minds. To "see" is for the original nature to awaken. There is no seen object apart from the seer and no seer apart from the seen. The original nature existing as itself – this is what is meant by "seeing one's nature." And this is precisely what is meant by "attaining Awakening" (literally, "becoming a buddha"). So, to become a buddha is to awaken to the Buddha-nature that is our own original nature. It is our awakening to the Formless, True Self, never our believing in or becoming the kind of buddha that is an "other" to us.

Because the saying I read before is a kind of Zen slogan, the lecture-master questions it. He asks whether the Three Vehicles' twelve divisions of teachings upon which he relies don't also elucidate Buddha-nature. He asks why Zen establishes itself as a principle of Buddhism apart from those teachings. Given the Chinese epoch in which Zen and its goal of direct awakening emerged, it is only natural that this doubt arose in someone rooted in the doctrinal tradition that had held sway up until then. Perhaps even today such doubts haven't completely disappeared. Those who think that Buddhism is clarified by relying on scriptures rather than by directly becoming a buddha independent of scriptures find it extremely hard to fathom a direct attainment of Buddhahood. For this reason, doubts start cropping up.

People invariably tend to rely on the scriptures of their religion or sect. As the sole basis of and criterion for truth, these writings constitute the final object of dependence. For example, in Tendai

(Ch. Tiantai) Buddhism, the *Dharma-lotus Sutra* is the single sutra to which people turn; in Pure Land Buddhism the so-called "three sutras"[73] are definitive; and in Kegon (Ch. Huayan) Buddhism the *Avataṃsaka-sūtra* is the scripture upon which adherents of that sect rely.

Zen, however, does not make any sutra a final criterion. The Zen criterion exists only in the source from which sutras emerge. That source is also the place of reliance, for peace of mind is never found apart from it. In other words, Awakening is the final, and only, place of reliance. This is why Zen admonishes us not to seek the Buddha apart from ourselves or take an "other" as the Buddha, for the "Buddha" is Awakening itself. Nevertheless, the lecture-master still wonders whether the Three Vehicles' twelve divisions of teachings don't elucidate Buddha-nature, just as the doctrinal approach, based on scripture, clarifies Buddhism.

In response, Linji chides him: "This weed patch has never been spaded." To Linji, the Three Vehicles' twelve divisions of teachings are like rampant weeds. Linji shows restraint in characterizing them this way, for in another talk he says, "The Three Vehicles' twelve divisions of teachings are all waste paper for wiping off privy filth." From his perspective, the wild weeds have already been spaded, or, rather, they fundamentally do not exist. Linji breaks through the lecture-master's Dharma-entanglement and points directly to the True Self by asking how he, a revered priest, could continue to nurture weeds rather than uproot them. Linji tells him it would be best to spade them out of the way. Linji clearly discloses the direction leading from the leaves and branches to the root of the matter. Actually, it isn't simply the direction but the very root that he is pointing to.

Up until now, the doctrinal study of Buddhism has harbored a pitfall: insofar as there are such things as voluminous sutras and elaborate commentaries, people get entangled in them. They grope about in darkness, become increasingly confused, and never rid themselves of this Dharma-entanglement. But, as an existential critique of the idea that investigation of the scriptures will lead one to a true understanding of Buddhism and the attainment of Buddhahood, Zen provides a living means of shaking free from Dharma-entanglement.

We sometimes hear the expression, "a nun who is ignorant even of a single passage of scripture."[74] Even if you don't know a single word of the scriptures, you can become a buddha. Why? Because "buddha" is our Original Face, our True Self.

In the FAS Society, F, the Formless Self, is the Original Face of all human beings. It is the true "I." Accordingly, the *Record* tells us again and again not to seek outside ourselves, for however long we may seek externally, we are heading in the wrong direction. The Self is *you*, and you certainly don't exist outside yourself. Perhaps you've heard the saying, "Missing themselves, all sentient beings chase after things."[75] When we lose ourselves, we chase after things and search farther and farther outside ourselves. This is a fatal mistake in direction. As you know, Linji often draws on the story of Yajñadatta, who ran wildly about looking for his head, only to realize that the seeker was the head. In referring to this story, Linji is warning us against seeking Buddha apart from ourselves. All true followers of the Way must realize this.

But the lecture-master says, "Surely the Buddha would not have deceived people." The Three Vehicles' twelve divisions of teachings are what the Buddha preached. It is insulting to call them toilet paper. What sacrilege! Without doubt they are Buddha's words. "Why would the Buddha deceive us?!"

To this Linji replies, "Where is Buddha?" You say Buddha this, Buddha that, but where is he? Tell me!" Though the lecture-master has read every line of the Buddhist canon, he can't even begin to answer this question about the Buddha's whereabouts. All he can do is refer to sections of the scriptures or, worse yet, state that the Buddha is a man named Śākyamuni who lived in India 2500 years ago, that he now resides in a western paradise called the Pure Land, or that he abides in a nirvanic afterlife.

In "The Existing-Place of the True Buddha," a section of my book, *Eastern Nothingness*, I tried to clarify what the True Buddha is, where Buddha must exist, and what "exist" means here. Linji doesn't listen to the priest's explanation of where the Buddha is. He wants the priest to give a direct expression of Buddha-nature by answering, "Buddha is here!" If the lecture-master were to awaken to Buddha-nature through Linji's direct pointing, he could answer on the spot. He could clearly and fully present Buddha-nature. But we cannot expect such a response from a lecture-master who searches for Buddha in sutras.

With things proceeding in this way, the lecture-master is left speechless. Were his muteness the same as Vimalakīrti's silence, it would be a magnificent self-presentation of the Buddha. But he is simply at a total loss for words. Only able to stand there dumbfounded, the lecture-master reveals the impotency of mere doctrinal study. Present-day Buddhologists need to be especially careful they don't end up like this priest.

We have gathered here today from far and near to take part in a seven-day retreat so that we may answer Linji's question. Of course, our central concern isn't limited to Linji's question. This is a question we must ask ourselves in total seriousness. It is the ultimate question a human being can ask another human being. But people tend to think of Buddhism as something remote from them, as a religion, philosophy, or cultural tradition transmitted with various changes from ancient India to the modern world. Because of this view, they fail to understand Buddhism in a direct way, here and now. They don't realize that Buddhism is the ultimate question we can't avoid asking ourselves. Another reason they don't grasp Buddhism as our ultimate problem is that Buddhism has become a matter of having people worship Buddha-images drawn on paper and sculpted from wood or metal, request things from those images, believe in a postmortem Buddha, or try to perceive Buddha as a transcendent entity other than themselves. As I continually stress, though, the Buddha is our Original Face, our True Self, which is never temporally apart from us for even a moment or spatially apart from us even an inch. If you search externally for the Buddha as some sort of object, you will only drift farther away from it. Linji is telling you that however much you study the scriptures and acquire correct knowledge, your knowledge will be "merely a beautiful display of words," not the true, living Buddha.

For this reason, we all must stop thinking of idols and scriptures as things significant for the afterlife and stop searching for Buddha apart from ourselves. We should investigate in the direction of the True Self. That is to say, we shouldn't investigate while worshipping Buddha-images or reading sutras – everything necessary is assembled in this five-foot body, this lump of red flesh. That which answers and that which questions never diverge from this lump of flesh, for I am the one who questions myself. The 80,000 Dharma teachings aren't things written on paper – they are all provided with this body. Accordingly, though this body is only five or six feet tall, it is never small; though its life spans only 70 years, it is in no way short. That is why I repeat that the Formless Self harbors the boundless world of All Humankind and envelopes the endless time of Suprahistorical History.

To study Buddhism for many years, perhaps even for a lifetime, and yet fail to manifest directly the Buddha in response to the question about the Buddha's whereabouts, can only be seen as pitiful. Such failure indicates that you haven't truly studied Buddhism. Of course, this question about the whereabouts of the Buddha would surely humble contemporary Buddhologists, for they, too, would end up as silent as the lecture-master. Even if you pile scriptures mountain-high, a true Buddhologist will not emerge. Nor will the True Self awaken. Indeed, the lecture-master's helplessness is quite regrettable.

Because of what has transpired, Linji says to the lecture-master: "You thought you'd make a fool of me in front of the Counselor." The Counselor is a man named Wang, and he is the Governor of Henan Province. At the Counselor's invitation, Linji is giving a Dharma talk. In the process, as we have seen, he turns to the questioning lecture-master and asks him if he thought he could make a fool of him in front of the Counselor. Linji yells at him: "Get out, get out! You're keeping the others from asking questions." Linji addresses the other people gathered for his talk, saying, "Today's Dharma assembly is concerned with the Great Matter. Does anyone else have a question? If so, ask it now!" And he warns them: "But the instant you open your mouth you are already way off. Why is this so? Don't you know? Venerable Śākyamuni said, 'Dharma is independent of words, because it is neither subject to causation nor dependent upon conditions.'" Linji has directly expressed that about which Śākyamuni hadn't preached a word for 49 years, that which words fail to reach. "The moment you open your mouth, you are already way off" – how do you receive this direct pointing? How do you come before him? If you realize your Formless Self, responding to him will be a simple task.

16

The Instant You Open Your Mouth You're Already Way Off

In my last talk I discussed how Linji responded to the lecture-master's notion that the Three Vehicles' twelve divisions of teachings reveal Buddha-nature. Confronting the standpoint of doctrinal study, Linji pointed to the source from which those teachings emerge. Yet the lecture-master could not enter directly into that source, so he ended up stuck in silence. Linji broke off their *mondō* by asking him to take his interest in trivialities and leave so that those with questions about the fundamental matter could step forward and ask their questions.

After driving him away, Linji proclaimed, "Today's Dharma-assembly is concerned with the One Great Matter. Does anyone else have a question? If so, ask it now!" Having received a request from Counselor Wang, the provincial governor, Linji set up this Dharma-assembly, which was a gathering for a lecture, so to speak, on the Dharma. Linji explains that the Dharma-assembly was being held for the sake of the One Great Matter. A passage in the *Dharma-lotus Sutra* claims that buddhas come into this world because of the One Great Matter of causes and conditions. Scholars offer varying explanations of what "One," "Great," and "Matter" each mean. In Linji's Zen monastery, the gist of the One Great Matter is for sentient beings to open up satori, and for more experienced practitioners to create conditions under which others can open up satori. One often hears the expression, "With one leap enter directly into the land of the Tathāgata."[76] This direct or abrupt entrance into the land of the Tathāgata – in other words, awakening directly to our Original Face or Buddha-nature – constitutes the One Great Matter. In the context of the FAS Society, the One Great Matter is our awakening to the Formless Self. This is crucial. In this awakening is established the True Self, the basis on which the world is unified and history is forever created freely and without hindrance. The One Great Matter is this fundamental formation of human beings, which in the final analysis is the expression of our Original Face.

At this point in history the primary challenge we face is how to awaken to the true human being that has broken through the blind spots of medieval theism and modern humanism, and from there to function freely and to live a true life extricated from living–dying (samsara). In short, we must find a way to awaken to the Formless Self, which in the FAS Society constitutes a true religious life.

The crux of Zen is to awaken to the Original Face, and one who has done so is a buddha. Any external Buddha or God we seek, entrust ourselves to, or believe in, falls short of the true buddha. Zen proclaims that the true buddha is nothing other than the self that has awakened to our Original Face. In the *Record* Linji refers to it as "person," for when we hear the word "buddha" we are apt to conceive of it as something to be believed in external to ourselves or as something on which to rely. In Buddhism, "buddha" tends to be construed as some sort of theistic entity other than oneself. Linji rejects this, for he has rid himself of theism. He speaks of the "person of the Way" who is "solitarily emancipated" and "non-dependent," the "true person," the true human in the sense of someone who is dependent on nothing, who stands in an absolute autonomy rather than heteronomous theonomy. This person is an "I" that is truly independent, and it diverges completely from the "I" in religions that speak of absolute reliance or absolute dependence.

This is not the kind of human being who seeks Buddha externally, who is caught up in living-dying, who is split between good and evil, who through being fractured has lost sight of the Self, who envisions some sort of true self as an ideal in the endless future. The human of whom Zen speaks is an ideal that is already actualized in the present and full of vitality. It is a human who has resolved the contradictions at the foundation of modern humanism. From the perspective of modernity, this is a new human arriving in the next epoch, an eternal human that is not restricted in time or space. This human is the true embodiment of humanity, extricated both from religion as it has existed up until now and from contemporary images of humanity. Diverging from medieval theism and modern humanism, this human is something new. Though I refer to it as "new," it is an embodiment of humanity that has existed fundamentally all along.

The awakening to this embodiment of the true human is the One Great Matter. More than anything, we must resolve this matter, because if we don't, we will lose ourselves – our subjectivity – forever, and we will never awaken to true human who is "solitarily emanci- pated" and "non-dependent." Regardless of how minutely or repeat- edly one reads sutras or even the entire canon, and regardless of the level of one's intellectual understanding, should the One Great Matter remain unresolved, one's accomplishment is trivial. This is why Śākyamuni spoke of the "One Great Matter of causes and conditions," in the sense of sentient beings opening up satori or of having other sentient beings open up satori. I am not saying that these words are venerable because they are Śākyamuni's, or that they are venerable because Linji uttered them. Rather, they are venerable because they proclaim the true human.

To say that these words are venerable because they come from Śākyamuni or Linji is to remain entangled in theism. We must sweep away all dogmas, criticize even rational objectivity, and seek that which is true. Then, from there, we regard whatever accords with it to be venerable and whatever does not to be mistaken. This free stand- point is the posture we take when we are truly seeking the Way, and it must be realized as the fundamental way of being human. In this standpoint, contrary to what one might expect, absolute objectivity that is in no way subjective is established.

Linji says that the assembly has been set up for the sake of the One Great Matter. He asks whether among you there is someone who wants to ask about it. If so, he wants you to step forward and ask a question, to come forward immediately and engage in an exchange of questions and answers (*mondō*). This is how Linji functions towards the audience.

In working on the assembly by inviting them to ask questions, Linji is revealing directly to them the severity of questions about the One Great Matter. He is vividly presenting the true way of being of ques- tions posed for the sake of the One Great Matter. If you have a ques- tion, ask it now! But the instant you open your mouth, you are way off. Though urging us to ask a question, Linji declares that we will be way off the second we open our mouths. To be "way off" means that whatever we say will be wide of the One Great Matter. What should we do? We are told to ask a question, but when we open our mouths, no true question will emerge. To ask in the way the lecture-master did is to fail to ask a true question. Nevertheless, the people assembled are prodded to ask a true question about the One Great Matter. Ordinary questions about the Three Vehicles' twelve divisions of teachings are blocked by Linji. So how should we ask? If you even begin to open your mouth you will be way off. How can you ask without opening your mouth? How do you do it?

Linji speaks here of opening the mouth, but he is not referring simply to the individual thing called the mouth. To open the mouth is to have a form, to become entangled in forms of all kinds. We cannot use any of the five sense organs or even the mind to ask questions about the One Great Matter. If we use them, we will be wide of the mark. If the mouth is of no avail, we might try asking by thrusting a hand forward, by moving the legs, or by using some sort of logic. But Linji is rejecting all possible uses of the body and mind when he speaks of our opening the mouth. Though Buddhism speaks of the eyes, ears, nose, tongue, body, and mind as the "six consciousnesses," we cannot ask the question with them or with their objects – colors, sounds, smells, tastes, touches, or thoughts. No matter which of these we use, we won't be able to ask the right question.

But if we ask without depending on any of the six consciousnesses or their objects, in our very questioning will lie an answer. As the saying goes, "Where there is a question there is an answer."[77] Unless we ask the question in that way, we can't respond to Linji's invitation: "Ask it now!" Linji asks the audience to step forward and ask a question without opening the mouth, and with this challenge he is blocking all trivial questions and thrusting forward the true answer. The words are few, but their meaning is beyond measure. "The instant you open your mouth you are already way off."

If we suddenly accord with that which does not open the mouth, if we accord with the kind of questioning that is formless, if we can do that kind of questioning, then Linji's words have achieved their goal: to deprive us of ourselves and thereby bring us to life. He is freely using the "sword that takes life and the sword that gives life," for he has a means of slaying all things and then bringing them back to life. This is found time and again in Zen *mondō*.

When we think shallowly we conceive of questions as things we ask with our mouths, but even our ordinary questions aren't ever limited in this way. There are many types of questions. A deaf and mute person can ask questions. Actually, a deaf-mute might be able to ask more concretely than we can, for his or her question will be less conceptual. The question I am discussing is no ordinary question you can conceive, for it diverges even from ways of questioning that do not use the mouth. If the eyes, ears, nose, tongue, body, and mind, together with colors, sounds, smells, tastes, touches, and thoughts, simultaneously asked a question, it would still not be the question needing to be asked here. The true question has to do with "dying the One Great Death and gaining new life."[78] Only in that question's causing us to die to ourselves do we find peace of mind. In this context we can speak of the "unlimited treasury in the midst of a not-a-single-thing."

Though things seem complete at this point, Linji asks yet another question: "Why is this so?" Thinking that those assembled did not easily understand what he said about opening the mouth, Linji explains it further, with the kindness of an old grandmother. "Why is this so? Don't you know?" He in effect says, "Is this not what Śākyamuni said? What I am telling you matches his words exactly." Śākyamuni said, "The Dharma is independent of words." The Dharma is not something that can be spoken of in this way or that, for it is prior to words, not something based on them, even though it gives rise to words. As indicated in the expression, "Verbal inquiry does not reach it," we can't express the Dharma in words. Why not? People often say things like "This feeling of mine can't be expressed in words," or "Words fail to capture the taste of this delicacy." There are many feelings in the world that cannot be expressed in words. But this is not what Linji is getting at here.

Because it is formless, the Dharma is independent of words. And it is separate from other things as well, for words aren't the only things with form. The 84,000 Dharma-gates – the Buddhist scriptures of the Tripitaka canon – are not the Dharma *itself*. The Dharma is independent of all sutras, of all words. The Three Vehicles' twelve divisions of teachings are words, as are speculation and the objects of speculation, thinking and the objects of thought. For this reason there is no Dharma in the Three Vehicles' twelve divisions of teaching. The Dharma is independent of them, though they are expressions of it and gain in it a true foundation. In no way can we, through these teachings, clarify the Dharma or realize the freedom of not being entangled in words coming from the Dharma.

So, whatever has form is not, as it is, the Dharma. Even the sutras, the talks on the Dharma issuing from Śākyamuni's "golden mouth," are not absolute. Buddha's talks were given in accordance with certain times and places, and past scriptures are not the only scriptures. To treasure these words after Buddha's death and say that they are his central teaching is to exhibit ignorance of the basic fact that the Dharma is independent of words. The Dharma is living in the present. New expressions and teachings may – and indeed must – emerge from it one after another. For words to emerge moment to moment from that which is independent of words and for those words eternally to take new forms – for this kind of scripture to continue coming forth – means that Buddhism or the Dharma is truly alive.

One who truly lives in the Dharma does not become entangled in words from Śākyamuni's "golden mouth." In fact, Zen speaks of "a transmission independent of doctrinal teachings and not dependent on words or letters." Zen uses sutras freely without being used by them. Never caught up in past sutras, the True Self freely creates new sutras and has them function. So even though words from scriptures are quoted here and there in Zen writings, Zen is using these words, not being used by them, for Zen is not a religion that believes in scriptures or in God. In this respect Zen displays a profound, autonomous subjectivity. Being independent of all forms and presenting all forms – this is the Dharma.

About the Dharma, Linji goes on to say, "neither subject to causation nor dependent upon conditions." According to a prevailing understanding, the fundamental Buddhist world view is that everything here is constituted and ruled by causes and conditions from which we cannot escape. For this reason the Buddhist world view is said to hinge upon a law of cause and effect. But the Dharma is neither subject to causation nor dependent upon conditions – it is beyond causes and conditions, and this constitutes the truly Buddhist world view. Causation and conditioning are a law that pertains to the way of being found in the world of phenomena. The Dharma, however, is extricated from conditioning, and for this reason we can speak of absolute emancipation. If we fail to consider this, the Buddhist world view will come to be seen as a type of determinism. Were Buddhism to claim that people cannot become extricated from the law of causation and conditioning and that a Buddhist life is to accord with and obey causes and conditions, all freedom would be lost and there would be no way people could speak of being "solitarily emancipated" and "nondependent." A true person is neither subject to causation nor dependent upon conditions, but completely emancipated, autonomous, and unobstructed. In the *Heart Sutra* we find the expression, "unobstructed." Encountering no obstructions, no hindrances, no obstacles, no restrictions by others or oneself – this is the truly free and autonomous self. For this reason, Buddhism is fundamentally the Dharma, the teaching and truth of non-dependent-coarising.

Linji continues: "Your faith in this is insufficient, therefore we have bandied words today." In several places in the *Record* Linji speaks of insufficient faith. People often say that religion is based on faith, and that a generic expression for religious people is "the faithful" or "believers." This wording derives from belief in God or Buddha. In believing objectively in God or Buddha, of course, one is not simply knowing God or Buddha, for faith is a kind of activity, a religious activity involving a religious heart (J. *shūkyōshin*), but this is not what Linji is referring to when he speaks of insufficient faith.

Insofar as faith is belief in an object, it is better not to have faith in the True Self. Given the nature of Awakening, it would be more appropriate to speak of not having faith in the True Self, Original Face, or the True Person. But this isn't what Linji is saying, either.

Nor is he referring to faith without an object, to faith in the sense of conviction. We need to have the conviction through which we act to the bitter end or probe ever deeper into the self, but this type of "faith," which is sometimes referred to as the root of faith and takes the form of self-confidence and will-power, falls short of the faith Linji claims is insufficient.

In Buddhism we hear the expression, "One can enter the great sea of the Buddha-Dharma through faith." This faith can be taken in various senses, too, but none of them corresponds to what Linji means by "faith." To him, Dharma itself, the Awakening of Dharma, is ultimate faith. Linji is in effect telling those assembled that they ramble on about this or that because they haven't penetrated or awakened to Dharma as their root-source. Because they have not awakened to it, Linji has "taken too much vine and rattan." This expression, "taken too much vine and rattan," refers to making too much use of words, which usually bind and restrain us from free activity. So when Linji says, "I have taken too much vine and rattan today," he is referring to how he tried to explain the Dharma in various ways because of the lack of faith of the assembled people.

When Linji earlier spoke of being invited perforce to give a talk on the Dharma in front of Counselor Wang, he said that if people could "enter with a leap" he would not have to offer an explanation of the Dharma. In effect he said, "I have been explaining the Dharma, but don't get entangled in my explanation! It would be best for you to go straight to the original place, for if you get tangled up in my words and explanations they will ensnare you." The Dharma is independent of words, so the explanation of the Dharma is an explanation aimed at having you get free from words, of having you get independent of the explanation. That is to say, the explanation of the Dharma aims at having you awaken directly to the True Self, and the explanation of the Dharma that frees us from the explanation is the true explanation.

After all these twists and turns in his talk, Linji exclaims, "I fear I am obstructing the Counselor and his staff, thereby obscuring Buddha-nature." He is afraid that he has hindered both the Counselor, who invited him to talk, and the accompanying officials. He fears he has sidetracked them from awakening to their Original Face. We run the risk of defiling Buddha-nature when we offer verbal explanations while at the same time arguing that the Dharma is independent of words and explanations. The Three Vehicles' twelve divisions of teachings are no exceptions to this. Linji expects people to "enter directly with one leap," to awaken immediately and truly to the Self, so he decides not to ramble on any longer, saying "I had better withdraw." Clearly, at this point he stops his talk on the Dharma, but to where will he withdraw? To the place he came from, to the place beyond all verbal explanations. Obviously, in this case "withdraw" differs from what people usually mean by the term. His withdrawing boldly displays his Original Face, the place to which he retreats from his talk.

Saying he must withdraw, Linji gives a shout: "*Kaah!*" This is a shout that emerges from where "the path of speech is cut off and all mental activity is destroyed." Linji isn't simply opening his mouth wide and yelling in a loud voice, for that would simply be a voice, however strong it might be. Again, as he puts it, the instant you open your mouth you are way off. If the shout does not come from the place in which the body-mind and all verbal explanations have dropped off, it can't be a true shout. The true shout isn't a shout that lasts an instant and then disappears. The true shout is a shout that extends from the eternally distant past to the eternally distant future.

Immediately after displaying that shout, Linji declares, "For those whose root of faith is insufficient, a final day will never come." Not to arrive at true faith is to roll around in rebirths across an endless future: In the final analysis this is like wandering aimlessly in a jungle. No matter how long you might look around in scriptures for solutions, you won't make any progress. A final day will never come, and this can only be called a false endlessness. "Do not seek outside yourselves!" "If you seek it you go against it." No matter where you seek you will go against it.

Linji concludes his talk: "You've been standing a long time. Take care of yourselves." He notes how long they have been standing there listening to the Dharma, and he closes with parting words, in effect saying, "Goodbye, and take care." He is aware of how long they have been standing, and I am aware of how painful your legs might be from sitting so long while listening to me. This parting remark, "take care of yourselves," weighs a thousand pounds. Let us stop here for today.

17

No Dividing into Categories

Today I will take up the three categories of inherent capacities Linji discusses at the end of the "Discourses" section of the *Record*. People have various capacities, and Linji divides them into three groups.

As for the students who come from every quarter, this mountain monk divides them into three categories according to their inherent capacities. If one of less-than-average capacity comes, I snatch away his surroundings but do not snatch away his Dharma. If one of better-than-average capacity comes, I snatch away both his surroundings and his Dharma. If one of superior capacity comes, I snatch away neither his surroundings, nor his Dharma, nor himself. But should a person of extraordinary understanding come, I would act with my whole body and not categorize him. Virtuous monks, when a student has reached this point, his manifest power is impenetrable to any wind and swifter than a spark from flint or a flash of lightning. The moment a student blinks his eyes, he's already way off. The moment he tries to think, he's already different. The moment he arouses a thought, he's already deviated. But for the person who understands, it's always right here before his eyes.

Virtuous monks, with your bowl-bag and your dung-sack slung from your shoulders, you rush up blind alleys, seeking Buddha and seeking Dharma. Do you know who it is who right now is running around searching this way? It is brisk and lively, with no roots at all. Though you [try to] embrace it, you cannot gather it in; though you [try to] drive it away, you cannot shake it off. If you seek it, it retreats farther and farther away; if you don't seek it, then it's right there before your eyes, its wondrous voice resounding in your ears.

If a person has no faith [in this], he'll waste his entire life. (p. 29, adapted)

Linji speaks of "students who come from every quarter," of those who come to seek the Way. Such students are also referred to as "people who study the Way" (J. *gakudō no hito*). Of course, this "study" is different from scholarship. Gathered here today in Kyoto are people who are wholeheartedly studying the Way in this pleasant spring season. Likewise, people have come to Linji from all around to seek the Way, and the mountain monk – Linji himself – divides them into "three categories according to their inherent capacities." The people have their own capacities, and Linji groups them.

The first type is "one of less-than-average capacity." This "less" does not indicate a lowest or inferior group – Linji does not bother to consider them – but rather those on the low end of the middle range of individuals. When such a person comes, Linji snatches away his or her surroundings but does not take away his Dharma. The word "surroundings" refers to the objective world, which for humans includes colors, sounds, odors, tastes, and physical sensations of touch. Linji will snatch away this objective world and leave the Dharma. When we sit *zazen* here we clear away various external hindrances and turn our minds inward. In terms of our strategy,[79] we snatch away the mind that directs itself outward and turn it inward toward the Dharma. Regardless of the external surroundings, we snatch that mind away so as not to get led astray by them. What remains is the subject, or subjectivity.

Earlier in the *Record* Linji talks about the "Four Classifications." The first is to "take away the person and not take away the surroundings"; the second is to "take away the surroundings and not take away the person"; the third is to "take away both person and surroundings"; and the fourth is to "take away neither the person nor the surroundings." What we are discussing today corresponds to the second classification, to take away the surroundings but not take away the person, for "person" here is synonymous with "Dharma."

Linji continues, "If one of better-than-average capability comes, I snatch away both his surroundings and his Dharma." He snatches away both the objective world and the subject. This point is not necessarily limited to Linji, for it appears with different wordings in Zen records and other Buddhist texts. To snatch away both is to "appear in all places." In terms of form and emptiness, the "surroundings" are form, and what is referred to here as "Dharma" is emptiness (Skt.

śūnyatā). Buddhism also speaks of the active and the passive, which are the activity and the object upon which one acts, the person and the surroundings.

Linji is talking about snatching away the inside and the outside. The person of better-than-average capability is someone who gets stuck on the inside, who dwells within, who stops in the Dharma, who lingers in subjectivity or the "active." From the perspective of Zen, neither attachment to objects nor attachment to the subject is the true way of being. When the surroundings and the person are snatched away, when form and emptiness are both emptied, there emerges a self that is not dependent on either the world of objects or the world of the subject. The subject and the objective world here are not a subject with contemplative knowledge and a mere object of knowledge. Rather, they concern life. If one is engaged in Zen practice, they amount to the one who practices and that which one practices. Perhaps it is more appropriate here to speak in terms of the one who acts and that upon which one acts, the one who lives and that which is given life.

Linji snatches away both subject and object. In this there is neither subject nor object, and this is the true unity of the two. Or, more fundamentally, this can be referred to as "prior to the separation of subject and object," and it is the fundamental Original Face, the "root-source," from which subject and object, the active and the passive, emerge. We return to that source, yet it is not the case that we unite two dualistic things there. Rather, the subject and object return to the source prior to separation, to their "Original Face." This is not simply word-play: it is the place in which subject and object have been snatched away and we awaken to the self that has become Oneness.

Zen makes much of the expression, "The myriad things return to one," depicting it with a circle. Zen artists often draw circles in their paintings, and this is the place in which subject and object have been snatched away. We see this in *Ten Pictures of an Ox*.[80] One caption reads, "Person and ox are both forgotten." It is to this place that those of better-than-average capacity go. Yet they stop on the side of the subject, and become attached to it, and for this reason the subject must be snatched away, too. The line of the *Heart Sutra*, "There are no eyes, ears, nose, tongue, body, or mind; no color, sound, odor, taste, touch, or thought," expresses this place in which body and mind have been snatched away.

The place where subject and object have been snatched away is the "mirror wisdom of the great circle." This circle is a great mirror with no cloudiness whatsoever. There is nothing reflecting and nothing reflected, for this stands prior to the separation of subject and object. This is an equality without distinction that exists beyond all distinctions. We must arrive at this place, for it is the True Self.

Zen says, "Prior to the separation of guest and host, subject and object are united," and this is my way of being, my form. Yet this "form" is a formless form, and it fills the ten directions of the world and the infinite future. Because it is formless it is free. Extricated from all hindrances, it is the true selflessness or no-self. People speak of "no-self" in various ways, but this is the true no-self. It is also the True Self. The "dropping off of body-mind" refers to this self, and "to see into one's nature" (*kenshō*) is to awaken to or become this self. This is the self that has snatched away subject and object. To "investigate matters of the self" (J. *koji-kyūmei*) is to investigate this self. In arriving at that self, all methods of investigation find their goal. To direct oneself upward, to enter nirvana, is none other than this. The Buddha is said to have awakened on the eighth day of the twelfth month under the Bodhi Tree, and the awakened Śākyamuni – the Buddha – is this Self. This is the Non-abiding Self, which is emancipated from all things and entangled in nothing. This is the person of superior capacity.

"If one of superior capacity comes, I snatch away neither his surroundings, nor his Dharma, nor himself." If such a person comes, there is no need to snatch away the surroundings or the Dharma. This statement is virtually the same as saying that one snatches away neither the surroundings nor the person. This corresponds to the fourth of the Four Classifications. "Not to snatch away" indicates that everything has already been thoroughly snatched away and that, at the same time, the surroundings and the person are freely present. This may mean a rebirth in which we die completely to our ordinary selves and awaken to the True Self, to true emptiness. Because a new, true self awakens, this is referred to as being reborn in death. Both the person and the surroundings that were snatched away are reborn. This holds a new meaning and a new life. In fact, this is where we find a Buddhist life, a religious life, as well as the Pure Land, the Western Paradise, and the world of nirvana. The person and the surroundings exist as the world of discriminations, established upon the truly emancipated formless self.

It is here that the A and S of FAS come into being. This is not merely the world or history in the usual sense. Rather, the Formless Self creates this world and history freely and without limits. Established in this is a religious world and a history that take the True Self as subject. This entails equality, not superficial equality in the usual sense of rights but the fundamental equality that exists in the true human way of being. So when we speak of all humankind we are referring to all sentient beings, to the entire world. It is here that one comes to stand in the standpoint of all humankind, the place where Linji snatches away neither the surroundings, nor the Dharma, nor the person.

Linji next speaks of what he would do "should a person of extraordinary understanding come." This extraordinary person is the Formless Self, and in some cases it becomes the person, in some cases the surroundings, in some cases the subject, and in some cases the object. And in some cases it is neither subject nor object. The person who functions freely in this way is extraordinary. If such a person were to come, "I would act with my whole body." This is the truly free functioning in which all things are one and this one is all things. When Linji faces such a person he is equal to that person, he comes forth in the same way, and he is truly an intimate friend.[81] Here there is no "dividing into categories," for no separation exists between them, and this is why Linji says he would "not categorize him." There is no way they can be separated. Both act with their whole bodies, both knowing the tune. No one else can get a word in edgewise or do anything. Here we can discern the true significance of a Zen *mondō*. In the *mondō* that occurs when one encounters Linji's snatching away of the surroundings, Linji advances his questioning as a living strategy.

Here Linji is dividing capacities into three levels, but he knows that in actuality they are fundamentally one, not three separate things. This is the "one" of acting with the whole body. Whether Linji gives a shout or wields the staff, when a person sizes up Linji that person encounters this total activity of the body. Ultimately, this is the coming of the person of extraordinary capacity, the person who crosses swords with Linji, who gives him an even fight, like when a dragon goes up against a tiger. No one can say which is superior. "Virtuous monks, when a student has reached this point, his manifest power is impenetrable to any wind ...." At this extreme point, the student of extraordinary capacity displays a power that even the wind cannot penetrate. There isn't the tiniest crack.

And that power is "swifter than a spark from flint or a flash of lightning." There is no time, no temporal gap in this, not even the instant of a spark from flint or a flash of lightning. A spark or a flash is too slow here. Not even a hair's breadth separates them. Such interaction appears throughout the *Record of Linji*. In the Zen of the Founding Teachers[82] monks do not ramble on about things in their discourses.

The ultimate state of *mondō* in this type of Zen does not have any cracks for the wind to penetrate or a temporal gap as long as the duration of a flash of lightning. We do not find such a *mondō* in the doctrinal study of Buddhism, or anywhere else in the world, for that matter. This is the distinctive Zen *mondō* of the "Founding Teachers." It is a kind of sumo between two people of Zen.

"The moment a student blinks his eyes he's already way off." When the eyes gaze around – blinking, stopping, and moving – a student of the Way is unsteady. What exactly does Linji mean by this? The "eyes" are the student's way of being, not merely eyes in the ordinary sense. The person does not become settled, does not arrive at the final stability of a giant boulder, does not penetrate the great peace of mind. When the Buddha, God, or death are taken to be external to oneself, the eyes are turned outward. If nirvana or the Western Paradise are thought of as external, the eyes will glance around and you will fall wide of the mark. This is what Linji meant when he said, "The instant you open your mouth you'll be way off." If your eyes glance around, any hope of attaining what you seek will be out of the question.

Linji next said, "The moment he tries to think, he's already differed. The moment he arouses a thought, he's already deviated." This expression, "tries to think," indicates the wobbling of the mind when one considers doing this or that. The mind directs its thoughts in certain directions, and no matter what it does, it "differs" from the true mode of being. The moment one arouses a thought, a myriad other thoughts follow, and this falls short of what is true. "But for the person who understands, it's always right here before his eyes." It's not found in a remote or deep place. It's right before your eyes. It does not part from right now and right here. Just as they are, here and now are the activity of the whole body.

Linji calls out, "Virtuous monks, with your bowl-bag and dung-sack slung from your shoulder." A bowl-bag represents a monk who begs with a metal bowl in which food is placed. The dung sack stands for the body, which carries excrement. Zen uses another pejorative expression: "clothes pole and rice bag." The human mind is part of a rack for hanging clothes, and the body is a bag for holding rice. "Clothes pole and rice bag" refers to the body-mind of someone who is a human being in form only. Such people "rush up blind alleys seeking Buddha and seeking Dharma." "Blind alleys" connotes houses other than one's own, into which such people run in search of Buddha or the Dharma outside themselves.

"Do you know who it is who right now is running around searching this way?" Linji asks if we know the person running around in confusion, looking around externally, unaware of what is inside or what is right before the eyes. Who is inside? What is right before us? It is the True Self, the Formless Self. Linji is in effect saying, "That which is always before your eyes is this person – don't you understand this?" This is "brisk and lively." It is splashing around in great vitality "with no roots at all." It is free and autonomous, with no root or stump in which to get stuck. It is a rootless tree that runs around freely in the "thousand vast worlds." The "rootless tree"[83] is a tree that is not a tree. You must be this rootless tree, for you will be in trouble if you are an "I" that cannot move because of entanglement in the roots called body and mind.

"Though you [try to] embrace it, you cannot gather it in; though you [try to] drive it away, you cannot shake it off." The expression rendered "embrace" here literally means to rake together, to gather things together. You cannot gather in the self, and if you try to drive it away, it will not scatter. "If you seek it, it retreats farther and farther away." To seek it is to head in the wrong direction. "If you don't seek it, then it's right there before your eyes." Not to seek it is crucial here.

Someone might ask how it can be obtained if one does not seek it. It is quite superficial to say "seek and it shall be given," because if one seeks it, it is not given. Linji in effect says, "Don't seek outside. It's right now, right here!" Linji in other places talks about "you who are listening to the Dharma." What is it that is sitting there right now listening? Isn't what you're seeking none other than what is listening? Isn't it precisely that which is looking? Linji is telling us above all else to take leave of the mind that runs around searching. "If you don't seek it, it is right before your eyes." It can't be hidden. It is fully and impressively presenting itself. Confucianism has an expression, "I hide nothing from you." Though this expression is apparently quite similar to what I'm getting at, here the connotation is different: there is nothing I hide from you, for it's right before your eyes.

It's right in front of you, with "its wondrous voice resounding in your ears." This wondrous voice is the sound of Linji's talk on the Dharma. It's the wondrous voice that acts with the whole body. What is it like when one hears this wondrous voice? There is no ear and no sound. Linji has snatched away the root of the ear, making this voice the voiceless voice, the soundless sound that fills heaven and earth. "If you don't seek for it then it's right there before your eyes, its wondrous voice resounding in your ears." Let's stop here for today.

18
The Four Classifications: A General Outline

Today I will discuss Linji's "Four Classifications." The text reads,

> At the evening gathering the Teacher addressed the assembly, saying, "Sometimes I take away the person and do not take away the surroundings; sometimes I take away the surroundings and do not take away the person; sometimes I take away both the person and the surroundings; sometimes I take away neither the person nor the surroundings."
>
> Then a monk asked, "What about 'to take away the person and not take away the surroundings'?"
>
> The Teacher said, "The spring sun comes forth, covering the earth with brocade; a child's hair hangs down, white as silken thread."
>
> The monk asked, "What about 'to take away the surroundings and not take away the person'?"
>
> The Teacher said, "Mandates of the Sovereign are spread throughout the world; the General has laid the dust of battle beyond the frontiers."
>
> Again the monk asked, "What about 'to take away both the person and the surroundings'?"
>
> The Teacher said, "No news from Bing and Fen, isolated away from everywhere."
>
> The monk asked, "What about 'to take away neither the person nor the surroundings'?"
>
> The Teacher said, "The Sovereign ascends [the throne in] the jeweled palace; aged rustics are singing." (pp. 6–7)

It goes without saying that the teacher here is Linji. For the group of people assembled at an "evening gathering" he gives a talk on the

Dharma. This was a regular practice, and at one such gathering Linji says that sometimes he snatches away the person yet does not snatch away the surroundings.

"Surroundings" here refers to the world of objects, and the "person" can mean either an ordinary person or a True Person. "Surroundings" is the objective world, which includes the external objects of the senses: colors, sounds, odors, tastes, and things touched. We also sense the objects of the mind, which Buddhists usually list with the eyes, ears, nose, tongue, and body as a sense organ. The world of the objects of the mind is evident when we construe something as, for example, "cute," "detestable," or "aggravating."

We sometimes hear the expression, "seeing, hearing, perceiving, knowing." That which stands against and objectifies the objects of seeing, hearing, perceiving, and knowing – subjectivity in a broad sense – is the "person" about which Linji speaks. "Person" can also be the subjectivity of the eyes, ears, nose, tongue, body, and mind, that which sees, hears, smells, tastes, touches, and knows in the usual sense. People are likely to believe that there is no person apart from this sort of person standing over and against the objects called color, sound, odor, taste, touch, and thought. Even in Zen people often speak of discerning the self without getting caught in objects, and in this way advise others to direct their attention toward that which sees, not that which is seen, with the True Self existing in that which sees. People might think that the sense of sight that sees a color or a form is the self.

More internally, people are likely to take as the self that which thinks or that which knows. Another possible assumption is that, differing from the subject behind each of the separate acts of seeing, hearing, sensing, and knowing, there is something that unifies the whole, and that this is the self, too. One could think that the unifying subjectivity that brings together all of our external and internal sensing is the self, the True Self, the True Person. This is often the case, and in opposition to this, a person of old said, "Students of the Way do not know the truth because they have hitherto identified their conscious mind with it. The very source of living-dying over incalculable eons of time they take to be the Original Person – this is the way of naming by an idiot."[84] They take their conscious mind to be the Original Person, but it isn't. Only when we break through the conscious mind does the True Person present itself, for the conscious mind is ultimately the root of our living-dying, the source of the delusion. If we don't slaughter it we can't really know what is true. This is why Zen warns us that the subject of our seeing, hearing, perceiving, and knowing is not the True Person, and why Linji tells us not to identify the conscious mind with the Original Person. This is a difficult point.

In the FAS Society we use the expression, Formless Self, to make this clear and to ensure that there'll be no mistake. It is the self and it is formless; it is formless and is self, and this is what Linji calls the True Person without Rank and the Sixth Founding Teacher calls the Original Face. But people are apt to be mistaken and take this person, this True Person, as the surroundings. In other words, that Person is apt to become an object. But any "True Person" we grasp as an object is hardly the True Person.

For that reason, when one speaks of taking away the person and not taking away the surroundings, if one does not take away the objectified "True Person" at the same time one takes away the person of ordinary seeing, hearing, perceiving, and knowing, one will not have completely taken away the person. The Formless Self itself is that which takes the person away. It is the ultimate agent of snatching away the self.

Linji says that in certain cases he does not take the surroundings away. This differs from what might usually be meant by taking away the surroundings. This expression usually connotes our being held captive by surroundings in the sense of the objective world, our being the captive of the colors, sounds, odors, tastes, touches, and thoughts of internal and external sensation. In this we lose ourselves in the negative sense. In contrast, the true loss of the self is the taking away of the person. The true loss of self is the true no-self, the Great Self, or what Linji calls the Person of the Way who is solitarily emancipated and non-dependent. What about this, everyone? We must all lose the self in this sense.

The taking away of the person is the absolute loss of self. But a loss of self in the usual sense is the exact opposite of this. The usual loss of self is when the self is merely taken away and one falls into a state of empty or false release, and without an identity one is spun around by surroundings. There is no subjectivity here, no independence or autonomy at all. One can't even call this an ordinary human being.

With this meaning, "not to take away the surroundings" isn't something to be affirmed. In the true sense, "not to take away the surroundings" is to extricate oneself from surroundings, not to be hindered, ruled, or restricted by them. Usually we must snatch our surroundings away. But the truth of the matter is that we don't need to. Just as people say that this is the world of the True Person in which every speck of dust emits light, the objective world of the True Person is that which the True Person makes use of freely and without hindrance. Zen has spoken of there being "no thing to be hated." Indeed, there is nothing that should be detested. Everything is affirmed. And not in a relative sense, for things are affirmed absolutely.

If A and S are not the A and S of "not to take away the surroundings," they will not be the true A and S. In their true sense, various buddha lands, such as Amida Buddha's "Pure Land," are this "not taking away the surroundings." In their midst, as the expression goes, "one disports oneself in a dense forest." One isn't hindered by anything. One is unobstructed and free. This is, as it were, the vigorousness of emancipation. Snatch away each and every surrounding in an absolute way – this is truly "not to take away the surroundings."

Let us for a moment consider somewhat superficially how, when we practice, we usually become the captive of external surroundings. We tend to get caught up in the world of objects experienced by the five sense organs. Unable to settle our minds, we direct our attention externally and become captives of the "outside." When we do this, there are surroundings but no person. Whenever we are directed only to the outside there is no person, and in this state of affairs it is impossible to be a human being. Something is lacking. This is a loss of self in the ordinary sense: there is no subjectivity, for one has flown off somewhere. In no way can a human bear such a situation. For this reason there naturally arises an impetus to return somehow to the inside, to the mind or self that has been caught by the outside. This is what happens in *zazen*. But even though one might be sitting, it is not real sitting, for the mind has flown away. To stop being held captive by the outside one must pull the mind back to the inside, to the person that is the inside.

Usually, however, people consider the inside to be the person or mind that is a subject standing over and against the external world, and on this basis they make efforts to bring this mind back inward. This is probably how it is when you sit *zazen*.

Take, for example, the first picture in *Ten Pictures of an Ox*: looking for the ox. The ox has been lost, and only the external world remains. The person looks around for the ox, but he doesn't even know what the ox is. He simply looks outside for something, anything, and there he discovers tracks of the ox. In these pictures, to chase after and seek the ox is to head inside, toward the subject.

In the inside exists the world of the objects of internal perception, so even if one does not get caught by external colors, sounds, odors, tastes, and touches, one still gets caught by the objects of internal sensation that rise up in droves. This is the internal world of the mind, of the person, that is different from the outside. Compared with pursuing things all over the place on the outside, in the inward shift one's subjectivity has been retrieved much more. But if the mind is now dragged about by the world of the objects of internal sensation, true subjectivity will not come forth.

We are yanked around not only when we feel anger, or when we find something detestable or cute, or when we like or dislike things, but also by affirmation and negation, good and evil, beauty and ugliness – polarities that are a valuable part of the content usually found in human psyches. When captured by such things, we have lost true subjectivity. The True Self gets pursued in this world of objects, and if we don't snatch that world away we won't become this pure Self. It is for this reason that we have an expression by the Sixth Founding Teacher: "Without thinking about good and without thinking about evil – when you are just so, what is your Original Face?" The Original Face is found where one thinks neither of good nor of evil. This does not pertain only to good and evil, for it holds for living and dying and arising and ceasing as well. When you neither arise nor cease, what about your Original Face? Where there is no living and no death – this is where the Original Face is found. That which undergoes living-dying isn't the Original Face or the True Person that has extricated itself from that process.

In Buddhism and other religions, Buddha or God is said to be something highly venerable. Such a thing, however, is usually an object, a part of the surroundings. In contrast to this, can we call the Buddha or God that is not part of the surroundings "Buddha" or "God"? That which is transcendent or immanent is usually said to be God or Buddha. More exactly, that which is transcendent externally or immanently is God or Buddha. But the subjectivity, person, or self that takes such a thing as God or Buddha to be part of its surroundings is not the true person. This is why Zen says there is no Buddha and no Founding Teachers. What is the Original Face that does not think about the Buddha or the Founders?

Linji tells us not to seek Buddha outside ourselves. When you find the kind of buddha or founding teacher that remains external to you, slaughter it. This killing should not be misconstrued in a negative sense, for it is precisely what needs to be done. Slay both the Buddha and the Founding Teachers. These severe words are not simply an expression that has been around since the beginning of Zen, for they express the true, final negation in Buddhism. Do not set up a buddha. Do not set up founding teachers. If that which is referred to by such terms as Tathāgata or nirvana remains an object or the surroundings, it will fall short of the true Tathāgata or the true nirvana. Only when we thoroughly kill the Buddha and the Founding Teachers do we find the truly final person and gain peace of mind. Insofar as the Buddha or Founding Teachers are still hanging around outside us and influencing us this way or that, we have not yet become truly composed or solitarily venerable. Legends report that right after he was born Śākyamuni said: "Above and below heaven only I am venerable." I need to point out that this state of being the only one above and below heaven who is venerable was the case even before Śākyamuni was born, not something that came about after his birth. It was like this prior to his birth, but not in the sense of 2500 years ago. "Prior to" indicates the present, here and now. To be the only one venerable is absolute independence, absolute autonomy, the True Person who is solitarily emancipated and attached to nothing. Linji wants to say here that it is not a matter of the infant's voice or the meaning of what he said – it is that which is living, your Original Face.

This autonomy is the gist of "not to take away the surroundings," realized when one snatches away all surroundings and leaves nothing to be disliked. In this one achieves rebirth after the Great Death. Here things are just as they are. That which is "just as it is" is not something fixed but something that arises in abundance. As indicated by the expression, "When the mind arises, various things arise," this is not a matter of things that already exist. In "not to take away the surroundings," limitless things come into being. It is only in this sense that Linji exclaims that the surroundings are not taken away.

From long ago Zen has said things like "The willows are green and the flowers red" and "Mountains are mountains and waters are waters." As ways of expressing the true Source, such expressions are fine. But if we think they are merely referring to things before us being as they are, we will be as wide of the mark as heaven is from earth.

In the expression, "Die the One Great Death and be reborn," to die the One Great Death is to snatch person and surroundings completely away. We cannot truly affirm person and surroundings without truly snatching them away. That which snatches away person and surroundings is the True Person. And only with that True Person does there emerge that which does not take either of them away, and this is the focus of the fourth of the Four Classifications.

If the snatching away of both is simply a matter of negating or eliminating them, the fourth classification of not taking away either will
end up being our normal human state of affairs. In that state there is
both a person and surroundings; because there is a person there are
surroundings, and because there are surroundings there is a person.
Linji doesn't need to set up the Four Classifications, but he does so to
have people awaken to the True Self. They are in no way four things to
be discriminated or analyzed. Awakening is a matter of non-discrimination, non-discriminating knowledge, or, as expressed in the "consciousness-only" school,[85] "the turning over of consciousness and the
attainment of wisdom."[86]

The wisdom attained in this turning over of consciousness is the
true human being. For this reason the world of consciousness, the
world of the eight consciousnesses,[87] is not the true world but simply
the world of normal human beings, the world where people are
caught up in causes and effects, in affirmation and negation, good
and evil. It is the basis of living-dying. Or, more specifically, the eight
consciousnesses are the basis of living-dying through infinite eons.
Hence the expression, "Cut down with a sword into the field of the
eight consciousnesses." We must take up the sword and slay the eight
consciousnesses.

The classification scheme I am discussing is not something that Linji
discriminated for the sake of discrimination, and the expression, "Four
Classifications," was coined not by him but by people later on.
Nevertheless, Linji's classification is wisdom, his wisdom, the wisdom
attained in turning over consciousness. I use the word "classification"
to connote Linji's living strategy to awaken others. This strategy is a
religious method, and it comes into play through Linji's being this
living strategy. Accordingly, it is clearly not derived from the kind of
discrimination that says, "It should be like this," or "It must be such
and such." This is a free and self-abiding discrimination, a classifying
that is a free activity transcendent of ordinary discrimination.

Linji says, "sometimes,"[88] but in no way does this refer to specifically
designated times. His "sometimes" is the time without time, the time-
less time. Herein lies the freedom of this "sometimes." Of course, this
"sometimes" is always some time, and it must be so. But this is not
simply time, for it ought to be "some place" as well. Where a certain
place cannot separate from a certain situation – this is where the true
way of being of the True Person exists. If time and place separate, there
is no True Person. Extinguishing time and place, temporality and

spatiality, the True Person is constantly now and here. Such is the True Person, the True Person without Rank, the Formless Self. This is FAS.

Starting today, we will conduct the fifty-first retreat of this organization. I want all of you to take as your objective the Self that has snatched away both person and surroundings. You must not be the self standing over and against what has been snatched as surroundings. Aim for the Self that has taken away both person and surroundings. Do not look outside yourselves.

19

The Four Classifications: First Half

The day before yesterday I offered a general outline of the Four Classifications. Today I will begin talking about each of them in turn.

Linji says to the assembly, "At certain times I take away the person and do not take away the surroundings; at certain times I take away the surroundings and do not take away the person; at certain times I take away both the person and the surroundings; at certain times I take away neither the person nor the surroundings." As soon as he says this a monk steps forward and asks, "What about 'to take away the person and not take away the surroundings'?" This monk is Kefu, one of Linji's famous disciples.[89] After Linji became heir to Huangbo's Dharma and established his own expression of the Dharma on the bank of the Hutuo River, this Kefu, together with a monk named Puhua, assisted Linji in his teaching. Known in Japanese as Fuke, Puhua was actually a disciple of Panshan Baoji. His conduct was highly eccentric, and he is often depicted in Chinese and Japanese Zen paintings. There is a painting of a venerable monk ringing a bell in the clouds, and the subject of this painting is Puhua. In Japan there are Fuke monks, otherwise known as Komu monks.[90] The Komufuke Sect started with Puhua, and it is said that the sound of his bell ringing in the clouds, radiating out across heaven and earth, is the origin of the bamboo flute (J. *shakuhachi*) and the source of sound. In any case, Puhua and Kefu took great pains to assist in the establishment of Linji's Dharma.

Stepping forward with a question, Kefu asks what sort of thing "to take away the person and not take away the surroundings" might be. On the spot Linji responds by conveying its meaning with a verse. Because this is a verse of the very thing expressed by "to take away the person and not take away the surroundings," if one does not clearly understand the first classification the verse will lose its life. It will be mere word-play. So, Linji answers Kefu by directly expressing in a verse the gist of the first classification. He says, "The spring sun comes forth covering the earth with brocade." The "spring sun" indicates warm, fair weather. When spring arrives, the sun begins to shine brightly and coaxes up grasses, trees, buds, and flowers. With this the fields come alive in an array of flowers – red, yellow, and white – and this brocade decorates the earth. As you have all probably surmised here, this sings the praises of "not to take away the surroundings" as opposed to "to take away the person." The surroundings have not been taken away, for they are presenting themselves just as they are: the earth blooms with myriad flowers.

But if we take this as simply an existing landscape or a spring scene, it will have no connection to the true "not to take away the surroundings" expressed by the verse. Herein lies the symbolic character of Zen verses, for this is not mere scenery but a symbol conveying a specific meaning. Yet if we take it merely as a symbol, our understanding will approximate the gist of Linji's verse but inevitably fall short. In saying "The spring sun comes forth, covering the earth with brocade," Linji has presented "not to take away the surroundings" in the true sense. In effect he throws it before the monk and says, "So, do you understand?"

Linji's statement is not simply a verse. Nor mere words. Nor merely an actual scene. It is an immediate presentation of truth (*genjō-kōan*). If we're not careful, we'll mistakenly take this to be an ordinary scene sketched by a poet who specializes in landscape description. And should we take it to be a verse from a poet who has given a symbolic expression to something internal, we'll end up viewing the verse only symbolically. Neither of these approaches is correct. Spring has fully arrived, and blooming flowers cover the earth – this is "not to take away the surroundings." It is, so to speak, a "certain time" of Linji's True Person without Rank. It does not separate from this Person, for it is that Person's self-presentation. This is how we must view Linji's verse.

He continues: "A child's hair hangs down, white as silken threads." The child is an infant, a baby, and its hair hangs down, "white as silken threads." As you may have guessed, this verse conveys the taking away of the person. But why? A baby doesn't have enough hair to hang down. And even if it did, it surely wouldn't be white. This child – as a kind of person – is being negated here. The person has been snatched away, and only the surroundings remain. The self has completely vanished into the surroundings, leaving not even a speck of anything that can be called "person." In a profound sense, this is the state that is cut off from the "delusion brought about by people" (J. *ninwaku*). At times the True Person becomes free in the "taking away of the person" that leaves nothing to be called the self. The Zen expression, "Mountains are mountains and waters are waters," expresses this "to take away the person but not to take away the surroundings." To what does this correspond in terms of F, A, and S? I want you all to investigate this. Is it F? Is it A? Or is it S? Which is it?

Kefu next asks, "What about 'to take away the surroundings and not to take away the person'?" In response Linji answers with the verse, "Mandates of the Sovereign are spread throughout the world; the General has laid the dust of battle beyond the frontier." "Mandates of the Sovereign are spread throughout the world" – is this to take away surroundings or not to take away surroundings? "Mandates of the Sovereign" refers to the person. The Mandates of the Sovereign are enforced throughout the realm. They control the realm and the realm submits to them. The realm is equivalent to the person, so this line also describes the situation of "not to take away the person."

The second line here, "The General has laid the dust of battle beyond the frontiers," refers to the situation in which the General is no longer fighting in outlying provinces to protect the realm. The dust of battle is the smoke of signal fires and the dust stirred up by horses in battle. Battles and chaos have now disappeared completely, and no confusion remains anywhere in the land. This line hence refers to the settling of tumultuous times into a state of peace and quiet, in which there is no thing at all. That is to say, the surroundings have been snatched away, leaving only the person, the self. Apart from this self there is nothing, so from a certain angle this is absolute solitude. Ordinary solitude differs greatly from "The General has laid the dust of battle beyond the frontiers," for in such solitude myriad things are swarming. Endless waves are surging in the mind. Though it may appear to be solitude, it really isn't. In contrast, true solitude is absolutely unique. It contains no "other," and it is entirely one. To be true, solitude must be this one.

I am not speaking only of Linji. When we arrive at the true Zen way of being we become the solitude, the self, that has no outside and no inside. There is a Zen expression, "The ten-thousand things return to one." We can view "things" here as the surroundings. The return of all things to one is the self of the dropping off of body-mind. When we arrive at this point, we do not feel anything like good feelings or a refreshed mood. When the Sixth Founding Teacher says, "Originally, not-a-single-thing," he is speaking of this Self, the Original Face. It is the self that is emancipated from all internal and external surround-ings. Solitude reaches its ultimate form here. There is no solitude like it.

In ordinary solitude the mind is highly composed and pure, and for this reason people often say they want to be solitary. When the world becomes obnoxious, everything seen or heard is repulsive. In response, people consider retreating to somewhere quiet, retiring from the sur-roundings in the world. From long ago people have discarded the world and renounced home, thereby becoming renunciates. Looked at from a certain angle, renunciates seem to be terribly lonely, miserable people. They have found the world to be a bitter place, and out of their alienation they want to be alone, even though being alone is miserable and lonely for them. Entanglement in these two sides of being human – the desire to be alone and the sorrow of being alone – follows those who have left home and renounced the world. Appearing in songs, dramas, and paintings, this ambivalence is treated as the subtle work-ings of human feeling and it moves the human heart. With people retiring into mountains away from the smoke and dust, Kumagaya Naozane's name has become a household word in Japan.[91] His, however, was not true solitude. "In heaven and earth there is only one person," and this person fills the universe. There are no hindrances and no loneliness. No anguish caused by the world, and no loneliness from being alone. This solitude is fulfilled. Is it not a wonderful solitude?

When Linji says that he takes away the surroundings but does not take away the person, he is referring to this type of person. If we don't become this person, we will never be able to extricate ourselves from anguish and loneliness. We will spend our days talking about how much anguish or loneliness we feel. True composure of the mind is not found here. The mind that is simply composed – or not composed – in the relative sense is not the true mind. In the true mind there is no security or insecurity, and only this can be called the mind that has true peace. A self that relies on an absolute being or the power of nature, that clings to an external entity like God or Buddha, is not the self that is truly and absolutely composed. The self or person that does not need the Buddha, the Founding Teachers, or the public world, and is no self to be called a "self" – this is the person of taking away the surroundings but not taking away the person.

The first classification of "to take away the person and not take away the surroundings" is the absolute world, while the second classifica-tion, "to take away the surroundings and not take away the person," is the absolute self. The latter is the "one" in "The ten-thousand things return to one"; the former is the ten-thousand things in "To what place does the one return? The one returns to the ten-thousand things."[92] We must be able to move freely in both of these two directions.

As conveyed by the expression, "the ten-thousand things return to one," all things return to a one. This one is not the oneness usually spoken of in philosophy, for it is the self. It is the one that is the self and the self that is the one, and to this the ten-thousand things return. At the same time Zen asks, "To what place does the one return?" And it answers, "The one returns to the ten-thousand things." If we fail to move freely in this direction, too, we will fail to grasp the "taking away of the person and not taking away the surroundings." I want all of you to try returning to this one by tackling the question, "To what place does the one return?" Then emerge in the place of "the one returns to the ten-thousand things." If you simply think about or imagine this with your heads, this one will become the surroundings or objects of our seeing, hearing, perceiving, and knowing, and such surroundings are not the true One. Realize that the true One is not a one conceived objectively as some sort of absolute, as the source of the world, or as the world's ultimate.

I want all of you to investigate this point carefully. From the perspective of Zen inquiry, this is extremely important. For this reason Linji at certain times snatches away everything and has the person awaken. At other times he snatches away the self and has it return to the world. Linji engages in this functioning vis-à-vis the "person," and with his discourses on the Dharma, his staff, and his shout he is executing a living strategy. He does these things because fundamentally all of us – not just Linji – are such a person. "The ten-thousand things return to one. To what place does the one return?" If you yourselves investigate this, Linji will be there.

20
The Four Classifications: Second Half

Starting today we will conduct the fifty-second retreat of the FAS Society. I am glad that all of you have come here from far and near to spend a week studying the Way even though you are busy as the end of the year approaches. At first a week seems like a long time, but I want this to be a retreat in which the week ends before we know it, in which each day is complete and fulfilled and you feel regret at its passing. Sometimes people grow impatient, wanting the stick of incense to burn down so they can release their attention and take their legs out of the lotus posture. Some people want the week to end quickly. Given that all of you have devoted precious time to being here at this retreat, I don't expect you to be like this, but I would like all of you to immerse yourselves in the investigation of the Self and make this a meaningful and fulfilling retreat.

None of Linji's Four Classifications is easy to understand. He says that at certain times he takes away the person but does not take away the surroundings. What is involved in truly taking away the person but not taking away the surroundings? Linji also says that he sometimes takes away the surroundings but does not take away the person. Usually we tend to get caught up in the surroundings, and it is extremely important for us to avoid doing this. For this reason, when Zen people of old encountered those of less-than-average capacity, they suggested snatching away the surroundings and preserving the Dharma, just as Linji in effect did to ordinary people before him when he said, "Cast aside all the hindrances of your surroundings."

People often speak of losing subjectivity or losing the self. What does this mean? We get tossed around by and caught up in our surroundings, and because of this the "protagonist" is lost. This protagonist might not get lost when we are in a quiet place, but as soon as it enters a slightly tumultuous place it is snatched by the surroundings and gets lost somewhere. As technological civilization becomes progressively complex, we get caught in our surroundings and lose autonomy. The human is lost, and only the surroundings remain. Actually, when the remaining surroundings are of the kind that exist upon the establishment of true subjectivity, they are more genuine than the protagonist separated from surroundings. Usually, however, this is not the case. Ordinarily, when only surroundings remain, subjectivity has been lost, in that the person is being chased around by surroundings. The anguish that accompanies this becomes deeper and deeper, and for this reason Linji takes away the surroundings yet does not take away the person. The person who is not chased around by surroundings is central here. Even if one is doing *zazen*, it is extremely hard not to get caught up in surroundings. Despite references to "koan samadhi," practitioners often are grabbed by their surroundings and fail to enter this samadhi. They may speak of "just sitting" (J. *shikantaza*), of truly sitting and cutting through, but they tend to get obstructed by surroundings and encounter various impediments. In the end they fail to sit completely. For this reason we must take away surroundings but not take away the person.

When the surroundings are taken away and the person remains, however, people then get caught up in that person. They adhere to it as if stuck in mud. They get bound up in the protagonist, losing all freedom in their surroundings. When doing *zazen* they may appear to be truly sitting without being hindered by anything and thereby finding some sort of protagonist, but as soon as they separate from *zazen*, the protagonist they went to the trouble of finding will run off somewhere. Obviously, this is not the true protagonist, and for this reason it must be snatched away. Simply put, we must not be caught up in the surroundings or in the person, so we need to take them both away.

Linji next tells the assembly, "Sometimes I take away both the person and surroundings." Here there is no person and no surroundings; otherwise there is no True Self and no true surroundings. Linji says he takes them both away. When we get to this point things get extremely difficult. It is often suggested that we rise quietly from *zazen* so the state of sitting will not be lost. This is something to keep in mind when rising from sitting, but if our sitting is such that our state of sitting is lost when we get up, it falls short of true sitting. For this reason I constantly stress that it is the sitting that rises. Sitting is true sitting when walking, standing, sitting, and lying are all sitting and this kind of sitting is not lost in our surroundings. If the protagonist is the protagonist only when we are sitting, it is obstructed and must be snatched away. Hence Linji says he snatches away both person and surroundings.

When people hear that Linji snatches them both away,they are apt to think that there won't be anything left. If nothing were left, we would end up in a mere negation, mere nothingness, void of person and surroundings. When we truly investigate things, however, we see that what remains is the very person that took away person and surroundings, the self that has slipped free of all entanglements, the self that isn't caught up in either the person or the surroundings. It takes neither the form of the person nor the form of the surroundings. Only when it is something formless and neither subject nor object can we say that it is the truely formless Self, what Linji calls the "One True Person without Rank." Buddhism at large argues that the Dharma-body (*dharma-kāya*) and nirvana are formless. In the "body of Awakening," which is not something that once awakened but rather that which is constantly awakening, there are no forms whatsover. This is what Linji is indicating when he speaks of taking away both the person and the surroundings.

In the last retreat I gave talks on the first two classifications, and today I want to look at Linji's third: "Sometimes I take away both person and surroundings." As I said last time, the "monk" who is questioning Linji at the evening gathering is Kefu. This time he asks, "What about 'to take away both person and surroundings'?" What does it mean to snatch away both of the two things? Linji exclaims, "No news from Bing and Fen, isolated away from everywhere." From the start Linji has been responding not with conceptual explanations but with symbolic couplets, with what people ordinarily might refer to as poetic verses. Often Zen figures will respond symbolically rather than conceptually, and this is a distinctive characteristic of Zen *mondō*. This method is not limited to answers, for Zen teachers often formulate questions with symbolic wording. Though not a few *mondō* are executed with words, that is, concepts, *mondō* are usually carried out in an extremely concrete form – in activity. For example, Zen speaks of "Raising the eyebrows and blinking the eyes." Such acts appear in a great number of *mondō* in the Zen of the Founding Teachers. This use of gestures rather than words is a distinctive facet of Zen *mondō*.

But there are *mondō* that use neither the body nor words. They are beyond the body, the mouth, and the mind as the three loci of karma.

If we don't take it to this level, we won't reach the true, ultimate *mondō*, or true Buddhism, for that matter. What sort of thing is "emancipation"? It is to surpass the body, mouth, and mind in the "dropping off of body-mind." If we haven't done this, we have not yet engaged in a true *mondō*. The question and the answer must be one, and it is only by surpassing the body, mouth, and mind that we can reach the point where the question is the answer and the answer is the question. This is the "transmission from Self to Self," and in it, prior to any expression, the question and answer are undivided. If you do not make it to this point, you won't penetrate the marrow of *mondō*.

You can't truly take away both person and surroundings if you haven't surpassed the three types of karma. Likewise, a *nenbutsu* or *daimoku*[93] that does not surpass the body, mouth, and mind is not a true one. Nevertheless, sometimes people stop in the place of verbal karma when they chant the *nenbutsu* or *daimoku*. This is an important point, and it is not limited to these practices. Practitioners who are working with Zen koans must extricate themselves from the body, mouth, and mind as well. Otherwise they will stop in the three loci of karma. And if you stop there, you won't be able to act freely.

If the Formless Self beyond the body, mouth, and mind as the three loci of karma has not presented itself, you have not passed decisively through the koan. "When the one is cut through, the many are cut through as well."[94] If anything remains at the end, the passing of the koan will not have been true *kenshō*. You must awaken to the Formless Self, and realize that it is the True Self.

Zen uses other expressions that correspond to Linji's statement, "I take away both person and surroundings." For example, the Sixth Founder said, "Fundamentally, not-a-single-thing." There is also an expression, "Worldly passions fallen away, holy intent is completely emptied."[95] With passions dropped off, and with no thoughts of the sacred, there is no Buddha and no person. Yet we tend to get caught up in the Buddha and nirvana, and so Linji tells us that when this happens neither that which is doing the catching nor that which is caught is the true Buddha. If the Founders and the Buddha are something fixed outside of us, we will get caught up in them, so as people have been saying from long ago, we must be the Self that has surpassed all forms. We must become the One True Person without Rank, the True Person who is solitarily emancipated and non-dependent.

Linji says, "No news from Bing and Fen, isolated away from everywhere." There is no news from two prefectures in remote, outlying areas. Occupied by Wu Yuanji (783–817), they no longer have any relations with the central government. All news has been cut off. The authority of the Imperial Court, of the Sovereign, has been lost in Bing and Fen, and the mandates of the sovereign are no longer in effect. For this reason, Bing and Fen, as surroundings, have been snatched away. And given that the orders of the Emperor are no longer carried out there, the person that is the master has been snatched away as well.

Linji expresses the taking away of both person and surroundings by presenting a verse about Bing and Fen. These prefectures had been occupied by Wu Yuanji, who had holed up in the Cai Castle.[96] This castle had walls so thick that it was impregnable, and it had never fallen. One day after a deep snowfall, however, the forces of the sovereign attacked and the castle was taken. Wu Yuanji was killed and the independence of Bing and Fen ended.

Dahui mentions this in a capping phrase he wrote about "to take away both person and the surroundings." He regarded Bing and Fen, which had been invaded, as the surroundings, and Wu Yuanji, who had been killed, as the person. His capping verse reads, "The Castle of Cai was toppled and Wu Yuanji was killed."[97] The Cai Castle was toppled, whereupon the two prefectures fell – this is to take away the surroundings. And Wu Yuanji was killed, so the person was snatched away, too. Dahui attaches his words to Linji's verse, "No news from Bing and Fen, isolated away from everywhere," and this is easy to comprehend. What he says is probably easier to understand than Linji's verse, but this is nothing special. One could create many expressions like Dahui's, and far better ones at that. But here we have no special use for things like that. Simply, "I take away both the person and the surroundings."

In praising an outstanding technique for riding horses, people often say, "Above the saddle no rider; below the saddle no horse." The ultimate technique of horseback riding is not simply a matter of there being no person or horse. One is caught up in neither the person nor the horse. But it is not simply an individual case of riders and horses, for all persons and surroundings must be snatched away together. The snatching must be general and total.

Just as people often speak of the "deep pit of emancipation"[98] in Zen, if the taking away of both person and surroundings ends up being a mere negation in which there is no person or surroundings, it will not be the true thing. If the True Self remains simply formless or finds cheap satisfaction with its formlessness, this will amount to falling into the deep pit of emancipation, otherwise known as "falling into a dark cave."[99] Not only Linji Zen but Zen as a whole warns us about this.

The true taking away of both person and surroundings functions in a vigorous and lively way, and it must be, so to speak, the body of functioning. This functioning is the body of awakening (J. *kakutai*), the Awakened body, a wondrous activity. Simply put, if *zazen* is something like being lost in meditation, it drifts far away from us.

In the FAS Society, F is the Self that is formless, yet free and unobstructed in its functioning. It must be that which, while functioning freely and without obstruction, is constantly formless and never caught up in the surrounding objects on which it is functioning. To convey the fact that this taking away of both person and surroundings does not fall into the pit of emancipation, Linji next says, "I take away neither person nor surroundings." This isn't a matter of not taking them away in the usual sense, for it is to "be reborn after death," and that which takes neither away is the true world.

At certain times the true world becomes the person, at certain times it becomes the surroundings, and at certain times it snatches away both person and surroundings. Only when "the person and the surroundings go and come freely" do the Four Classifications become something true and become one. The Four Classifications must be one classification, and this must mean that the person and surroundings are free and independent. This is not simply a matter of "extraordinary capacity," for the Four Classifications must become that which has no stages.

> The monk asked, "What about 'to take away neither person nor surroundings'?" The teacher said, "The Sovereign ascends [the throne in] the jewelled palace; aged rustics are singing."

Linji is asked what the taking away of neither person nor surroundings is all about, and he answers, "The Sovereign ascends the throne in the jewelled palace; aged rustics are singing." The Sovereign is the person, and the jewelled palace is the surroundings. The aged rustics – the populace – are singing. The singing is the surroundings, and the aged rustics are the person. And neither is taken away here. This is the world in which both person and surroundings are affirmed.

21
On the Way and at Home

Taking the high seat in the hall, Linji said: "One person is endlessly on the way, yet has never left home. Another has left home, yet is not on the way. Which one deserves the offerings of people and devas?"

Then he stepped down. (p. 5)

Today I want to consider this talk by Linji from the high seat in the hall. He says there is a person who is endlessly on the way yet has never left home. For many eons, this person has been on the way, on a pilgrimage or traveling. Though on the road, the person is said not to have left home. What is Linji driving at here?

The person is "on the way yet has never left home." It would seem that if the person were on the way, he or she would have left home, and if the person were at home it seems impossible for the person to be on the way. Yet Linji says that for a long, long time the person has been on the way and yet has not left home.

If we take Linji's statement only at the verbal level, it can be construed in various ways. If we locate the home "over there" and think of the person as on the way to it, as in the middle of returning to a house, "on the way" means "on the path of return" or "on the way home." In this situation, one's home is constantly on one's mind as one advances in that direction. This is one instance of being on the way yet not having left home. To set up an ideal and then for many long years press on along a single path in that direction is to be on the way yet never to have left home. From beginning to end one's home is on one's mind, yet one has not arrived there. Linji's statement thus might be interpreted as meaning that one was previously at home, left, and now is on the way back. Here the home clearly exists as "my home," in which one is living, and it is one's source, the place from which one emerges. One leaves that house and then returns to it.

We can also interpret Linji's statement to mean that one does not yet clearly know where one's home is, yet one is searching for it. After asking around, one arrives at or truly returns to it, and for the first time one confirms its existence with one's own eyes. Inevitably such a home is verified clearly, and it must become a real existence, an actuality.

In some cases though, no matter how much time passes, this home does not come fully into existence. The farther one goes, the farther away the home becomes. Or one eternally pursues the home without verifying it, and as a result the home never becomes a real existence. From a certain angle, this, too, is an instance of being on the way and, with the home constantly on one's mind, never leaving it. One has not left, but no matter how much time passes one will not grasp what sort of thing the home is, and one will simply keep pursuing it along a single path. In this scenario lies a connection between the home that has not been verified, the home that is no more than an idea, and "on the way." This state of affairs is something we constantly experience in our daily life. It is quite common.

We can also imagine the scenario in which the person on the way has clear evidence of the existence of the home, a firm proof of the home's existence, and is heading for this confirmed home. However, the "home" here is known by the person as a teaching that is based on proof. By means of this teaching the person is on the way home. The person is not going around aimlessly, for he or she clearly is going to arrive there. Because the home has been confirmed with certainty, through the teachings the person will return there and directly confirm the home's existence.

The "on the way" I have just discussed appears, for example, in Jōdo-shinshū[100] as the "going aspect." One is on the way to the true realization, to actual corroboration. In the deepest sense, this home is nirvana, the elimination of suffering (J. *metsudo*). In terms of the three bodies of the Buddha, this is the Dharma-body (Skt. *dharma-kāya*). It is what is true. We may be "going" there, but as indicated in the Jōdo-shinshū expression, "Return to the capital of the Dharma-nature," to go here is actually to return.

Accordingly, instead of "go," Kegon Buddhism uses the expression "return to the source." One returns, as it were, to the source that is confirmation. Even in this case, although one is on the way there and hence has not yet attained it, one isn't separate from the attainment. One is in the process of practice, on a pilgrimage, and will arrive at true satori. Confirmation here is to realize satori, and in Zen terms it is to awaken to one's Original Face, which is one's home. One returns to this home through the guidance of the teachings. This differs from being lost without an aim, for the destination is clearly fixed, not something hazy. Yet because one is on the way and has not yet confirmed it, one has not yet emerged from the confirmation, the home. One is going *to* the home, to satori, and this sort of relationship between the home and "on the way" is extremely different from the previous case of being on the way yet never having left home.

And there is yet another possible case: on the basis of confirmation, one is clearly at home and the home is the source. This is an "on the way" in which one is in the home that is the source and that from which one sets out. There is no need to follow a path home, for the "going home" emerges from the house, from the confirmation. The previous going was a going to the confirmation, a pilgrimage. But this is a pilgrimage *from* the confirmation.

Usually there is no one who does not have a home. We leave the home and then return to it as something clearly discerned. In this case, our being on the way can be highly composed. We have a home and we have set out from the home. So to return to it is nothing special. When we leave home, our trip is quite composed, unlike that of those who do not have a set home. We are not on a trip of wandering.

Humans find their home in the Original Face, the One True Person without Rank, the functioning of what this Society calls the Formless Self, to which we awaken, or, better yet, which awakens in us. Our usual home is apart from us when we are "on the way," but when the Formless Self that is our Original Face functions, it truly is on the way yet has never left home. The home is always on the way, and one is on the way without leaving home. This "on the way" cannot separate from home, because the home is the subject of functioning. For one to awaken to the Original Face and for this awakening to become the source of our living is the true meaning of "on the way yet has never left home," as well as the true living of human beings. As long as you are still searching for home and have not yet arrived there, you are not yet living the life of home, the life of the true human.

This true living differs from idealism and from the Buddhist living called the "going aspect." This is practice upon attainment, our being reborn in total death. We must experience this. Our usual "on the way" must become our returning to the home one time, getting composed, and leaving on a trip from there with peace of mind. It must turn into our "dying the One Great Death and being reborn." There must be what the Consciousness-Only School refers to as "turning over the eight consciousnesses and giving rise to the four wisdoms."[101] But usually, even in Buddhism, this doesn't happen. Though speaking of Buddhist living, people tend to run around aimlessly pursuing ideals, and in this way they handle living.

If your being on the way does not involve a truly existent home as your aim, it will fall short of truly being on the way. And insofar as it is the "going aspect" or the "aspect of returning to the source," it cannot be called a true Buddhist living. The issue here goes beyond simply whether it is a Buddhist way of living, for it concerns whether your living will be truly settled. What Linji is referring to when he says, "on the way yet has never left home," is the "going" – the practice – that emerges upon confirmation. If we have confirmed it, there is no past, present, or future. Confirmation is beginningless and endless, and it is unborn and unceasing.

People might take "beginningless and endless" to be something vague, but it isn't. It entails a beginninglessness and endlessness that transcends time and space while encompassing them. This is the true eternity. It is an eternity that is neither a temporal eternity nor a spatial infinity. That which surpasses time and space is the formless True Self. This is the character of what is called the Original Face.

"Original Face" is interpreted in many ways. Suchness (Skt. *tathatā*) and nirvana receive various interpretations as well. Yet in the FAS Society, what we refer to as F must be the True Human, the True Self, and the A and S are the "on the way" existing upon the F as their home or subject. This is the meaning of "on the way yet has never left home." But, if we take A and S to be heaven or the paradise of the Pure Land, they will diverge from what I mean by A and S.

We must be "endlessly on the way yet never left home," endlessly functioning in time and space. The eternal, Formless Self must be functioning eternally, unhindered by living-dying or good-evil. Only when one is the Formless Self can one function infinitely without being hindered by arising-ceasing or good-evil. Therefore, "on the way yet has never left home" is for A and S never to leave F.

Linji next says, "Another has left home, yet is not on the way." The person has separated from home yet is not on the way. What sort of thing is this? If one is not home one ought to be on the way, and if one is not on the way one ought to be home, so what does it mean to be neither at home nor on the way?

This way of being is hard to imagine. The person is neither in actuality nor in the source of actuality – what does this entail? Both places have been completely negated. This is a way of being that cannot be called a "way of being" in the ordinary sense. What sort of person has left home and yet is not on the way? In our practice we must work on this question.

In his earlier statement, "on the way yet has never left home," Linji mentions "on the way" first. As with the person who has left home and is on the way, "on the way" is the primary consideration. In this, functioning comes out into the open from the home as its source. At this time the person is not at home, and the emphasis is on the temporal and spatial way of being that is found in traveling. Of course, what has emerged from the home is, in the language of Jōdo-shinshū, the "return aspect," or in the language of Kegon Buddhism, the "arising and moving" or the "arising of one's nature." The emphasis here is on arising. This "arising," however, must also have the connotation of returning to the home. There is an "on the way" in which the person has left home and yet is not separate from it, and this includes going back home. In this case, the "on the way" is a return aspect, what Jōdo-shinshū calls the "going aspect" and Kegon Buddhism calls the "return to the source."

Thus there are two types of "on the way." There is, as it were, a circular type in which one leaves home, then returns, and then leaves again. The source here is the home. Though the person leaves home and then returns to the home, the home is constantly there. It is the source of functioning from which one leaves, to which one returns, and then from which one leaves again. Whether one is returning or going, entering or leaving, the house is central. In fact, this is a moving house, a functioning house. For this reason, whether one is returning or going, one is never outside the house. What is more, the house is leaving and entering, too.

Hakuin's *Zazen wasan*[102] includes the line, "Going and returning both occur in no other place." By "no other place" Hakuin means one's home. Going is one's home and returning is one's home – from beginning to end one does not leave home. The home doesn't get caught up in going and returning, nor in being on the way. We must become this subjectivity, expressed by the statement, "has left home yet is not on the way." To be neither at home nor on the way – this is the true Original Face.

When people speak of "on the way" or "home," they are usually placing emphasis on one of the two and getting caught by it. The person who emphasizes the functioning gets caught up in it, despite the fact that this isn't something we would expect to happen. The person whose main consideration is the home ignores "on the way," and when a person's being at home splits off from being on the way, the person is not exhibiting the true way of being. Failing to embody the true way of being, people tend to be on the way and forget the home, or tend to be at home and forget "on the way." They cling to nirvana. They cling to functioning. They get caught up in expressions like "wondrous activity," "subjectivity," or "body of awakening." Fundamentally, none of these is anything to get caught up in. To be at home and to be on the way, to leave and enter freely – we must reach this point.

What I am saying here is that to have left home yet not be on the way isn't some sort of middle ground between the way and the home. Bringing the expression "middle way" to this situation would be an outrageous setback. That which has left home and yet is not "on the way" is the truly free, independent, ultimate Self. It goes to paradise and to hell. It leaves hell and enters paradise and leaves paradise and enters hell – it is free in living-dying, good-evil, and leaving-entering.

Contrary to what people usually say, this is not a matter of a different or lofty dimension. It isn't something lifted up high as an ideal we must attain. Rather, it is the present. It is actuality. It is me. It is my living.

So Linji says, "One person is endlessly on the way yet has never left home. Another has left home yet is not on the way. Which one deserves the offerings of people and devas?" Which receives the offerings of people and devas? Which is worshipped as a sacred person? Which do you look upon as the person to take as your ideal? Which is the True Person?

Linji asked this question and then "stepped down." He suddenly came down from the high seat. What is the gist of his stepping down from the high seat? It is no mere explanation. It is no mere way of questioning. It is clearly presenting itself. Let's stop here for today.

22
The Buddha-Dharma is Deep and Mysterious

Followers of the Way, true sincerity is extremely difficult to attain, and the Buddha-Dharma is deep and mysterious, yet a good measure of understanding can be acquired. The mountain monk explains it exhaustively all day long for others, but you students give not the slightest heed. Though a thousand times, nay ten-thousand times, you tread it under foot, you are still in utter darkness. It is without a vestige of form, yet distinct in its solitary shining.

Because your faith [in yourselves] is insufficient, you students turn to words and phrases and from them create your understanding. Until you've reached the half-century mark, you'll continue drag-ging [your] dead bodies up blind alleys and running about the world bearing heavy loads on shoulder poles. The day will come when you'll have to pay for the straw sandals you've worn out. (p. 28)

"Followers of the Way" – this is a call to all of you who study the Way. In Zen, "true sincerity" refers to the Original Face, to what our FAS Society calls the Formless Self. To see with the eyes, hear with the ears, touch with the body, and think with the mind is an everyday occur-rence, and there is nothing difficult here. But we do not find it at all easy to awaken to the Original Face or Formless Self that surpasses all seeing, hearing, perceiving, and knowing. This is what is "true" and "sincere" for Linji, not what people normally take to be true and sincere. As such, it is exceedingly difficult. If we don't drop off body-mind and become the Original Face or Formless Self, it will be hard to attain. Unless we truly die the One Great Death and become reborn, it will be far from easy. But "true sincerity" is our true identity, our true Self.

Linji speaks of that which is "distinct in its solitary shining." It is clearly presenting itself here, beyond any particular here and now. To think it is difficult to attain is actually a bit strange. It's nothing special. It is just as it is (J. *sono mama*). It is that which is ordinary. But because people are wrapped up in and hindered by the myriad internal and external things connected with the eyes, ears, nose, tongue, body, and mind, with colors, sounds, odors, tastes, touches, and thoughts, they can't awaken to it. But in terms of easiness there is nothing easier than this.

Linji next says that the "Buddha-Dharma is deep and mysterious." "Deep" (J. *yū*) indicates that which is dim, misty, refined, and with deep interiors. "Mysterious" (J. *gen*) refers to what is black, but it does not simply mean black, for it indicates profundity. The Buddha-Dharma is deep and refined. But it is deep and refined from the perspective of that which is wrapped up in this, while from the perspective of the Buddha-Dharma itself it is actually clear, "distinct in its solitary shining." There is nothing hidden. It is boldly revealing itself.

Usually, however, the Buddha-Dharma is deep and refined and one can barely arrive at it. "Yet a good measure of understanding can be acquired." Linji says that it will be good if we understand. It will be a fine thing, and "every day will be a good day."[103] But because we do not fully understand, it is extremely difficult, extremely inapproachable. If we gain some understanding of it, however, this extreme difficulty will change into extreme ease. If we die completely and are reborn, if we drop off body-mind, things will be good.

"The mountain monk explains it exhaustively all day long for others." The mountain monk is Linji himself, and each and every day he gives discourses on the Dharma for others. But he exclaims, "You students give not the slightest heed." Linji is working hard to explain things, but the students give no thought to what he is saying. They listen absentmindedly. He in effect says, "Don't you understand this simple matter? I'm tossing it before your very eyes!" Nevertheless, they don't understand.

"Though a thousand times, nay ten-thousand times, you tread it under foot, you are still in utter darkness without a flame." Even though a thousand or even ten-thousand times they step firmly on the place of the Buddha-Dharma, they are still in the dark. Things are black and nothing is clear. In Linji's idiom, they float in "a boundless expanse of darkness."

The word "black" connotes this total darkness, and in Dongshan's Five Ranks there is the rank of the straight depicted by a black circle. This is nirvana, *tathatā*, what we call the Formless Self, the Self that has surpassed all distinctions. It is nothingness in the true sense. By nothingness I do not mean "does not exist," for it is the source from which all distinctions appear, the source that surpasses distinctions. Distinctions are expressed in terms of the rank of the leaning (or discernment, depicted with a white circle). They are bright. The source is that which is prior to the appearance of distinctions, and from the perspective of distinctions this is "prior to the birth of one's parents." When distinctions appear, they are bright; before they appear, things are dark. Though it is referred to as dark, this is the darkness that is the source of brightness, not the darkness of the dichotomy between brightness and darkness. The *Heart Sutra* expresses this darkness:

> O Śāriputra, all things here are characterized with emptiness: they are not born, they are not annihilated; they are not tainted, they are not immaculate; they do not increase, they do not decrease. Therefore, O Śāriputra, in emptiness there is no form, no sensation, no perception, no dispositions, no consciousness; no eye, ear, nose, tongue, body, mind; no form, sound, smell, taste, touch, objects; no realm of vision, till we come to no realm of consciousness; there is no ignorance and no extinction of ignorance, till we come to no old age and death and no extinction of old age and death; there is no suffering, no cause of suffering, no cessation of suffering, no path; there is no knowledge, no attainment [and] no realization, because there is no attainment.[104]

Though one might read the *Heart Sutra*, it is exceedingly difficult to be able to read it in the true manner. When we read as the Formless Self, the *Heart Sutra* is words from the Self, words emerging from the "golden mouth." That which emerges from Śākyamuni's mouth are a buddha's direct words, and in Zen this "golden mouth" isn't limited to Śākyamuni alone. All the words that emerge from anyone's True Self or Formless Self are from a "golden mouth." For this reason, black in the sense of dark and of not understanding something is extremely different from the black of the "rank of the straight."

In the phrase, "utter darkness, with all flames extinguished," "extinguished" indicates that no traces are left. It expresses the freedom of true functioning. One walks, but there are no traces of walking. One sits, but there are no traces of sitting. One talks, but there are no traces of talking. One listens, but there are no traces of listening. All traces have vanished. That which gets caught by nothing, and is nothing, is the true vanishing of traces. Similarly, a flying bird leaves no traces. "Extinguished" has this meaning as well, but from Linji's mouth it connotes something utterly dark and incomprehensible. Linji says that even though people step on it a thousand or ten-thousand times, nothing is clarified. This is truly pitiful.

"It is without a vestige of form, yet distinct in its solitary shining." Before a single word or half a phrase is uttered, it is shining brightly. "Because your faith (in yourselves) is insufficient, you students turn to words and phrases and from them create your understanding." The students are those who are seeking and studying the Way. "Faith is insufficient" – the formless Original Face has not truly awakened. As I always say, the faith here is not faith in some external object. It does not connote an inability to have faith in the Buddha objectively as some sort of object of faith, for not to have faith means not to realize satori or awaken to the True Self. Because the students cannot awaken to the Formless Self, they get stuck on words. When things are expressed with words, students take only the meaning of the words. On the basis of seeing, hearing, perceiving, and knowing, they may acquire understandings of this and that, but they fail to get at the true entity expressed by them. Words are a predicate describing true reality, and only in the context of true reality are words comprehended. Nevertheless, the students get caught up in the words and fail to grasp what they express.

There ceasing to be seeing, hearing, perceiving, and knowing is the very reason they exist. Even though giving a discourse on the Dharma or exhaustively explaining it means surpassing seeing, hearing, perceiving, and knowing, the students try to understand on the basis of the four modes. In the expression, "Enter directly into the realm of the Tathāgata with a single leap," one leaps over seeing, hearing, perceiving and knowing into the realm of the Tathāgata. One awakens directly to the Formless Self. And if you proceed to this point, true insight appears independently and displays itself in one's seeing, hearing, perceiving, and knowing. Usually, however, people keep running around in circles, unable to leap into that which is true. In contrast to Jōdo-shinshū horizontal transcendence, Zen often speaks of a vertical transcendence, which involves a leap directly into the source. If one leaps directly into the underground water that keeps bubbling up, a limitless spring will gush forth. In general, however, people just stand by a puddle on the ground, lost in vacant loitering. No matter how long they do this, they can't get to the source. They need to make a vertical leap.

Linji exclaims, "Until you've reached the half-century mark, you'll continue dragging [your] dead bodies up blind alleys." Linji says that though they are approaching fifty, they still drag their bodies up blind alleys. Without penetrating the source of the self, they wonder where the true thing might be, and end up looking outside themselves, walking around completely lost. With this remark, Linji seems to be saying, "What's the good of all this coming and going?!" People walk around lost here and there and never arrive at their original home-town. Linji declares that the Original Face is not outside of us: it is right beneath your feet. Zen speaks of shedding light on what is under one's legs, and this simply indicates that the Original Face is the funda-mental place right where you are. However long you may look outside, you'll be heading in the wrong direction. Linji often cites the story of Yajñadatta. One might think that the head is outside and wander aim-lessly here and there asking about it, but that which asks is the very head!

Linji calls out to "You listening to this talk on the Dharma." Isn't the listener the True Self?! With his words Linji is telling you that it is right beneath you. Realizing this calls for an abrupt awakening. Unless it is abrupt, you cannot get there, for that which is not abrupt is not true. This is the "on the way" that I discussed in my previous talk. People take this "on the way" to be their home and continue dragging dead bodies. Despite the fact that it is directly beneath their heels, they go around seeking it externally.

Such people are "running about the world bearing heavy loads on shoulder poles." The heavy load consists of various sutras, letters, or, at present, old-case Zen koans. From long ago, Zen has spoken of "a trans-mission separate from doctrinal teachings, independent of words and letters." This expression conveys the marrow of the Buddha-Dharma. Nevertheless, Zen itself came to compose writings that are no different from scriptures, and at present the tradition is dragged around by them. Zen in this way clings to letters and old-case koans, and its fol-lowers bear this load as they walk around lost, seeking here and there in heaven and on earth.

"The day will come when you will have to pay for the straw sandals you've worn out." Even though it is right beneath your feet, you search around outside yourselves, lost, and the expense of your straw sandals will mount up as you get caught in wasteful expenditure. You must enter directly into your original home. What you must do is awaken directly to the Formless Self. With his incisive discourse on the

Dharma, Linji tell us not to idle away our time creating understandings, not to look apart from ourselves.

For one week all of you have worked hard, day and night, in your practice here. As Linji says, the very thing that practices is the True Self. Don't search apart from yourselves. If you awaken to the thing that practices, yours will be the practice based on confirmation and every day will be a good day. Without limit you will make the world and create history, and yet you will not have left home. You will be on the way yet never have left home, and you will be home yet always on the way. You can freely and independently be on the way or at home, and you will neither be at home nor on the way. Presenting itself here is a life that leaves no trace.

Notes

1. J. Rinzai Gigen, c. 810–66.
2. J. Sanshō Enen, n.d.
3. *The Record of Lin-Chi*, tr. Ruth Fuller Sasaki (Kyoto: Institute for Zen Studies, 1975), p. 1. Henceforth, all page numbers will refer to this translation, portions of which have been adapted here.
4. Here the Sanskrit word *dharma* seems to mean reality as it is, expressing itself as a living truth that is free from the distinction of expresser and expressed. See Talk 8.
5. J. *daiki-daiyū*.
6. Hisamatsu uses the date indicated by the extant Linj-lu text, the source of which is an 1120 revision by Yuanjue Zongyan (J. Engaku Sōyen, n.d.) of earlier versions. In *The Record of Lin-chi* (p. 63) his final date is given as the tenth day of the first month in the 8th year of Xiantong during the Tang dynasty, which corresponds to 18 February 867. (Cf. Iriya, note 235, in *The Record of Lin-chi*, p. 88) Recent philology follows the date offered by sources earlier than the *Linji-lu* text edited by Yuanjue Zongyan, such as the *Zutang-ji* (J. Sodōshū, compiled in 952), volume 19, *Song gaoseng-zhuan* (J. Sō kōsō-den, 982), volume 12, *Jingde chuandeng-lu* (J. Keitoku dentō-roku, 1004), volume 12, and *Tiansheng guangdeng-lu* (J. Tenshō kōtō-roku, 1036), volume 10. These sources claim that Linji died on the tenth day of the fourth month in the 7th year of Xiantong during the Tang dynasty, which is 27 May 866.
7. J. Shōgen Sūgaku, 1132–1202. His second generation dharma-heir, Xutang Zhiyu (J. Kidō Chigu, 1185–1269) taught a Japanese Rinzai Zen monk, Nanpo Jōmyō (1235–1308), who is regarded as the initiator of a new line of Dharma-transmission in Japan.
8. J. Ōbaku Kiun, d. 850(?).
9. As a student of the *Diamond Sutra*, Deshan Xuanjian (J. Tokusan Senkan, 782?–865) at one point set out to refute the Zen teaching of Huineng, which contended that a person could be a buddha by directly grasping his or her true nature. On his way to Longshan, the mountain where the Zen master Longtan Chongxin (J. Ryōtan Sūshin, n.d.) lived, Deshan stopped at a roadside teahouse for a snack (J. *tenjin*, "refreshing the mind"). The old woman working there asked, "What are you carrying on your back?"

    Deshan answered, "My commentaries on the *Diamond Sutra*."

    "They are indeed," said the woman. "May I ask you a question? If you can answer it to my satisfaction, you will have your snack for free; but, if you fail, you will have to go somewhere else."

    Deshan agreed, whereupon the old woman continued, "I read in the *Diamond Sutra* that the mind is not attainable in the past, or in the present, or in the future. If so, which mind do you wish to refresh?"

This question from an old woman stumped Deshan, despite his scholarship and the commentaries on the *Diamond Sutra* that he carried on his back. (Adapted from D.T. Suzuki, *Essays in Zen Buddhism*, Second Series (London: Rider and Company, 1974), pp. 49–50.) The earliest recounting of this story appears in the record of Master Deshan in the Korean Gaoli version of the *Jinde chuandeng-lu* (1004), vol. 15. But it is the *Liandeng huiyao* (1183) that reports that Deshan burned his commentary on the *Diamond Sutra*.

10. Huineng; J. Enō, 638–713.
11. J. Nangaku Ejō, 677–744.
12. J. Baso Dōitsu, 709–788.
13. J. Hyakujō Ekai, 749–814.
14. The hall for *zazen*.
15. Ch. *canchan*; literally, joining, entering, or taking part in Zen. In the context of the *Record of Linji*, this term can be rendered, "engaging in Zen practice." This term appears once in the *Record*, and Sasaki renders it "practicing meditation."
16. Literally, "questioning and answering."
17. Ch. *Wumenguan*, J. *Mumonkan*.
18. The term *buddha-dharma* means reality as it is, awakened to and expounded as a living truth. It can be rendered as "the awakened way of being."
19. Skt., *anutpattika-dharma-kṣānti*, a key term in many Mahāyāna texts.
20. The Four Schemes of Thought are 1. a concept, A; 2. its opposite, B, (not-A); 3. both A and B; 4. neither A nor B.
21. J. Daigu, n.d.; Dayu practiced under Guizong Zhichang (J. Kisū Chijō, n.d.), and like Huangpo he was a second-generation Dharma-heir to Mazu Daoyi.
22. When Huijue was asked by a monk the preceding question about reality, he responded by repeating the question. This interaction is seen in the final, one-hundredth case of the *Congrong-lu* (J. *Shōyō-roku*; *Taishō* 48:291c). Langye Huijue (J., Rōya Ekaku, n.d.) was a disciple of Fenyang Shanzhao (J. Fun'yō Zenshō, 947–1024).
23. Weishan Lingyou (J. Isan Reiyū, 771–853).
24. J. Myō Jōza, usually known as Huiming (n.d.).
25. A short staff symbolic of office.
26. The Chinese term *xin-fa* (J. *shinpō*; Skt. *citta-dharma*), literally "mind dharma," usually means "the element called mind." In this case both mind and dharma indicate a conceptual mode of being that should be transcended by awakening to true reality.

Around 513 CE, when Bodhiruci, one of the three translators of the Sanskrit text of the *Laṅkāvatāra-sūtra* into Chinese, translated *citta* in the sense of normal conceptualizing, he used the Chinese expression *xin-fa*. (The *Laṅkāvatāra-sūtra*, ch. 10, verse 249c: *tathatā citta-niruktam*, *Taishō* 16:571a.) Bodhiruci also used this Chinese expression for rendering a completely different expression, *citta-dharmatā*, which means "the original, awakened nature of mind," in a sense, "the Mind as the Dharma" (chapter 10, verse 252b: *cittasya dharmatā śuddhā*, *Taishō* 16:571b; also, verse 270b: *tathatā citta-dharmatā*, *Taishō* 16:571c). Around 700–704 CE,

Śikṣānanda, another translator, insisted on rendering citta-dharmatā as xin-xing or xin-fa-xing, to distinguish it from the ordinary xin (citta) or xin-fa (citta-dharma) (Taishō 16:629b and c).

Chan figures, including Huangpo and Linji, seem to have adopted Bodhiruci's second use of xin-fa. In other words, they use xin-fa not as citta-dharma or "the element called mind" but as citta-dharmatā, the "original, awakened nature of the mind."

In some texts, citta is identified with the ālaya-vijñāna and is regarded as working with manas (the thinking faculty) and mano-vijñāna (the discriminatory faculty). It is sometimes identified with the latter two, and it is always the source of discrimination. According to the Laṅkāvatāra-sūtra, the four-fascicle Chinese version of which Bodhidharma purportedly recommended to Huike as the best reference for practice at their time in China, this same citta works as the source of discrimination because it is not awakened to its original way of being (svajāti-lakṣaṇa). The original way of being of citta has nothing to do with discrimination; it is nirvana free from non-awakening. However, no citta realizes its original way of being until it realizes its own ignorance. More specifically, it believes its own discriminative faculty is ultimate, but once it realizes its ultimate ignorance it comes to know the true way in which the discrimative faculty should work. The same citta realizes that its own authentic way of being is no-citta.

This seems to be what Linji calls the mind-dharma (xin-fa), the mind that is awakened to its original way of being. It has ceased to be the source of discrimination and has come to be the true source of creation. It is Mazu's "calm and constant mind." Readers may take note that the translators of Hisamatsu's talks follow Hisamatsu's lead and often use "Self" instead of "mind" for xin, to indicate the mind's original way of being. See note 72.

27. The story of Yajñadatta is found in an esoteric Buddhist scripture that advocates jianxing (J. kenshō, "seeing one's nature"). According to what is written next to the title, this text appeared in the Tang dynasty as "a translation made in 705 from a Sanskrit original brought from Nalanda, India." The title is Dafoding-rulaimiyin-xiuzheng-liaoyi pusa-wanxing-shoulengyan-jin (abbreviated as Lengyan-jing; J. Ryōgon-kyō): "Śūraṃgama-sūtra, as Lofty as the Buddha's Great Head-Excrescence, the Ultimate Teaching for Practice and Attainment as the Tathāgata Secret Cause, Provided with Millions of Bodhisattva Practices," vol. 4, Taishō 19:12b.

28. Yunmen Wenyan (J. Unmon Bun'en, 864–949).

29. Some translators have rendered the Chinese expression here "shit-wiping stick."

30. The "five ranks" (J. go-i) clarify the relationship between religious Awakening and its functioning to awaken the world. They have been attributed to Dongshan Liangjie (J. Tōzan Ryōkai, 807–69), but they appear to have been devised by his Dharma-heir, Caoshan Benji (J. Sōzan Honjaku, 840–901). These Chan masters were later regarded as the co-founders of the Caodong (J. Sōtō) sect.

The oldest extant text that introduces "Dongshan's Verses on the Five Ranks" is the Chanlin-sengbao-zhuan (J. Zenrin-sōbō-den) by Juefan Huihong (J. Kakuhan Ekō, 1071–1128); see chapter 1 on Caoshan Benji.

Two terms and one concept are central to the five ranks: "the rank of straight" (Ch. *zhengwei*; J. *shōi*), "the rank of leaning" (Ch. *pianwei*; J. *hen'i*), and "returning to each other" (Ch. *huihu*; J. *ego*). The term "straight" means freedom from discrimination, or nirvana, while the term "leaning" means discerning, as the function of nirvana, and these two are viewed as "returning to each other." The five ranks discussed in the Linji lineage and adopted by Hisamatsu are as follows:

1. the rank of the straight with the leaning inside;
2. the rank of the leaning with the straight inside;
3. the rank of coming from inside the straight;
4. the rank of arriving at the inside of the leaning;
5. the rank of having arrived at the non-duality of the straight and the leaning.

To Hisamatsu's way of thinking, the first and the second ranks portray the characteristics of Awakening and its functioning as being inseparable from each other. The third shows how the two ranks, as one, begin to function through the original vow innate to all buddhas. The fourth shows how the first two ranks, as one, function in reality. The fifth shows the realization of the two ranks functioning as our True Self.

In the *Shōbō-genzō* fascicle titled "*Shunjū*," Dōgen (1200–53), founder of the Japanese Sōtō sect, rejected as misleading the traditional belief that Master Dongshan devised the five ranks as something essential for guiding practitioners. According to Dōgen, people should approach Master Dongshan directly through the living truth of his Awakening, i.e., *shōbō-genzō* (see p. xlvii, n. 5), instead of through such a circumlocution as the five ranks. Hakuin (1685–1768), a Japanese Rinzai master in the Edo period, made much of the five ranks and devised his unique koan, "the sound of one hand," in close connection with them. In 1960 Hisamatsu criticized Dōgen in the eight lectures on the five ranks he gave for participants in FAS Society retreats. Those lectures are recorded in the sixth volume of Hisamatsu's collected writings, together with his lectures on Master Linji, lectures on the *Dasheng-qixin-lun* (Treatise on the Awakening of Mahāyāna Faith), lectures on the *Vimalakīrti-nirdeśa-sūtra*, and lectures on *Ten Pictures of an Ox*.

31. The translators have adapted this section of the Sasaki translation while consulting *The Zen Teaching of Rinzai*, tr. Irmgard Schloegl (Berkeley: Shambhala, 1976), pp. 24–5.

32. Hisamatsu is referring to the well-known verse of the Buddha toward the end of the *Diamond Sutra*:

> Those who have seen me by form, and
> Those who have followed me by voice,
> Being devoted to wrong efforts,
> Those people will see me not.

33. Zongmi (J. Shūmitsu, 780–841) attributed this remark to Bodhidharma, though with a different third phrase: "making the mind like the wall." (In an article entitled "On *Zazen*," Hisamatsu attributes these words to Huike, Bodhidharma's disciple.) In the *Erru-sixing-lun* (J. *Ni'nyū-shigyō-*

ron, On Two Enterings with Four Practices), the earliest Chan text from Dunhuang, Bodhidharma states that one attains the Way when one realizes that the ordinary mind is originally empty of any self-nature, though it manifests itself as something external. Bodhidharma compares the mind to pieces of wood or pebbles that appear in a magician's art. For this comparison, see the *Laṅkāvatāra-sūtra*, ch. 10, verses 618 and 619, with Bodhiruci's Chinese rendering, *Taishō* 16:580a.

34. Nanquan Puyuan (J. Nansen Fugan, 748–834), a Dharma-heir to Mazu Daoyi.

35. A collection of poems by the hermit Hanshan (J. Kanzan) begins with an introduction by a possibly fictitious official Lu Qiuyin (J. Ryo Kyūin) of the Tang dynasty in the first half of the seventh century. According to the introduction, Hanshan used to utter these words when he came out to join priests at the Guoqing-si (J. Kokusei-ji), a well-known temple dedicated by Emperor Yang of Sui (J. Zui no Yōdai) to Zhiyi (J. Chiki, 538–97) a few years after this Tiantai master's death. The poet, who had come from his hermitage in the depths of Hanshan ("Cold Mountain"), returned to hide himself there.

Hakuin took up Hanshan's utterances in his commentary on this poetry, *Kanzanshi sendai-kibun* (Hanshan's Poetry Heard and Commented upon by a Heretical Buddhist):

"Bah! Bah! Transmigrating in the threefold world!" These words are extremely difficult to believe, extremely hard to realize. You should not easily take them in or swallow them. If you penetrate them as clearly as you see [a fruit] in your palm, you will immediately be meeting Hanshan, getting thoroughly free from the threefold world, and promptly realizing the deepest meaning of Hanshan's poetry. If you want to read his poetry, you must necessarily consult these words, and you will certainly have the sutra-minding eyes. As for long-consulting practitioners, they will see upon a glance. As for those who are used to discriminative knowledge, at any age they won't see even in their dreams.

36. The Sanskrit term *dharma*, according to Vasubandhu, connotes two things: 1. as far as conventional truth is concerned, it connotes that which bears its own characteristics or form; 2. as far as ultimate truth is concerned, it connotes nirvana, which is free from any characteristic or form, particular or common.

37. According to Asaṅga's *Mahāyāna-sūtrālaṃkara* (chapter 19, *Bodhi*), the awakened one's four wisdoms or discernments are *ādarśa-jñāna* (wisdom like a mirror), *samatā-jñāna* (wisdom of equality), *pratyavekṣā-jñāna* (wisdom of inquiry or attention, inspection, examination), and *kṛtya-anuṣṭhāna-jñāna* (wisdom of doing what is to be done). Buddhist philosophers after Asaṅga offer explanations of how the eight consciousnesses turn over into the four wisdoms. The turning over or transformation entails four facets. The mirror wisdom is the *ālaya-vijñāna* (the True Self unawakened, remaining as "undefiled source consciousness") trans-

formed; the wisdom of equality is the *manas* (ego) transformed; the wisdom of inquiry is the *mano-vijñāna* (consciousness) transformed; and the wisdom of doing what is to be done is the fivefold perception transformed. See note 86.

38. Hakuin (1685–1768) used this term late in life, as seen in the *Yaemugura* ("cleavers," a kind of wild grass), volume 1, written in 1759 at the age of 75. The eighth consciousness (*ālaya-vijñāna*) is the True Self to which one has yet to awaken and which has turned into the source of all delusive thoughts and discriminations. Hakuin mentioned it in expressions like "the dark cave of the eighth consciousness" and "the neglected field of the eighth consciousness." Hisamatsu misattributes the term to Zhaozhou.

39. Yuanwu Keqin (J. Engo Kokugon, 1063–1135). This expression is not found in the *Biyan-lu* (J. *Hekigan-roku*, the Blue Cliff Record, which is a collection of comments made by Yuanwu Keqin upon one hundred "cases" (koans) and related verses in a text by Xuedou Chongxian (J. Setchō Jūken, 980–1052) titled *Xuedou Songgu*), the *Yuanwu-lu* (J. *Engo-roku*), or the *Jijie-lu* (J. *Gekisetsu-roku*, Yuanwu's comments on Xuedou's *Niangu*, a collection of one-hundred verses (other than the *Biyan-lu*); Yuanwu referred to his comments as "keeping the beat" (*jijie*) in harmony with the rhythm of Xuedou's collection, so as to show his appreciation of those verses). Several expressions resembling Hisamatsu's quotation appear in these works by Yuanwu. In the *Biyan-lu*, one of Yuanwu's short comments on four lines of Xuedou's verse seems close. Xuedou writes,

> In the river country no spring winds have begun to blow;
> Partridges cry deep in thick flowers.
> Waves surging at three levels, fish have turned into dragons.
> Fools still draw water at the night embankment
> [in a futile attempt to empty the river].

Yuanwu responds to the last line:

> If a monk does nothing but places a hand on a hedge, gropes along a wall, pushes a gate, and stands by the door, *what's the use of the monk's functioning*? He would be no different from the guy who stands by a stump waiting for more hares to come [and run into the stump and die]. (emphasis added)

But the statement highlighted here has nothing to do with the expression Hisamatsu highlights.

The *Yuanwu-lu* has expressions that have the same meaning as Hisamatsu's quotation:

> A monk asked: "At the time when the days pass the winter solstice, spring weather arises. What happens when people of moral integrity develop their ways of life?" The master [Yuanwu] said, *"Among Chan monks there is nothing complicated."*

The questioner further said, "I've immediately accepted that." The master replied, "A sharp sword was wielded through the air." (*Taishō* 47:718c)

> The master said: "'An immediate realization of a fundamental koan' [see note 43] – still less do I use such a thing. Why? Because even immediately cutting off everything is not satisfactory; *the Buddhist truth originally doesn't have that much.* If you are free of mind, free of memory, free of things, free of action, free of comparison, and free of discrimination in matters like wearing clothes and eating meals, how will you ever move even a tiny bit? You could decisively lower the heads of buddhas in transformation, while you won't even begin to give rise to the view that you are on the side of Buddhist truth." (*Taishō* 47:769c–770a, emphasis added)

(Though the translators of Hisamatsu's talks have rendered these passages into their own English translation, they have referred to Thomas and J.C. Cleary, trs, *The Blue Cliff Record*, 3 vols. (Boulder: Shambhala, 1977) for the translation of certain terms.)

40. J. *Shinjinmei*, "Inscriptions on Faith and Mind," attributed to the third founding teacher of Chinese Chan, Sengcan (n.d.).

41. Dharmākara is not an historical person but a Way-seeker mentioned in the *Larger Sukhāvatī-vyūha* (see note 73). He is said to have attained great awakening by realizing his Original Vow to have every sentient being that meditates on him attain rebirth in the land of bliss or the so-called Pure Land. In this way, Dharmākara gave expression to nirvana's functioning as ultimate purification. After he awakened, his name became the "Infinite-Life-and-Light" (*Amitāyus-amitābha*), or Amida Buddha.

42. J. Issan Ichinei (1247–1317).

43. Ch. *xiancheng gongan* (J. *genjō-kōan*). This expression literally means "a presentation of a complicated legal case." As a Zen term it means "an immediate realization of [what Hisamatsu called] a fundamental koan." A prominent term in the writings of Dōgen, it appears earlier in a talk by Yunmen:

> Master Yunmen told practitioners: "You see, as soon as he saw a monk come up, Master Deshan dragged a staff and ran. As soon as he saw a monk enter the gate, Master Muzhou said, 'Here is a ready presentation of a complicated legal case. I shall let you go with thirty blows.'"

This appears in the section on Master Yunmen Wenyan in the *Jingde chuandeng-lu*, vol. 19.

44. J. Fuke, n.d.

45. J. Banzan Hōshaku, n.d. His words are quoted from the *Jingde chuandeng-lu*, vol. 7. See the *Biyan-lu*, case 37.

46. See note 30.

47. Luopu Yuan'an (J. Rakuho Gen'an, 834–98). Variants of the first character appear in texts that give his name as Laopu or Lepu.

48. Shide (J. Jittoku) was another hermit-poet who wrote in the Hanshan style of poetry. In his introduction to Hanshan's poems, Lü Qiuyin wrote that Shide saved the leftovers from the Guoqing temple for Hanshan, and that when Lü Qiuyin, who was a local official, directed the temple priests to follow and pay due respect to the two hermits, Shide disappeared in a cave with Hanshan, never to appear again.

49. For the date and place of Bodhidharma's death, the *Record of Linji* follows the information in the *Baolin-zhuan* (J. *Hōrin-den*, compiled in 801). According to the earliest source for information about Bodhidharma's death, the *Xu gaoseng-zhuan* (J. *Zoku kōsō-den*; by Daoxuan (J. Dōsen, 596–667), vol. 16, Huike buried his master's body where he died by the Luo River. That was some time before 534, when Huike, who had once wanted to bury himself beside the master's body but changed his mind, went north to Xin Ye, the capital of Eastern Wei, and began his own religious activities. The *Xu gaoseng-zhuan* makes no reference to Emperor Wu of Liang (r. 502–549) in connection with Bodhidharma. Reference to Mount Xioner as the place of burial for the "Founding Teacher" is first seen in the *Lidai-fabao-ji* (J. *Rekidai-hōbō-ki*), which was compiled between 775 and 800.

50. Kishū is present-day Wakayama Prefecture. Ippen (1239–89), personal name Chishin, first studied Tendai teachings and then the Pure Land *nenbutsu*, which emphasized the unity of believers and Amida Buddha. Through *nenbutsu* practice he realized Pure Land rebirth in one moment of *nenbutsu*. As a result of his confinement at the age of 36 at Shitennōji in Osaka, then on Mt. Kōya, and finally at the Kumano shrines, he received a revelatory message. Thereafter, he called himself Ippen ("one, universal") and continued his peregrinations. To the people he met during his itinerant preaching through the country to recommend the *nenbutsu* practice, he distributed paper slips with the handwriting, "*Namu-amida-butsu* ensures Pure Land Rebirth for all people" (literally, rebirth for "600,000 people," referring to the many people in the roughly sixty provinces at the time). (Dennis Hirota, *No Abode: The Record of Ippen* (Kyoto: Ryūkoku University, 1986), p. 17.) Ippen also devised the *odori nenbutsu* (dancing *nenbutsu*) upon the model of Kūya (903–72), and people called him *Sute-hijiri* ("a saint who has given up everything"; *Iwanami Bukkyō Jiten* (Tokyo: Iwanami Shoten, 1989), pp. 41–2.)

   Hottō Kokushi is Shinji Kakushin (1207–98), founder of the Hottō (or Hōtō) sect of Rinzai Zen. He received the bodhisattva precepts from Dōgen, went to China (1249), practiced Zen under Wumen Huikai (J. Mumon Ekai, 1183–1260), returned to Japan (1254), and then presided over Kōkoku-ji (1264) until his death. Emperor Kameyama asked him for instruction on the Dharma, and after Hottō's death the emperor praised him with the posthumous title, Hottō Zenji. Later, Emperor Godaigo praised him with the posthumous title, Hottō-enmyō Kokushi. Kakushin has been called Founder of the Fuke-shū, for he admired Puhua (J. Fuke) of Zhenzhou and played a bamboo flute. Komazawa Daigaku Jiten Henshūsho, eds., *Zengaku Daijiten* (Tokyo: Taishūkan, 1978), p. 152.

51. This story is usually quoted from the *Biyan-lu*, case 1. The first part of the story reads as follows:

> Q: "What is the ultimate meaning of the Noble [Fourfold] Truth?"
> A: "Vastly empty, and nothing noble."
> Q: "Who faces [me] the sovereign?"
> A: "Not knowing."

The first case in Xuedou's text and by extension the *Biyan-lu* lack the second part of the story, where Bodhidharma answers, "No merit," to the emperor's question of what merit he might have accrued for having been devoted to the Buddhist monastic order. The first and second parts of the exchange appear in several earlier Chan records: the *Zutang-ji* (J. *Sodōshū*, compiled in 952), the *Jinde chuandeng-lu* (J. *Keitoku dentō-roku*, 1004), and the *Tiansheng guandeng-lu* (J. *Tenshō kōtō-roku*, 1036).

The story of Bodhidharma meeting Emperor Wu of Liang was first introduced by Shenhui (J. Jinne, 670–762), who, by rejecting the group of practitioners gathered around Shenxiu (J. Jinshū, 606–706), kept insisting on the authenticity of Dharma-lamp transmission by Huineng (J. Enō, 638–713). Emphasizing how Huineng kept his distance from royal influence, Shenhui rebuked Shenxiu and his disciples for accepting imperial favors. To Shenhui, Huineng was another Bodhidharma who, unlike Shenxiu, made nothing of worldly power. Shenhui's version of Bodhidharma's exchange with Emperor Wu contains only the second part, in which Bodhidharma rejected Emperor Wu's idea of meritoriousness.

Regardless of Shenhui's objective when he disseminated the story of Bodhidharma's exchange with Emperor Wu, the story seems to have strongly appealed to Chan practitioners. Whether fictional or not, the story conveys a characteristically Chan way of thinking.

52. This is part of the verse by Xuedou attached to the first case in the Xuedou-Yuanwu text (*Biyan-lu*). The verse reads as follows:

> "Vastly empty, and nothing noble."
> When can the target be identified?
> "Who faces me?"
> He says, "Not knowing."
> Then he secretly crossed the river.
> How could thorn bushes be kept from growing deeply
> [after each of his steps]?
> "Not even if the whole country chased him would he return."
> They would in vain think of him forever.
> Stop thinking of him!
> With a cool breeze blowing all over the earth, what limit will there be?

Appearing right after these lines is the following exchange, recorded by a disciple of Xuedou:

> The master [Xuedou] looked around and said, "Is the Founding Teacher still here?" The master himself replied, "Yes, he is." The master continued, "Then call him forward and let him wash my feet."

53. This is a line from the *Zhengdao-ge* (J. *Shōdō-ka*, "Song of the Way Attained"), attributed to Yongjia Xuanjue (J. Yōka Genkaku, 675–713), a dharma-heir to Huineng, the Sixth Founding Teacher. The line appears in a nine-part section:

> When awakened, it's finished; no effort is exerted.
> Nothing composite of the world is like this.
> Practicing charity, form-abiding brings about celestial happiness.
> It's like aiming and shooting an arrow up in the sky;
> Its force being exhausted, the arrow falls back.
> It invites a future birth that turns out against one's wishes.
> How could this be equal to the non-composite gate of real form,
> Through which in a single leap one directly enters the Tathāgata stage?
> Once the root is attained, there's no need to worry about the branch.

54. This is a line of verse attributed to a Song dynasty poet, Su Dongpo (J. So Tōba, 1036–1101). He practiced Chan under a Linji-line master.
55. These words appear in the *Jingde chuandeng-lu*, vol. 15.
56. The text referred to is *Dunwu-rudao-yaomen-lun* (J. *Tongo-nyūdō-yōmon-ron*). Dazhu Huihai (J. Daishu Ekai, n.d.) was a Dharma-heir to Mazu Daoyi.
57. This is an utterance by Yantou Quanhe (J. Gantō Zenkatsu, 828–87) to criticize his fellow practitioner, Xuefeng Yicun (J. Seppō Gison, 822–908), both of whom were practicing under Master Deshan Xuanjian. Xuefeng confessed to Yantou that he was far from steady in his way of being, even after many years of practice under masters, including his present master Deshan, and even after receiving a verse from a master confirming his attainment. In response to this confession, Yantou shouted, "Don't you know that it has been said, 'That which comes in through the gate is not the family treasure'?" Xuefeng then asked, "What should I do hereafter?" Yantou said, "Hereafter, if you want to propagate the great teaching, take whatever flows out of your own chest and cover the heaven and the earth with it." Upon these words, Xuefeng opened satori, made a bow, and repeatedly shouted, "Dear brother, today for the first time at Aoshan I attained the Way." Aoshan (J. Gōzan) was the name of the place where, on their trip from Master Deshan's temple, the two men had to stay because of heavy snow. Xuefeng was the name of the place where Xuefeng Yicun later resided and, until his death, attracted many superb practitioners, including Xuansha Shibei and Yunmen Wenyan. This anecdote appears in the *Xuefeng-yulu* (J. *Seppō-goroku*). See *Shike-goroku, Goke-goroku, Furoku Hōkoji-goroku, Seppō-goroku*, ed. by Yanagida Seizan (Kyoto: Chūbun Shuppansha, 1974), p. 248.
58. The expression, "human mind" (Ch. *renxin*, J. *ninshin*), could be rendered "humanity's True Self." The expression first appeared in Huangbo's talks, *The Essentials of Transmitting the Mind-Dharma*:

> A monk Ming caught up with the Sixth Founding Teacher at the pass in Mt. Dayu. The master said, "What are you here for? Are you here for the robe or for the Dharma?" Ming said, "Not for the robe – it's

only for the Dharma that I'm here." The master said, "In that case you may collect your thoughts for a while, and keep away from all thoughts of good and evil." Ming accepted this. The master then said, "Not thinking of good, not thinking of evil, just at that time return to me your Face that is not yet born of your parents." Ming, upon hearing the words, instantly had a realization in silence, and with a bow he said, "As a person who drinks water knows for himself whether it is cold or hot, I now realize all my efforts over thirty years under the Fifth Founding Teacher have been made in vain, and I repent that wrong." To this the Sixth Founding Teacher said, "You are right." Through consideration of all this we come to realize that the Founding Teacher's coming from the west was for directly pointing to humanity's True Self (Ch. *zhizhi-renxin*; J. *jikishi-ninshin*), which enables one to see into one's own nature and attain Buddhahood, and is not for verbal exposition. (*Zen-no-Goroku*, vol. 8, Japanese translation and annotations by Iriya Yoshitaka (Tokyo: Chikuma Shobō, 1969, p. 85.))

As indicated in Huangbo's remarks, by the term *renxin* (J. *ninshin*) he meant the core (Skt. *hṛdaya*) of humanity, instead of the human mind (Skt. *citta*). Hence the above translation of his statement.

59. An expression used by Mazu Daoyi (709–88): *pingchang-xin shi dao*. The expression *ping-chang* (J. *heijō* or *byōjō*, "calm and constant") is currently used in the sense of "common" or "ordinary." But one cannot be truly "ordinary" unless one is "calm and constant." Mazu used the term *pingchang-xin* (J. *heijōshin* or *byōjōshin*) in its authentic meaning, i.e., the mind (or self) of no defilement and no discrimination, and he contrasted it with another term, *shengsi-xin* (J. *shōji-shin*, "the life-and-death mind (or self)"), which to Hisamatsu is nothing other than defilement. Critics of Mazu's thought fail to see this point.

60. Yunmen Wenyan (J. Unmon Bun'en, 864–949) told the practitioners: "I won't ask you how you are before the fifteenth day [of the month, when the moon gets full]. How are you after the fifteenth day? Say it in one sentence." On their behalf he said, "Every day is a good day" (Ch. *riri shi haori*; J. *hibi kore kōjitsu* (or *kōnichi*)).

61. In response to the question, "During the twelve divisions of a day how should I take care of myself?" Zhaozhou Congshen (J. Jōshū Jūshin, 778–897) said, "You suffer as the twelve divisions of a day employ you; this old monk makes free use of the twelve divisions (Ch. *shide shi'er-shi*; J. *jūniji o tsukaietari*). About which time are you asking?"

62. This is an utterance attributed to an Indian *dhyāna* teacher, Manura, the twenty-second figure in the Zen lineage, counting from Mahākāśyapa. The *Linji-lu* (Sasaki p. 27) quotes it from the *Baolin-zhuan*, vol. 5.

63. A central statement of the approach of the FAS Society, the Vow reads,

> Keeping calm and composed, let us awaken to our True Self, become fully compassionate humans, make full use of our gifts according to our respective vocations in life, discern the agony both individual and social and its source, recognize the right direction in which history

should proceed, and join hands without distinctions of race, nation, or class. Let us, with compassion, vow to bring to realization humankind's deep desire for Self-emancipation and construct a world which is true and happy.

64. The Chinese character here has several connotations: "meaning," "purpose," "intention," and "will."
65. For the term "mind-dharma," see Talk 8 and note 26.
66. Zhaozhou asked Nanquan, "What is the Way?" Nanquan said, "The ordinary mind is it." Zhaozhou inquired, "Can I aspire after it?" Nanquan said, "When you seek it you turn against it" (Ch. *ni ji guai*; J. *giseba sunawachi somuku*). Zhaozhou said, "Unless we intend, how could we know it is the Way?" Nanquan said, "The Way does not belong to knowing or not knowing. Knowing is false awareness, and non-knowing is only what is still indistinct. Once you truly attain the indubitable Way, it is like great space, empty, wide, and open. Why bother to speak of right and wrong?" Upon these words Zhaozhou immediately realized the subtle purport, and his mind was like the bright moon. (From the *Zhaozhou-lu*, case 1; see *Jōshū-roku*, rendered into modern Japanese and annotated by Akizuki Ryōmin, *Zen no goroku*, volume 11 (Tokyo: Chikuma-shobō, 1972).)
67. In his *Zazen wasan* (Hymn in Praise of Zazen, a short hymn in Japanese, consisting of 44 phrases over 22 lines; composed by Hakuin (1685–1768) for recitation by practitioners of *zazen*; the exact date of composition is not known), Hakuin refers to the impoverished, vagrant son of a wealthy merchant described in a story in the *Dharma-lotus Sutra*, ch. 4. The son did not recognize his father, who succeeded in bringing his son back to his mansion without telling the young man that he was his father. It was only on his deathbed, after many years of hard work through which the son grew up to be a competent merchant himself, that the old merchant proudly introduced his son to the people who had gathered.

In the *Dharma-lotus Sutra* it was Kāśyapa who on behalf of his fellow disciples told this story to express their gratitude for the Buddha's assuring Śāriputra, one of their fellow practitioners, that he would attain Buddhahood. Kāśyapa realized that, like Śāriputra, the *śrāvakas*, who had been satisfied with being arhats and given up ultimate awakening, were competent enough to attain Buddhahood.
68. A renowned Shingon priest (1718–1804).
69. J. *inka-shōmei*. The term *yinke* (J. *inka*) is seen in Kumārajīva's translation of the *Vimalakīrti-nirdeśa-sūtra*, vol. 3, where Vimalakīrti criticizes Śāriputra for his formal understanding of the term "complete absorption" (Skt. *pratisaṃlayana*, which can also be rendered, "complete retirement for the sake of meditation"). Vimalakīrti says, "When they practice complete absorption in the way I mentioned, the Buddha tells them that they practice complete absorption." Kumārajīva translates this as follows: "If they sit that way, the Buddha will *yinke* them." *Taishō* 14:539c. The two characters *yin* and *ke* respectively mean "to confirm" and "to approve." When a master admits a practitioner to be fully mature, the master gives the practitioner something to certify that maturity (J. *inka-shōmei*),

though not necessarily a written document. With that certification the practitioner is considered to be a qualified master. In the Kamakura period Dōgen criticized the easygoing formal practice of *inka* in China and Japan, saying that no one except a buddha could certify another as a buddha. Dōgen wanted to advocate an authentic way of *inka*, which he located in the Caodong (Sōtō) tradition.

70. The Vehicle of the Śrāvakas (*Śrāvaka-yāna*) indicates those who gather to form the sangha to study and practice the Awakened One's teaching, strive to become arhats, and, after attaining arhatship, seek to remain in the sangha. The Vehicle of the Pratyekas (*Pratyekabuddha-yāna*) refers to Buddhists who have understood the Awakening of Buddhahood to be a matter of individuals who are not connected to the world and history and who have been practicing individually apart from the sangha. The Vehicle of the Bodhisattvas stands for the Great Vehicle (*Mahāyāna*).

71. The term Dharma-gate (*hōmon*) refers to Buddhist teachings.

72. The single Chinese character *xin*, which is rendered here as "Self," has several meanings: 1. the heart; 2. mind, feeling, intention; 3. center, core. (*The Chinese–English Dictionary* (Hong Kong: Shangwu-yinshu-guan, 1979), pp. 765–6.) The same character in Japanese has two pronunciations, *shin* and *kokoro*. With the first pronunciation (*shin*) the character connotes center, core, and sometimes the heart, and with the second pronunciation (*kokoro*) it connotes heart, mind, feeling, and intention. In Sanskrit, as in Japanese, *citta* (mind) is distinguished from *hṛdaya* (center, core, essence), just as *kokoro* is distinguished from *shin*. According to the *Laṅkāvatāra-sūtra*, what is seen as external is nothing but mind itself (*svacitta*). Further, mind is empty of any self-nature. In other words, the essence (*hṛdaya*) of mind (*citta*) is no-mind (*acitta*). No-mind is mind as truth (Ch. *xin-fa* or *xin-fa-xing*). Considering all this, the present translators render the Chinese term *xin* at times as "mind" and at other times as "Mind" or "Self." (See note 26.)

73. The three sutras are 1. The Larger *sukhāvatī-vyūha-sūtra*, "Sutra on Supernal Manifestation as the Land of Bliss" (J. *Muryōju-kyō*, "Sutra on Amitāyus"); 2. The *Guan-wuliang-shou-jing* (J. *Kanmuryōju-kyō*, "A Sutra on the Comtemplation of Amitāyus"; the assumed original title of the text, whose Sanskrit version has not been discovered, is *Amitāyur-dhyāna-sūtra*); and 3. The *Smaller sukhāvatī-vyūha-sūtra* (J. *Amida-kyō*, "A Sutra on Amitāyus").

74. This phrase appears in one of the letters by Rennyo (1415–1499) that have been included in his *Letters Addressed to Lay People*. Rennyo was the eighth abbot of the Honganji temple, founded by the great-grandson of Shinran (1173–1262) as one of the centers of the Shin or True Pure Land Sect. Through his lifelong efforts to propagate Shin faith, Rennyo made the Honganji sect flourish and stand out among other sects. Rennyo wrote 221 letters between the ages of 57 and 84, and they are grouped in five collections. While all the letters of the first four collections have dates, none of the letters in the fifth collection has any date. The words Hisamatsu quotes are from the second of the 22 letters in the fifth collection. The beginning of that letter reads, "It is said, you know, that even with all the knowledge of the eighty-thousand teachings of the Dharma Treasure, those who are ignorant of their afterlives are fools, whereas a

nun or lay priestess who is ignorant of even a sentence from the teachings but who knows her afterlife is a person of wisdom."

75. In the *Biyan-lu*, 46, Jingqing Daofu (J. Kyōshō Dōfu, 866?–937) quotes this sentence with a slight change from the second fascicle of the *Lengyan-jing* (J. *Ryōgon-kyō*, Skt. *Śūraṃgama-sūtra; Taishō* 19:111c). The original text reads, "All sentient beings, since beginningless time, have lost themselves, taking themselves for things. Being lost and unaware of their original Self, they have had things move them."

76. See note 53.

77. An allusion to this is seen, for example, in a negative comment by Yuanwu on an utterance in *mondō* that Xuedou pulls from the *Yunmen-lu* (*Taishō* 47:552c) as the thirty-ninth case of the *Biyan-lu*:

> A monk asked Yunmen, "What is the Buddha's clean and pure Dharma-body?"
> Yunmen said, "Peonies in full-bloom in a fence."
> The monk said, "Even when that is the case, what do you mean by it?"
> Yunmen said, "A golden-haired lion."

On the first answer by Yunmen, Yuanwu comments:

> *"Where a question is not genuine, an answer comes that is crude and rash.* One being clogged up, the other bumps against it. What is bent cannot hold what is straight in itself." (emphasis added)

78. Yuanwu makes this remark in his "Appraising and Singing" (Ch. *pingchang*, J. *hyōshō*) after the forty-first case of the *Biyan-lu*:

> Zhaozhou asked Touzi, "How is it when a person who has died the great death has come to life?"
> Touzi said, "While you are not permitted to go by night, you must be there by dawn."

Yuanwu remarks on this:

> People who have died the great death are all free of the Buddha-Dharma, free from its principles and its abstruseness, free from gain and loss, right and wrong, merit and demerit; they have reached here and rest in this way. An ancient [Yunmen] made this remark: "On the level ground are innumerable dead people; those who can pass through the woods of thistles and thorns are passed masters." This can be attained only by going through that boundary. However, nowadays it is hard for people to reach this sort of field. If they have anything to rely on or any comprehension, they will have no approach…. It can be attained only after *dying* a *great death one time and coming to life*. Master Yongguang of Zhezhong [J. Setchū no Yōkō Oshō, Dharma-heir to Yunju Daoyong, J. Ungo Dōyō, 835?–902] said, "If the sword of words misses the mark, you'll be tens of thousands of

miles away from your native soil. For your agreement and acceptance, you just need to let go with the hands while hanging from a cliff. If you *come to life after death*, no one could deceive you. Who could conceal an extraordinary truth?" (emphasis added)

79. Ch. *zuolüe*, J. *saryaku*.
80. See note 95.
81. Ch. *zhiyin-di*, J. *chiintei*.
82. Ch. *zushi-chan*, J. *soshizen*.
83. The expression, "the kind of tree that is rootless" (Skt. *amūlā nāma vṛkṣa-jātiḥ*), refers to a resolution to attain a buddha's wisdom; this analogy appears in a chapter on Maitreya in a sutra entitled "Entering the Dharma World" (Ch. *Rufajie-pin*, J. *Nyūhokkai-bon*; Skt. text, *Gaṇḍavyūha*, "Supernal Manifestations as a Rhinoceros"), part of the *Buddhāvataṃsaka-sūtra* (Ch. *Fahuayan-jing*, J. *Butsukegon-gyō*; "Sutra on the Buddha's Garland"). The entire passage in the *Gaṇḍavyūha* (*Buddhist Sanskrit Texts*, No. 5, ed. By P.L. Vaidya (Darbhanga: Mithila Institute, 1960) reads:

> Maitreya Bodhisattva said to Sudhana, "For example, son of a good family, there is the kind of tree termed 'rootless.' Its root-basis is unobtainable, whereas all the branches, foliage, and blossoms are fully manifested and become net-like on these trees. Likewise, the root basis for a resolution to attain [a buddha's] ommiscience is unobtainable, whereas it is seen having all the good work, wisdom, and supernatural faculties fully developed and as having become the network of a great vow in all the modes of life."

84. This is an utterance in verse by Changsha Jingcen (J. Chōsha Keijin, n.d.), who together with Zhaozhou Congshen was a Dharma-heir to Nanquan Puyuan (748–834). Quoted from the *Jingde chuandeng-lu*, vol. 3.
85. The Yogācāra School of Buddhism, which advocated *vijñapti-mātratā* (J. *yuishiki-shō*), "the unobtainability of anything that makes itself known as something."
86. In his final chapter on Effected Wisdom, Asaṅga states in the *Mahāyāna Saṃgraha* (Tibetan text, ch. X, section 5; *Shōdaijōron*, vol. 2, Japanese translation and annotations by Nagao Gadjin (Tokyo: Kōdansha, 1987), p. 108) that the Awakened One's Dharma-body attains fivefold self-abidingness by turning over each of the five basic constituents (*skandhas*) of a human being. Through the turning over of the fifth constituent, the *vijñāna* group, it attains the four wisdoms: the "wisdom like a mirror," "wisdom of equality," "wisdom of inquiry," and "wisdom of doing what is to be done" (see note 37). In Xuanzang's Chinese translation of Vasubandhu's commentary on this part (vol. 11, section 1, *Taishō* 31:1597), the eight *vijñānas* are said to be turned over into the four wisdoms.
87. This refers to the Yogācāra classification of consciousness. (See note 37.)
88. Ch. *you-shi*, J. *aru toki*.
89. J. Kokufu, n.d.
90. *Komusō*, literally "monks of empty nothingness."

91. Kumagaya Naozane (1141–1208) was warrior for the Minamoto clan who killed young Taira Atsumori in the decisive battle of Ichi-no-tani in 1184. Despondent over killing a person about the same age as his own son, Kumagaya renounced the world and became a monk.

92. This statement appears in the *Zhaozhou-lu*, case 222 (see note 66):

> Question: "The ten-thousand things return to one. To what place does the one return?"
> The master: "When I was in Qing Province I made a hempen robe; it weighed seven *jin* [one *jin* is 600 grams]."

After Xuedou, Yuanwu took this up as the forty-fifth case in the *Biyan-lu*.

93. The practices of reciting the name of Amida Buddha (*Namu-amida-butsu*) and the name of the *Dharma-lotus Sutra* (*Namu-myōhō-renge-kyō*) in Pure Land and Nichiren Buddhism, respectively, as the expression of one's devotion.

94. Expressions in Yuanwu's foreword to case 19 in the *Biyan-lu* (on "Juzhi's (J. Gutei) Finger-Chan") might be the source of the phrase quoted by Hisamatsu here. The first half of the foreword to that koan reads as follows:

> A speck of dust moves, and the great earth is put away. A flower opens and the world starts. But when no speck of dust has moved, when no flower has opened yet, how do you see it? Hence the expressions: "It's like cutting off a thread; one being cut off, all are cut off. It's like dyeing a thread: one being dyed, all are dyed."

95. These are the first two phrases from the foreword by Ciyuan (J. Jion, n.d.) to the verse and the picture of an empty circle that convey the eighth stage, "both the ox and the person are forgotten," in *Ten Pictures of an Ox (Shi'niu-tu, J. Jūgyū-zu)*. The ten verses and pictures were prepared by Kuo'an (J. Kakuan), also known as Liangshan Shiyuan (J. Ryōzan Shion, n.d.), a Dharma-heir to Dasui Yuanjing (J. Daizui Genjō, d. 1135).

96. In the capital city of Cai Prefecture in Henan Province, Wu Yuanji took his stand against the Tang Court. The two prefectures, Bing and Fen, are in Shanxi Province, far north of the Yellow River, whereas Cai Prefecture is located far south of the river. Although the administrative officers of the two northern prefectures also revolted against the court, there is no record that Wu Yuanji occupied those regions.

Despite these historical facts, the two events were traditionally identified in interpretations of Linji's phrases; hence Hisamatsu's interpretation. For the two events and their relations, see the note by Yanagida Seizan in *Butten kōza* (lectures on Buddhist scriptures), vol. 30, *Rinzairoku* (Tokyo: Daizō Shuppan, 1972), pp. 70–1.

97. *Chan Master Dahui's Chronicle*, compiled in the tenth year of Shaoxing (1141), includes the account that to the aid-de-camp (*shilang*), Zhang Jiucheng, Tahui showed the two phrases, "The Castle of Cai was toppled and Wu Yuanji was killed", in place of Linji's verse, "Person and surroundings are both taken away." According to Yanagida, later people

> may have misunderstood this to mean that Linji's verse, "No news from Bing and Fen," points to the Wu Yuanji incident.

98. A phrase quoted by Baizhang Huaihai (J. Hyakujō Ekai, 749–814) from a Mahāyāna text.
99. Hakuin often used the expression, "the dark pit of *ālaya-vijñāna.*"
100. The True Pure Land Sect.
101. See note 37.
102. See note 67.
103. See n. 60.
104. D.T. Suzuki, "English Translation of the Shingyō," *Manual of Zen Buddhism* (New York: Grove Press, 1960), pp. 26–7; partially adapted here.

Index

Asaṅga, 146–7, 156
Avataṃsaka-sūtra, xxix, xxx, 92
Awakening, xx, xxix, xlvi, l, 6, 7, 13, 17, 27, 35, 58, 66, 87, 91, 102
Awakening of Mahayana Faith, see *Dasheng-qixin-lun*

Baizhang Huaihai (J. Hyakujō Ekai), 9, 27, 142, 158
Bashō, xlix
Biyan-lu (J. *Hekiganroku*, Blue-Cliff Record), xvi, xxviii, xxx, 147, 148, 150, 155
bodhi, 77
Bodhidharma, xxiii, 5, 47, 54, 69–70, 73–4, 82–3, 87, 144, 145–6, 149–50
bodhisattva, 66, 90, 154
Buddha, xxix, xli, xliv, xlv, xlvi, 4, 29, 32, 38, 39, 41, 44, 46, 47, 48, 51–2, 58, 61–2, 76, 79, 81, 89, 91, 115, 122
Buddha-Dharma, see Dharma
Buddha-nature, 39, 87, 91, 93, 103

Caoshan Benji (J. Sōzan Honjaku), 144
certification (Ch. *yinke*, J. *inka*), 88, 153–4
Changsha Jingcen (J. Chōsha Keijin), 156
Chuanxinfayao (J. *Denshin-hōyō*, Essentials of Transmitting the Mind-Dharma), xvi, xvii, xxi, xxv, xxxi, xxxv, xxxviii, 39, 151
Confucianism, 110
Consciousness-Only School, see Yogācāra School

Dahui Zonggao (J. Daie Sōkō), xlviii
daimoku, 127, 157
Daitō Kokushi, 37
Dasheng-qixin-lun (J. *Daijō-kishin-ron*, Awakening of Mahāyāna Faith), xxxii, xxxiii, xxxiv, xxxv, xl, xlviii, 145

Dayu (J. Daigu), 16–19, 143
Dazhu Huihai (J. Daishu Ekai), xvii, 78, 151
Demeveille, Paul, xxxvi, xxxviii
Denshin-hōyō, see *Chuanxinfayao*
Deshan Xuanjian (J. Tokusan Senkan), 8, 15, 60, 142, 151
Dharma, xv, xxix, xxxv, xxxix, xl, xliv, xlv, xlvi, xlviii, 3, 11, 13, 15, 20, 21, 25–6, 28, 38, 43, 47, 53–5, 58, 61–2, 64–5, 75, 77, 79, 81–5, 87, 100–1, 102, 104, 136–7, 146
dharma-kāya, l, 30, 39, 126, 131
Dharma-lotus Sutra, xl, l, 92, 96, 153
Dharmākara, 55
dhyāna, 42
Diamond Sutra, 8, 36, 39, 59, 142, 145
Dōgen, xlvii, 54, 145
Dongshan Liangjie (J. Tōzan Ryōkai), 64, 137, 144–5
Dunwu-rudao-yaomen-lun (J. *Tongo-nyūdō-yōmon-ron*), xvii, xxxviii, 78, 151

eight consciousnesses, 49–50, 117, 133, 146, 156
Emperor Wu (Wu-zong), xliii, xlv
Emperor Wu of Liang, 47, 69, 78
emptiness (Skt. *śūnyatā*), 105–6
Essentials of Transmitting the Mind-Dharma, see *Chuanxinfayao*

FAS, xi, xv, xviii, xxi, xxvi, xxxii, 35, 92, 96, 107–8, 114, 118, 121, 133, 136, 152
five grave sins, xlvi, l, 20
five paths, 43
Five Ranks, 36, 64–5, 137, 144
Formless Self, xvi, xviii, xx, xxi, xlvi, 20, 31, 48, 53–6, 58, 71, 74, 94–5, 96, 110, 113, 118, 136, 137, 139, 140
Founding Teacher, 76, 81
Four Classifications, xx, 105, 111–29

159

One True Person without Rank, see
True Person without Rank
Ordinary Mind, 42, 152
Original Face, xxiii, 4, 6, 65, 76, 90,
94, 97, 113, 115, 116, 132–4, 136,
139–40
Original Nature, 21

Panshan Baoji (J. Banzan Hōshaku),
63, 119, 148
Platform Sutra, see *Liuzu-tanjing*
pratyeka, 90, 154
precepts, 9, 23, 37, 43, 55, 77, 78
Puhua (J. Fuke), 63–8, 119
Pure Land Buddhism, xxx, 36, 92, 157

Record of Yunmen, see *Yunmen guang-lu*
Rennyo, 154

Śākyamuni, xxx, 1, 5, 28, 42, 55, 98,
100, 116
samadhi, xv, xlvi, 11, 22, 72–3, 125
sambhoga-kāya, 39
sangha, xliv, xlv, xlvi, 154
Sansheng Huiran (J. Sanshō Enen), 3
sanzen, 11
Sasaki, Ruth Fuller, xxxvi, xxxviii
satori, 21, 30, 39, 43, 61
Second Founding Teacher, see Huike
Shandao (J. Zendō), xlvii
Shenhui (J. Jinne), xxxviii, 150
Shenxiu (J. Jinshū), xl, xlix, 150
Shide (J. Jittoku), 68, 149
Shinran, xxxvii, xlix, 154
shōbō-genzō, xxvi, xlvii–xlviii, xxx, xliv
Shōbōgenzō, xlvii
six consciousnesses, 99
Sixth Founding Teacher, see Huineng
Song gaoseng-zhuan (J. *Sō kōsōden*, Song
Records of Eminent Buddhist
Priests), xliv, xlix
Songyuan Chongyue (J. Shogen
Sūgaku), 5, 142
śrāvaka, 1, 90, 154
Suzuki Daisetsu, xvii, xxxvi, xxxviii

Tathāgata, 39, 77, 96, 116, 139
tathatā, xxxiii, xxxiv, 9, 10, 46, 133,
137

teikō, xv, xviii, xxxii
teishō, xv, xxii, xxxvi, xxxvii
Ten Pictures of an Ox, 106, 114, 145,
157
Tendai, see Tiantai
three essentials, 11
Three Vehicles, 55, 89–90
Tiantai Buddhism, xxix, xxx, xxxiv,
91
Transmission of the Lamp, see *Jingde*
chuandeng-lu
Treasury of the True Dharma Eye, see
shōbō-genzō
True Person without Rank, xv, xxiii,
xxxiv, 4, 5, 21, 23, 29, 31, 33–4,
37, 46, 71, 112–13, 117–18, 126,
132
True Pure Land Buddhism, see
Jōdo-shinshū
True Self, xvi, xxi, xxiii, 4, 10, 17, 26,
32, 35, 39, 41, 46, 48–9, 51–2, 54–5,
60, 79–80, 83, 86, 91, 94, 95, 96,
101, 107, 110, 112, 115, 151–2

upāya, xxix, xxx

Vasubandhu, 55, 156
Vimalakīrti, 93
Vimalakīrti-nirdeśa-sūtra, xvi, xxxii,
36, 145, 153
Vow of Humankind, 81, 152–3

Weishan Lingyou (J. Isan Reiyū), xliii,
26, 143
Wumenguan (J. *Mumonkan*, Gateless
Barrier), xvi, 12, 22

Xinxin-ming (J. *Shinjinmei*,
Inscriptions on Faith and Mind),
50, 148
Xuedou Chongxian (J. Setchō Juken),
147, 150, 155
Xuefeng Yicun (J. Seppō Gison), li,
151

Yajñadatta, 34, 41, 62, 78, 86, 93,
144
Yantou Quanhou (J. Gantō Zenkatsu),
151